D0209158

Social History in Perspective
General Editor: Jeremy Black

Social History in Perspective is a series of in-depth studies of the many topics in social,
cultural and religious history.

PUBLISHED

John Belchem *Popular Radicalism in Nineteenth-Century Britain*
Sue Bruley *Women in Britain Since 1900*
Anthony Brundage *The English Poor Laws, 1700–1930*
Simon Dentith *Society and Cultural Forms in Nineteenth-Century England*
Joyce M. Ellis *The Georgian Town, 1680–1840*
Peter Fleming *Family and Household in Medieval England*
Ian Gazeley *Poverty in Britain, 1900–1965*
Kathryn Gleadle *British Women in the Nineteenth Century*
Harry Goulbourne *Race Relations in Britain since 1945*
Anne Hardy *Health and Medicine in Britain since 1860*
Tim Hitchcock *English Sexualities, 1700–1800*
Sybil M. Jack *Towns in Tudor and Stuart Britain*
Helen M. Jewell *Education in Early Modern England*
Alan Kidd *State, Society and the Poor in Nineteenth-Century England*
Peter Kirby *Child Labour in Britain, 1750–1870*
Arthur J. McIvor *A History of Work in Britain, 1880–1950*
Hugh McLeod *Religion and Society in England, 1850–1914*
Donald M. MacRaild *Irish Migrants in Modern Britain, 1750–1922*
Donald M. MacRaild and David E. Martin *Labour in Britain, 1830–1914*
Christopher Marsh *Popular Religion in the Sixteenth Century*
Michael A. Mullett *Catholics in Britain and Ireland, 1558–1829*
Richard Rex *The Lollards*
George Robb *British Culture and the First World War*
R. Malcolm Smuts *Culture and Power in England, 1585–1685*
John Spurr *English Puritanism, 1603–1689*
W. B. Stephens *Education in Britain, 1750–1914*
Heather Swanson *Medieval British Towns*
David Taylor *Crime, Policing and Punishment in England, 1750–1914*
N. L. Tranter *British Population in the Twentieth Century*
Ian D. Whyte *Migration and Society in Britain, 1550–1830*
Ian D. Whyte *Scotland's Society and Economy in Transition, c.1500–c.1760*
Andy Wood *Riot, Rebellion and Popular Politics in Early Modern England*

Please note that a sister series, *British History in Perspective*, is available,
covering key topics in British political history.

Social History in Perspective
Series Standing Order
ISBN 0–333–71694–9 hardcover
ISBN 0–333–69336–1 paperback
(*outside North America only*)

You can receive future titles in this series as they are published by placing a standing order.
Please contact your bookseller or, in case of difficulty, write to us at the address below with
your name and address, the title of the series and the ISBN quoted above.

Customer Services Department, Macmillan Distribution Ltd
Houndmills, Basingstoke, Hampshire RG21 6XS, England

Child Labour in Britain, 1750–1870

PETER KIRBY

First published 2003 by
PALGRAVE MACMILLAN
Houndmills, Basingstoke, Hampshire RG21 6XS and
175 Fifth Avenue, New York, N.Y. 10010
Companies and representatives throughout the world

PALGRAVE MACMILLAN is the global academic imprint of the Palgrave Macmillan division of St. Martin's Press, LLC and of Palgrave Macmillan Ltd. Macmillan® is a registered trademark in the United States, United Kingdom and other countries. Palgrave is a registered trademark in the European Union and other countries.

ISBN 0–333–67193–7 hardback
ISBN 0–333–67194–5 paperback

This book is printed on paper suitable for recycling and made from fully managed and sustained forest sources.

A catalogue record for this book is available from the British Library.

Library of Congress Cataloging in Publication Data
    p.   cm.
Includes bibliographical references and index.
ISBN 0–333–00000–0

10   9   8   7   6   5   4   3   2   1
12   11   10   09   08   07   06   05   04   03

Printed in China

Contents

List of Tables and Figure

Figure

Preface

This book arises from a need among students and teachers of economic and social history for a general synthesis of the child labour market between 1750 and 1870. The author hopes it will prove useful as a teaching aid as well as a guide to potential research topics in the field. The text has benefited greatly from the comments and suggestions of D. E. Martin, S. H. Rigby, M. E. Rose and an anonymous reader for Palgrave Macmillan. Invaluable assistance on specific points was provided by the late P. E. H. Hair, Jack Langton, Jim Oeppen and Bob Woods. Generous financial assistance was provided by the Arts and Humanities Research Board. The book is dedicated to my wife Carmel and to Calum, Rose, Theo and Ruth.

Introduction

For many people, the term 'child labour' conjures up thoughts of young children toiling in harsh and dangerous conditions in dark 'satanic' mills and mines. For much of the twentieth century, child labour was portrayed by historians as little more than a 'social problem' of the Industrial Revolution. Condemnation of child labour formed part of the standard critique of early industrial capitalism. This view owed much to early works on the development of factory legislation by historians such as Hutchins and Harrison and to the efforts of early labour historians such as the Hammonds, who went as far as to claim that 'during the first phase of the Industrial Revolution the employment of children on a vast scale became the most important social feature of English life'.[1] Later, during the Cold War, heated debates over the relative merits of communism and Western capitalism led to further interest in the social effects of industrialisation, and generated studies that were highly critical of capitalist development. Left-wing intellectuals and commentators argued that a major feature of early industrial capitalism had been a widespread deployment of child labour. E. P. Thompson asserted that during the Industrial Revolution 'the exploitation of little children...was one of the most shameful events in our history' and Brian Inglis argued that in 'the early part of the nineteenth century, child labour came to be used on a scale it had never been used on before'.[2] Others went still further, arguing from small samples of evidence that factory owners and overseers commonly inflicted serious physical assaults upon children. Walvin, for instance, claimed that 'thousands of pathetic [factory] children were beaten awake, kept awake by beating and, at the end of the day, fell asleep too exhausted to eat'.[3] For a large part of the twentieth century, therefore, social historians were preoccupied with the conditions of

1

child workers in large industrial processes and tended to overlook the much larger numbers of children in areas such as domestic service, small workshops and agriculture.[4] Such approaches established children's employment as a socially negative aspect of British economic growth.

Other historians have argued that the 'pessimistic' interpretation of child labour was exaggerated. Hartwell, for instance, observed that the pessimists' view was based upon a small number of examples of ill-treatment drawn from state reports. Chaloner noted that such sources had originally been drawn up for overtly political ends and warned historians against 'the danger of accepting at face value statements made in the course of the bitter social and economic agitations which enlivened the 1830s and 1840s'.[5] Moreover, the desire to depict child labour in an excessively dreary light, it was argued, disclosed more about the ideological motivations of historians than it did about the social conditions of child workers themselves. Hartwell noticed that there was a strong element of moral judgement in the debate and identified similarities in the way historians dealt with emotive issues such as slavery and child labour. He argued that

> some historians in writing...about slaves and children, argue as though the issue at stake is *not* what happened, but is the moral issue, not only of the wickedness of plantation and factory owners, but also that of the historians...Slavery and child labour in the past were 'proved' immoral and were abolished, and those historians today who in any way challenge this orthodoxy, are also 'immoral'.[6]

Hence, for much of the twentieth century, the debate over child labour in history was couched predominantly in terms of an underlying dispute over the ethics of child labour.

In recent years, however, the diminishing importance of rigid ideological approaches in social history has compelled a new generation of historians to reassess traditional narratives of child and family labour. It is increasingly clear that the focus upon child labour in large industries – although of immense importance to the history of child welfare – has seriously distorted our picture of the historic child labour market.[7] This view is supported by research on the character of the Industrial Revolution which has shown that large-scale industrial production was confined to only a few highly developed regions.[8] Most of Britain remained rural or semi-rural, and the typical site of production until the late nineteenth century was the farm, the domestic workshop or small factory. Such findings have highlighted the diversity of the British labour market and have rendered it more difficult to generalise about the employed child in history. Research into the historic social structure and the household economy, moreover, has shown how the very coherence of family life often depended upon the economic contributions of children.[9] In the early 1830s, about 40 per cent of the population was aged below 15 and the resultant high levels of child dependency almost certainly led to children earning their living at earlier ages.[10] In the case of very poor families, the earnings of children might provide a higher standard of living compared with households in which children did not work. Studies of the household economy in history have revealed a rich and varied market for family labour. Anderson's work in the early 1970s highlighted the effects of industrial and urban development upon the structure of mid-nineteenth-century families. Further research has extended the enquiry to specific regions and sectors. Kussmaul's investigation of agricultural service, Snell's examination of the agrarian labouring poor and Dupree's study of family structure in the Potteries have stressed the importance of the strategies adopted by families in the face of changing external local labour market demand.[11] The examination of surviving household accounts has shown the complex distribution of incomes and benefits within poor families, whilst research into ages at leaving home has offered an insight into the rates at which rural children became independent of parental support.[12] It is also understood that most eighteenth- and early-nineteenth-century parents regarded the *unemployment* of their children with trepidation. As Coleman has pointed out, 'far from thinking it was morally wrong, contemporaries thought it wholly right that children, especially those of the poor, should be put to work and kept out of mischief by being given employment, preferably by doing useful jobs within their own capabilities'.[13]

Economists too have argued for a greater stress to be placed upon the functions of the household economy. The classical economists recognised that there were links between the fortunes of the economy and the incidence of women's and children's work. McCulloch, for instance, thought that a drop in real wages encouraged women and children 'to quit their homes, or to engage in some species of employment'.[14] In the mid-1960s, Becker developed an economic model which he called 'the household production function' which regards the household as a unit of active production as well as passive consumption.[15] Becker argued that there was little economic difference between work done inside or outside of the household and that the well-being of households was maximised by the optimum allocation of the time and labour power of family members based upon decisions made largely within the household.[16] Tasks carried out by children within the home such as childminding, cooking and cleaning, for example, were very important in permitting a reallocation of the time of mothers and older siblings to work in the wider labour market. McKendrick has argued that rising earning capacity among women and children actually led to rising consumer demand and resulted in increased economic growth during early industrialisation; and, more recently, de Vries has suggested that the 'Industrial Revolution' so beloved of economic historians might be re-named an 'industrious revolution' to take account of fundamental changes in the organisation of time and labour among household members.[17] The labour strategies of families also mirrored profound macro-economic changes of the period 1750–1870. Levine has argued that the demographic structure of early industrial society was inextricably linked with economic growth and that the flow of incomes within families responded to changes in demand in the wider labour market.[18] Factors as diverse as variations in soils, access to markets, raw materials supplies, wage levels and technological innovation in industry also influenced levels of child and female employment across the labour market.[19]

Despite the wealth of studies of the household economy, few historians have chosen to investigate the long-term relationship between social and economic change and the child labour market. Research into individual employment sectors (lace-making, straw-plaiting, agriculture, textiles, potteries and mining, and the changing labour contract for apprentices and servants) have demonstrated the enormous potential for comparative approaches to child labour.[20] The major problem for historians, however, remains the provision of a general explanation of how Britain was transformed between 1750 and 1870 from a society employing large numbers of children to one in which children remained employable only at the margins of the economy.[21] This book provides a discussion of how historians have approached that fundamental problem. A further priority is an investigation of the universal transition from the extreme dependency of childhood to the relative economic independence of early adulthood. Very few children below 10 were ever engaged in productive labour whereas the vast majority of people had embarked upon a life of labour by the age of 16.[22] Hence, the focus of this study is upon the numerically important group of child workers aged 10 to 15 and upon how the transition from dependency to work changed over time and under different forms of economic development.

Children's employment was a fundamental aspect of the interaction between households and the labour market, and each of the chapters investigates a major question arising from that process. First, what are the sources of knowledge about child labour in the past and what problems exist in the interpretation of evidence? Second, why did so many working-class families rely upon the labour of their children? Third, how did changes in the structure and location of the workplace influence the types of work available to children? Finally, how did the state respond to children's employment? The present study does not seek to contribute significantly to the debate about the ethics of children's employment in the past (though many of the debates are addressed in the various chapters). Instead, this book offers a broad empirical analysis of how the work of children was integrated with the major economic and occupational transformations of eighteenth- and nineteenth-century Britain.

Notes

1. B. L. Hutchins and A. Harrison, *A History of Factory Legislation*, 3rd edn (1926). See also A. H. Robson, *The Education of Children Engaged in Industry in England, 1833–1876* (London, 1931) and M. W. Thomas, *The Early Factory Legislation: A Study in Legislative and Administrative Evolution* (London, 1948). J. L. Hammond and B. Hammond, *The Town Labourer, 1760–1832: The New Civilisation* (London, 1966), p. 145.
2. E. P. Thompson, *The Making of the English Working Class* (Harmondsworth, 1968), p. 384; though Thompson (p. 367) also admitted that 'Child labour was not new. The child was an intrinsic part of the agricultural and industrial economy before 1780 . . . The most prevalent form of child labour was in the home or within the family economy.' B. Inglis, *Poverty and the Industrial Revolution* (London, 1972), p. 30.
3. J. Walvin, *A Child's World: A Social History of English Childhood, 1800–1914* (Harmondsworth, 1982), p. 64. Walvin's chief source was a collection of brief extracts from E. Royston Pike, *Human Documents of the Industrial Revolution* (London, 1966).
4. Agriculture formed the single largest employer of boy labour at the time of the Great Exhibition but the Hammonds devoted 46 pages of *The Town Labourer* (1917) to child miners, chimney-sweeps and factory workers, whereas their *Village Labourer, 1760–1832: A Study of the Government of England Before the Reform Bill* (London, 1911) contained only a single index entry for agricultural children.
5. W. H. Chaloner, 'New Introduction' to W. Dodd, *The Factory System Illustrated: In a Series of Letters to the Rt Hon. Lord Shaftesbury* (London, 1968), p. vi.
6. R. M. Hartwell, *The Industrial Revolution and Economic Growth* (London, 1971), p. 392.
7. Davin has argued that it was 'easy to accept uncritically what we were all taught at school: in the bad old days there was child labour, but through heroic campaigning by humane and farsighted leaders . . . successive reforms during the course of the

[nineteenth] century eliminated this barbarism and civilized ideas came to prevail . . . it is important to confront and put aside this set of assumptions if we are to conduct an historical . . . examination of questions relating to family and labour': A. Davin, 'Child Labour, the Working-Class Family and Domestic Ideology in Nineteenth-Century Britain', *Development and Change*, 13 (1982), p. 650.

8. S. Pollard, *Peaceful Conquest* (Oxford, 1981); J. Langton, 'The Industrial Revolution and the Regional Geography of England', *Transactions of the Institute of British Geographers*, 9 (1984); P. Hudson, *The Industrial Revolution* (London, 1992); E. A. Wrigley, *Continuity, Chance and Change: The Character of the Industrial Revolution in England* (Cambridge, 1988).

9. O. Saito, 'Labour Supply Behaviour of the Poor in the English Industrial Revolution', *Journal of European Economic History*, 10 (1981); J. S. Lyons, 'Family Response to Economic Decline: Handloom Weavers in Early Nineteenth-Century Lancashire', *Research in Economic History*, 10 (1981).

10. B. R. Mitchell, *British Historical Statistics* (Cambridge, 1988), p. 15; M. Anderson, 'The Social Implications of Demographic Change' in F. M. L. Thompson (ed.) *The Cambridge Social History of Britain, 1750–1950* (Cambridge, 1990), vol. 2, p. 47; D. C. Coleman, 'Labour in the English Economy of the Seventeenth Century', *Economic History Review*, 2nd ser., 8 (1955–56), p. 286; E. A. Wrigley and R. S. Schofield, *The Population History of England, 1541–1871* (Cambridge, 1981), table A3.1, pp. 528–9.

11. M. Anderson, *Family Structure in Nineteenth-Century Lancashire* (Cambridge, 1971); A. Kussmaul, *Servants in Husbandry in Early Modern England* (Cambridge, 1981); K. D. M. Snell, *Annals of the Labouring Poor: Social Change and Agrarian England, 1660–1900* (Cambridge, 1985); M. W. Dupree, *Family Structure in the Staffordshire Potteries, 1840–1880* (Oxford, 1995); see also M. Berg, *The Age of Manufactures* (London, 1985); J. D. Holley, 'The Two Family Economies of Industrialism: Factory Workers in Victorian Scotland', *Journal of Family History*, 6 (1981); D. Levine, 'The Demographic Implications of Rural Industrialisation: A Family Reconstitution Study of Shepshed, Leicestershire, 1600–1851', *Social History*, 1 (1976). Notable earlier studies of the household economy include F. Collier, *The Family Economy of the Working Classes in the Cotton Industry, 1784–1833*, ed. R. S. Fitton (Manchester, 1964); I. Pinchbeck, *Women Workers and the Industrial Revolution, 1750–1850* (London, 1930); M. Hewitt, *Wives and Mothers in Victorian England* (London, 1958); N. J. Smelser, *Social Change in the Industrial Revolution* (London, 1959).

12. C. Shammas, 'Food Expenditures and Economic Well-Being in Early Modern England', *Journal of Economic History*, 43 (1983); S. Horrell and J. Humphries, 'Old Questions, New Data, and Alternative Perspectives: Families' Living Standards in the Industrial Revolution', *Journal of Economic History*, 52 (1992); S. Horrell, and J. Humphries, '"The Exploitation of Little Children": Child Labour and the Family Economy in the Industrial Revolution', *Explorations in Economic History*, 32 (1995); R. Wall, 'The Age at Leaving Home', *Journal of Family History*, 3 (1978); R. Wall, 'Leaving Home and the Process of Household Formation in Pre-Industrial England', *Continuity and Change*, 2 (1987).

13. D. C. Coleman, *The Economy of England, 1450–1750* (Oxford, 1977), p. 19. William Pitt stressed 'the advantage of early employing them in such branches of manufactures as they were capable to execute . . . If anyone would take the

trouble to compute the amount of all [children's] earnings...he would be surprised, when he came to consider the weight which their support...took off the country'. Jonas Hanway, the noted philanthropist and campaigner on behalf of climbing boys, urged that the children of the poor should be put to service at ten or eleven years, for 'where young people are not early in servitude, under the eye of a good master...they had better be dead than in idleness or vice': I. Pinchbeck and M. Hewitt, *Children in English Society* (2 vols, London, 1969; 1973), vol. 2, p. 390; Snell, *Annals*, p. 332; see also H. Cunningham, 'The Employment and Unemployment of Children in England c.1680–1851', *Past and Present*, 126 (1990).

14. Quoted in Saito, 'Labour Supply Behaviour', p. 634. It is probable that changes in the production of goods and services between 1750 and 1870 were the most important factors bearing upon the secular decline of child labour.

15. G. S. Becker, 'A Theory of the Allocation of Time', *Economic Journal*, 75 (Sept. 1965), pp. 493–517; G. S. Becker, *A Treatise on the Family* (Cambridge, MA, 1981).

16. Nardinelli has more recently attempted to apply this model to the historical study of child employment: C. Nardinelli, *Child Labor and the Industrial Revolution* (Bloomington, IN, 1990), pp. 36–45.

17. N. McKendrick, 'Home Demand and Economic Growth: A New View of the Role of Women and Children in the Industrial Revolution' in *idem* (ed.) *Historical Perspectives: Studies in English Thought and Society* (London, 1974); de Vries, 'The Industrial Revolution and the Industrious Revolution', *Journal of Economic History*, 54 (1994), pp. 249–70.

18. D. Levine, 'Industrialisation and the Proletarian Family in England', *Past and Present*, 107 (1985). See also F. Mendels, 'Proto-Industrialisation: The First Phase of the Process of Industrialisation', *Journal of Economic History*, 32 (1972); H. Medick, 'The Proto-Industrial Family Economy: The Structural Function of Household and Family during the Transition from Peasant to Industrial Capitalism', *Social History*, 1 (1976). Dupree has argued that 'Family employment patterns are the result of employers' demand for labour combined with family decisions as to which members supply labour inside and outside the home': Dupree, *Family Structure*, pp. 150–1.

19. K. D. M. Snell, 'Agricultural Seasonal Unemployment, the Standard of Living, and Women's Work in the South and East, 1690–1860' *Economic History Review*, 2nd ser., 34 (1981); P. Kirby, 'The Historic Viability of Child Labour and the Mines Act of 1842' in M. Lavalette (ed.) *A Thing of the Past? Child Labour in Britain in the Nineteenth and Twentieth Centuries* (Liverpool, 1999). Nardinelli has argued that rising real wages and changes in production technology greatly reduced household dependence upon child labour during the early- to mid-nineteenth century: C. Nardinelli, 'Child Labor and the Factory Acts', *Journal of Economic History*, 40 (1980).

20. P. Horn, 'Pillow Lace-Making in Victorian England: The Experience of Oxfordshire', *Textile History*, 3 (1972); P. Horn, 'Pillow Lace and Straw Plait Trades of Victorian Buckinghamshire and Bedfordshire', *Historical Journal*, 17 (1974); H. V. Speechley, 'Female and Child Agricultural Day Labourers in Somerset, c.1685–1870', PhD thesis (Exeter, 1999); Nardinelli, 'Child Labor and the Factory Acts'; Dupree, *Family Structure*; Kirby, 'Viability of Child Labour'; D. Simonton, 'Apprenticeship: Training and Gender in Eighteenth-Century England' in

M. Berg (ed.) *Markets and Manufacture in Early Industrial Europe* (London, 1991); K. D. M. Snell, 'The Apprenticeship System in British History: The Fragmentation of a Cultural Institution', *History of Education*, 25 (1996). Traditional approaches to industrial child labour continue, however: see for example C. Tuttle, *Hard at Work in Factories and Mines: The Economics of Child Labour During the British Industrial Revolution* (Boulder, CO, 1999), and P. Bolin-Hort, *Work, Family and the State: Child Labour and the Organisation of Production in the British Cotton Industry, 1780–1920* (Lund, 1989). One historian has offered the novel suggestion that there was widespread 'unemployment' among children in British society from the early modern period to the mid-nineteenth century: Cunningham, 'Employment and Unemployment'; see also P. Kirby, 'How Many Children were "Unemployed" in Eighteenth- and Nineteenth-Century England?', *Past and Present* (forthcoming).

21. Some attempt has been made recently to develop such questions, notably H. Cunningham, 'The Decline of Child Labour: Labour Markets and Family Economies in Europe and North America Since 1830', *Economic History Review*, 2nd ser., 53 (2000).

22. Or, as Laslett put it, 'the point at which offspring begin to be as big in body and as strong as those who gave them birth': P. Laslett, *Family Life and Illicit Love in Earlier Generations* (London, 1977), p. 214.

Chapter 1: *Sources for the History of Child Labour*

Any study of child labour in history must begin with an assessment of the limitations of the primary evidence upon which our knowledge is based. In recent decades, historians have shown how the norms and values of dominant social groups in the past influenced the collection and reporting of vital statistics.[1] The mere survival of an historical source provides no assurance that its subjects were typical of a wider population, and even the most prodigious of sources provide only a partial picture of the composition of past society. Large-scale social surveys such as the nineteenth-century censuses, for example, were largely accurate in their recording of the occupations of adult heads of households, but they were much less precise in recording the work of wives and children. Major government reports into child labour were also uneven in their coverage, focusing predominantly upon children in industrial occupations. The early social inquiries treated child labour as a 'social problem' and their function was to investigate the plight of groups of children who were deemed at risk of exploitation, violence or poverty.[2] As a consequence, the work of hundreds of thousands of children in agriculture, in small workshops, in domestic service or in casual and seasonal occupations escaped detailed scrutiny. The stark absence in historic sources of children engaged in the broad category of 'servant' (who, as Laslett observed, formed the largest child occupation group in the early modern period) demonstrates clearly the problems encountered in

9

dealing with a spatially disparate and subordinate group of workers.[3] Children who worked in the remote and informal farm service sector appear only fleetingly in Poor Law records or in general surveys of agriculture. Moreover, a majority of young female servants were employed as solitary 'maids-of-all-work' in small households that had no tradition of keeping formal accounts. Hence, although agricultural workers and domestic servants constituted the largest groups of child workers in the past, they have left behind the least evidence. The wide range of domestic tasks undertaken by young females in the home (cooking, cleaning and child-minding) are also poorly represented. Their work was not regarded as an 'occupation' by the General Register Office and thus remains one of the most poorly recorded features of social history.[4] The work of young children in important ancillary tasks such as carrying tools, cleaning under machinery, fetching wood and water, making tea, stoking stoves, carding and spinning, carrying outwork pieces and fetching their fathers' dinners, also remain largely invisible in census and other official listings.

To the problems presented by the irregular survival of evidence might be added the great variety of definitions of a 'child' in the past. Eighteenth- and nineteenth-century social commentators were by no means consistent in their use of the term and this reflects, in part, the persistence of diverse historic customs attaching to the child labour market.[5] Apprenticeships, for example, tended to commence at 14, but most apprentices were not thought of as 'adult' workers until they had emerged from their terms aged between 21 and 24. Similarly, agricultural servants lost their 'juvenile' status at around 16 but did not receive an adult income until they were about 20.[6] More generally, in agrarian society, people were not regarded as fully 'grown up' until they were married, by which time most of them had been absent from the parental home and occupied for many years.[7] A further conceptual difficulty for the historian is that childhood itself was of longer duration in the past. Eighteenth- and early nineteenth-century children achieved biological maturity about two years later than modern children and this almost certainly influenced contemporary understanding of the stages of child development.[8] Such perceptions were important, since the achievement of physical maturity seems to have been a crucial influence upon the entry of children to the labour market. In traditional society, puberty, leaving home and starting work were often regarded as more or less coincident events in the lives of children.[9] Hence, the transition from dependency to working life formed part of a major life-cycle change.

Quantitative Sources

Perhaps the single most serious obstacle to the historian of child labour is the paucity of reliable quantitative evidence. It was not until 1841 that census enumerators were required to record the occupations of individuals. Prior to this, the major demographic sources are largely silent in respect of children's work.[10] Even in 1841, the census abstracts do not provide an accurate count of child workers, affording only aggregate occupation statistics for the age-groups '20 years of age and upward' and 'Under 20 years of age'. Moreover, the enumerators of 1841 were instructed that the 'profession &c. of wives, or of sons or daughters living with and assisting their parents but not apprenticed or receiving wages, need not be inserted'.[11] This certainly led to widespread under-recording of the resident working kin of farmers and probably of children engaged in home-based manufactures. Such under-recording of children's occupations in the 1841 census has been confirmed in research undertaken at district level into the mining and pin-making industries.[12] The earlier censuses were far less detailed in their coverage of occupations. The employment tables contained in the 1831 census, for example, related almost entirely to persons aged over 20, and the censuses of 1801, 1811 and 1821 provided no systematic enumeration of children's work.[13]

The first moderately reliable national survey of occupations took place at the census of 1851 when just under 2 per cent of children aged five to nine and nearly 30 per cent of children aged 10–14 were recorded as having an occupation. However, the census is thought to have seriously underestimated the numbers of working females and children. The work of girls, in particular, was under-represented.[14] In England and Wales, 40 per cent of the enumerated male population aged between 10 and 14 had an occupation as against only 23 per cent of females. In Scotland, 33 per cent of 10–14-year-old males had a recorded occupation compared with only 24 per cent of females. This shortfall in the enumeration of the occupations of female children can almost certainly be explained by the tendency of more females to work in the domestic sphere.[15] The proportions of working children declined at each enumeration subsequent to 1851. In 1871, the figures for children occupied at ages five to nine and 10–14 were 0.7 and 26.4 per cent, respectively.[16] Indeed, the employment of very young children in mid-nineteenth-century society appears to have been exceptional, and by 1881 the census had ceased to count the numbers of occupied children aged below 10 on the grounds that their numbers had become insignificant to general employment statistics.[17]

Agricultural occupations (the single largest employer of child labour) posed serious problems for census enumerators. It has been suggested that between one- and two-thirds of farm servants were omitted from the census of 1831 and Speechley has shown that the occupations of large numbers of children entered in farm wage books in 1851 remained unrecorded in the census schedules.[18] Springtime enumerations also failed to count the many thousands of rural children engaged at harvest-time.[19] Indeed, the census was timed 'expressly to avoid the movements of the population during summer and the harvest season'.[20] Moreover, some agricultural or handicraft jobs remained so marginal that they were to all intents and purposes 'statistically invisible'.[21] In addition, many young agricultural and domestic servants lived in the households of their employers, and distinctions between their various 'indoor' and 'outdoor' roles proved problematical for the census takers.[22] Research by Anderson has shown, for example, that around a quarter of female general servants worked in the households of farmers and it is thought that about half of these worked in some capacity in agriculture.[23] In 1831, the progenitor of the modern census, John Rickman, voiced doubts about 'whether a Female hired by an Occupier of land, and resident in his family is to be deemed a Household Servant, or an Agricultural Servant.'[24] It was Rickman's view that such females should be accorded the occupation 'household servant'. It is doubtful, however, whether the enumerators employed such fine distinctions in the collection of their data, and youthful female servants continued to be recorded 'through-out the returns as house servants, maid servants, maids of all work, and under a dozen or more other names and grades down to plain "servant"'.[25] Other omissions from official listings were even more substantial. For example, the entire population of farmers' working children aged below 15 were omitted from the 1851 summary occupation tables.[26] Even at the very end of the period under discussion, therefore, national statistics of the child labour force tended to under-represent the incidence of child labour in society. The evidence for the eighteenth century, moreover, is too sparse to allow the compilation of national statistics of child labour.[27]

Early social surveys were also affected by a reluctance on the part of many parents to supply information about their children's occupations. Such reticence may have arisen simply from irrational or unfounded fears associated with the inquiries of middle-class investigators. In one case, a survey by the Statistical Society conducted in Wales shortly before Christmas in 1840 was seriously disrupted by a rumour (spread allegedly by local Chartists) that the inquirers intended to kill all the young children or to recruit them into the army.[28] Parents may also have structured the information they provided to some perceived advantage – to escape restrictive child labour laws, or to conceal the employment of their children from Poor Law authorities.[29] There is little evidence of improvement in the enumeration of children's occupations in the later nineteenth-century censuses.[30] However, as employment moved away from the domestic sphere, problems associated with the classification of children's occupations may have declined for both enumerators and parents. The emergence of compulsory education at the end of the nineteenth century probably provided some short-term inducement for parents to conceal the employment of their children but by that time employment opportunities for children of school age had fallen to very low levels.

Government Reports and Reports of Inspectors

In addition to the national counts of population, the state conducted a number of investigations into child labour in discrete industrial sectors. The reports and evidence of these inquiries survive in the printed parliamentary papers (or 'blue books'). Among the best known are the Factory Commission of 1833 and the Children's Employment Commission of 1842. However, numerous other reports survive from royal commissions, select committees and various *ad hoc* inquiries.[31] State reports contain many thousands of pages of evidence with direct relevance to the history of child employment. Moreover, the minutes of evidence appended to many of the reports contain voluminous first-hand testimony of working-class children together with valuable insights into their work environments.

The earliest state inquiries were conducted on a very small scale and dealt mainly with occupations that were thought to be harmful to children or to society at large. The 1819 Lords report and the oft-quoted Sadler Committee of 1831–32, for example, together took evidence from only about a hundred factory workers.[32] Moreover, many of the state commissioners harboured strong opinions about the problems affecting the working classes and so permitted their own values and beliefs to colour their reports. Often, the same people would be engaged on successive commissions and this led to the continuation of strategies and assumptions from one inquiry to the next.[33] The gathering of quantitative evidence was also defective in that many of the statistics that appear in the final reports were drawn from questionnaire returns completed by employers whose workplaces were never formally inspected.[34]

A further consequence of increasing state scrutiny of child labour during the nineteenth century was the establishment of inspectorates to deal with the implementation of industrial legislation. The factory inspectors appointed from 1833 collected statistics of child labour and produced frequent reports. However, a stringent budget forced inspectors to rely for their information predominantly upon larger urban manufacturers who were usually more co-operative and generally supportive of the regulation of child labour.[35] Smaller employers operating at the margin in more remote areas (who often employed larger proportions of children) tended to escape inspection. The statistics of industrially employed children were also affected by difficulties over who was legally responsible for employing children. Some children who were employed directly by factory operatives were deemed not to be in the employ of factory owners and were thereby frequently excluded from the inspectors' returns.[36] Even in industries carried out on a large scale and subject to greatest scrutiny, therefore, there is considerable doubt about the reliability of statistical evidence.[37] The inspection of coal mines was carried out on an even more limited scale. Although a Mines Act was passed in 1842, only one inspector was appointed for the entire country and inspection was hampered by a serious shortage of funds. After 1850, mines inspection was placed upon a more formal footing but the priority of the inspectors from the mid-century shifted towards the investigation of pit accidents rather than the collection of statistics relating to child labour.[38]

Articles in periodicals such as the *Westminster Review, Blackwoods, The Edinburgh Review, The Gentleman's Magazine* and *The Quarterly Review* often reported and analysed the findings of official inquiries; and from 1838, the *Journal of the Statistical Society* published articles relating to the child labour force and education. Other sub-national statistical evidence can be gathered from the surviving records of national and local non-governmental charitable organisations such as Dr Barnardo's or the Ragged School Movement which frequently sought to find work for orphaned or destitute children.

Health Records

The factory reform lobby of the 1830s and 40s placed great emphasis upon the health problems that were supposed to have arisen from industrial production. Deformities reported by former operatives such as William Dodd (the famous 'factory cripple') were held to have arisen from children standing for long periods whilst operating textiles machinery.[39] However, surprisingly little statistical evidence exists before the last quarter of the nineteenth century to allow comparisons to be made between groups of employed and non-employed children. General medical inspections were not introduced into factories until 1867 and medical examinations were not extended effectively to work-shops until 1906.[40] Moreover, no comprehensive surveys of children's health were carried out prior to the establishment of the School Medical Inspection Service in 1907.[41] Evidence of children's occupational health contained in early parliamentary reports can also be highly misleading since it often emerged from politically charged campaigns for reform. The nine doctors who gave evidence on occupational health to Peel's Factory Committee of 1816, for example, provided little more than 'a mass of abstract opinions' and six of them admitted to having never visited a factory.[42] Moreover, the 'full and leading questions put to London medical witnesses' before the Sadler Committee of 1831–32 'tended to limit their responses to mere affirmations'.[43] The identification of occupational ill-health among children is probably impossible to isolate against the very high background levels of urban illness and mortality in eighteenth- and early nineteenth-century Britain. It is probably safe to assert, however, that excessive infant and child illness and mortality recorded in industrial towns resulted overwhelmingly from environmental, rather than occupational, causes. As Chadwick noted of Manchester in 1842: 'opinion is erroneous which ascribes greater sickness and mortality to the children employed in factories than amongst the children who remain in such homes as these towns afford to the labouring classes ... more than 57 per cent die before they attain five years of age; that is, before they can be engaged in factory labour, or in any other labour whatsoever'.[44] Indeed, where statistical evidence has survived, it has proved ambiguous about the effects of occupations upon children's health. Studies of children's heights have shown that differences in stature are evident between different occupations but that these were much less significant than the variations that existed between rural and urban environments.[45] Public health records also tended to record only cases of death rather than illness and did not produce any useful figures linking occupations with ill-health. The absence of civil registration prior to 1837 prevents the historian from developing anything more than an impressionistic view of the effects of occupations upon children's health.

Business Accounts

Another unsatisfactory aspect of the historical record is the sparseness of evidence relating to children's daily work and pay. Business wage books sometimes contain lists of working children and evidence of their occupations and, more rarely, show the hours and days of the week upon which children worked.[46] Such records, however, seem to have had only short-term importance to firms and it is likely that many were destroyed when they had outlived their immediate usefulness. The failure of such evidence to survive has rendered it extremely difficult to estimate the extent to which changes in the composition of households (the death of a breadwinner, for example, or the departure from the home of an older, working, child) affected the day-to-day labour-force participation of children.[47] Most of the evidence of wage payments that has survived relates to the earnings of adults and provides scant information about the contributions of younger household members. Children's wages were often included in the pay of parents or older siblings and almost invariably went unrecorded in pay records. In addition, many rural workers received part of their remuneration in the form of money wages and part 'in-kind' in the form of housing, farm produce, fuel and other consumables.[48] For many employed children, payment in kind could constitute the whole of their income. Child agricultural servants, for instance, were sometimes paid no wages at all, the masters undertaking merely to maintain them within their households until they became old enough to become productive workers.[49]

Household Accounts

At various times during the eighteenth and nineteenth centuries, social investigators collected working-class household accounts in order to demonstrate the earnings and expenditure patterns of families. These accounts have been used by historians to estimate the welfare of members of families who were not household heads.[50] The surviving accounts are intrinsically interesting in the information they supply about family consumption and income. Moreover, they survive for periods when other evidence is sparse. One of their major drawbacks, however, is that they are often highly unrepresentative of the population at large. This is a problem that remains even after 'weighting' of the evidence to render the sample more representative of the national occupation structure because the poorest families in any occupation group are more likely to have been targeted by social inquirers eager to present the most pessimistic case to their readers.[51] Poorer households tended to rely disproportionately upon the incomes of children and thus their household accounts show a higher incidence of child labour.[52] In fact, the amount of detail in surviving household accounts is surprisingly small. Only 35 per cent of a sample of accounts collected by the most recent researchers in the field actually record the sex of children.[53] More seriously, the accounts reveal very little about the jobs that children actually did and this has led to their occupations being inferred from that of their fathers. Moreover, the accounts contain virtually no evidence of the ages at which children started work or left home.[54] Hence, the finding that children in industrial households seemed to work more than those in agriculture might be explained by the simple fact that children in urban and industrial areas tended to leave home much later than agriculturalists and were therefore much more likely to have a job whilst still resident in the parental home. Furthermore, when the accounts are broken down by fathers' occupations and by age-groups, they produce sample sizes (sometimes single figures) that are far too small to provide meaningful averages. This means that differential demand for child labour between sectors cannot be measured with accuracy using these sources.[55]

Apprenticeship and Service

Where the relationship between child workers and masters existed on a statutory footing, the keeping of official records was often a requirement. In principle, the hiring of any servant was bounded by the Statute of Artificers of 1563 and the annual statute sessions usually formed the legal occasion of hiring. However, few records have survived from the statute or 'hiring' fairs.[56] Research into settlement examinations has revealed the seasonality of agricultural labour and the geographical mobility of young farm servants, but the surviving records do not permit reliable estimates of the numbers of child agricultural or domestic servants for periods prior to the mid-nineteenth century. The most important surviving statutory records are the apprenticeship registers (now held in the Public Record Office) which were kept from the early eighteenth century. Since the registers were kept for taxation purposes, they suffer from attempts by masters to evade registration. However, the returns from several English counties do provide a large amount of evidence of the ages, terms of employment and the trades to which apprentices were bound.[57] Moreover, records of court proceedings arising from violations of indentures provide further evidence of the social conditions of apprentices and highlight ill-treatment and neglect as well as the difficulties faced by masters and apprentices in declining trades.[58] In contrast to skilled craft apprentices, the binding of children to unskilled occupations was often an informal matter and was rarely marked by a written record, though indentures and papers relating to the binding of pauper children by Poor Law overseers may often be found in parish chest collections.[59] By the nineteenth century, the statistical evidence relating to apprenticeships in general became 'extremely inexact'.[60] The problems of studying nineteenth-century apprentices arise partly from the structure of the census (whose emphasis moved away from traditional handicraft designations and towards an increasingly polarised distinction between 'employer' and 'employed'[61]) and partly from a progressive decline in the popularity of formal apprenticeships during the later eighteenth century which contributed to its abolition in 1814 as a statutory requirement for practising skilled trades.

Non-Quantitative Sources

Among the more important non-quantitative sources on the lives of working children are the autobiographies and diaries of the working class.[62] Autobiographers commonly provided a special place in their accounts for their childhood experiences and, from these, historians have learned much about ubiquitous child jobs such as bird-scaring, child-minding and domestic work that were not recorded in official statistics. One drawback is that the autobiographers were predominantly male (only half a dozen autobiographies by working-class women have been discovered from the first half of the nineteenth century).[63] Another drawback is that autobiographies and diaries supply information only about a small, literate, minority of society.[64] Although autobiographies do not contribute to a quantitative understanding of the child labour force, however, they do provide unparalleled glimpses into many of the private aspects of family life and labour.

In contrast to autobiographical accounts, nineteenth-century novels form an extremely poor source of information about the lives of working children. Many mid-nineteenth-century novelists were deeply influenced by the sentiments of the anti-child-labour campaigns and their works of fiction were bought and read chiefly as a means of affirming middle-class concerns about social problems. As Neff observed, 'By 1850 fiction was in a harness of moral obligation.'[65] The majority of fictional works about child labour, therefore, exaggerated both the scale and intensity of child labour and were focused upon a very narrow range of industrial child occupations. They were in the main written by individuals who had never actually visited factories or mines and who drew heavily upon government reports to supply a context for their pessimistic narratives. Indeed, the high point in the production of novels dealing with the privations of industrial child workers occurred in the wake of the publication of the first major royal commissions on child labour. There is little hope of deriving much useful evidence about the general conditions of child labourers from such evidence, though such novels do provide a great deal of information about the beliefs and aims of their (mainly) middle-class authors.[66]

Despite such problems of bias and omission, it is possible to develop an equitable approach to the study of child labour in the past. Since the employment of children formed an integral part of the overall social and economic structure, such an approach requires the examination of a much wider range of demographic and labour market sources than those dealing solely with child employment.

Notes

1. M. Anderson, *Family Structure in Nineteenth-Century Lancashire* (Cambridge, 1971); M. Anderson, 'Households, Families and Individuals: Some Preliminary Results from the National Sample from the 1851 Census of Great Britain', *Continuity and Change*, 3 (1988); E. Higgs, *A Clearer Sense of the Census* (London, 1996); E. Higgs, 'Women, Occupations and Work in the Nineteenth-Century Censuses', *History Workshop*, 23 (1987); H. V. Speechley, 'Female and Child Agricultural Day Labourers in Somerset, c.1685–1870', PhD thesis (Exeter, 1999).
2. Chimney-sweepers' apprentices, for example, loom large in the popular historical imagination but were very small in number. Much of their high visibility resulted from the campaigning of Jonas Hanway in the eighteenth century and Lord Shaftesbury and Charles Kingsley in the nineteenth. See C. Kingsley, *The Water Babies*

(London, 1863). In 1841, the number of sweeps' apprentices aged below 10 in London was estimated by Mayhew to be 370 (at a time when London's population numbered 2.2 million). Hanway estimated that in 1785 there were 400 to 550 climbing boys in London, and an estimate from seven years later supposed their number to be 500: G. L. Phillips, *England's Climbing-Boys: A History of the Long Struggle to Abolish Child Labour in Chimney-Sweeping*, (Boston, MA, 1949), p. 3; B. R. Mitchell, *British Historical Statistics* (Cambridge, 1988), p. 25. According to the census of 1851, there were 1107 British chimney-sweeps aged below 15 in Britain: Parliamentary Papers (PP) 1852–53, LXXXVIII, pt.I, tables xxv, xxvi.

3. P. Laslett, *Family Life and Illicit Love in Earlier Generations* (London, 1977), p. 35.

4. A. Davin, 'Working or Helping? London Working-Class Children in the Domestic Economy' in J. Smith, I. Wallerstein and H. Evers (eds) *Households in the World Economy* (London, 1984). The General Register Office was the government body responsible for the collection of social statistics.

5. Early nineteenth-century government inquiries attempted to establish definitions of 'childhood'. The Children's Employment Commission of 1842, for example, regarded those aged below 13 as children and adopted the term 'young persons' for those aged 13–18, and the factory inspectors adopted a similar classification for much of the nineteenth century: *Children's Employment Commission*, PP 1842, XV, 'Supplemental instructions to the Sub-Commissioners', p. 269; *Copy of Regulations issued by Leonard Horner, Esq., Inspector of Factories*, PP 1836, XLV, p. 4; D. T. Jenkins, 'The Factory Returns, 1850–1905', *Textile History*, 9 (1978), p. 59. A statute of 1903 defined a 'child' as a person 'under the age of fourteen years': *An Act to make better Provision for Regulating the Employment of Children*, 1903, 3 Edw. 7, c.45, s.13.

6. A. Kussmaul, *Servants in Husbandry in Early Modern England* (Cambridge, 1981), p. 37.

7. Laslett, *Family Life and Illicit Love*, p. 163. Speechley observes that 'In the social reality of the rural population in the eighteenth century, domestic status took precedence over actual age': Speechley, 'Female and Child Agricultural Labourers', p. 153.

8. J. M. Tanner, 'The Secular Trend toward Earlier Maturity', *Education and Physical Growth* (1961), pp. 113–19.

9. Laslett, *Family Life and Illicit Love*, p. 163.

10. Child occupations do not feature in baptismal or marriage registers and the low mortality rates of working-age children ensure their relative absence from burial registers. Where children's deaths were recorded in burial registers the entry often contains a reference to the occupation of the deceased child's father: P. H. Lindert, 'English Occupations, 1670–1811', *Journal of Economic History*, 40 (1980), esp. p. 691. Wall has used parish registers in conjunction with a small number of surviving household and occupation listings to establish the numbers and ages of children who were absent from the parental home and thereby to estimate ages at leaving home. R. Wall, 'The Age at Leaving Home', *Journal of Family History*, 3 (1978); R. Wall, 'Work, Welfare and the Family: An Illustration of the Adaptive Family Economy' in L. Bonfield, R. M. Smith and K. Wrightson (eds) *The World We Have Gained* (Oxford, 1986), p. 264.

11. Higgs, *Clearer Sense of the Census*, p. 103.

12. P. Kirby, 'Aspects of the Employment of Children in the British Coalmining Industry, 1800–1872', PhD thesis (Sheffield, 1995), app. C, pp. 313–17.

D. A. Gatley, *Child Workers in Victorian Warrington: The Report of the Children's Employment Commission into Child Labour* (Stoke, 1996), pp. 9, 11.

13. E. A. Wrigley, 'Men on the Land and Men in the Countryside: Employment in Agriculture in Early Nineteenth-Century England' in L. Bonfield, R. M. Smith and K. Wrightson (eds) *The World We Have Gained* (Oxford, 1986), p. 304.

14. M. Anderson, 'What Can the Mid-Victorian Censuses Tell Us About Married Women's Employment?', *Local Population Studies*, 62 (1999); P. Kirby, 'How Many Children were "Unemployed" in Eighteenth- and Nineteenth-Century England?', *Past and Present* (forthcoming).

15. H. Cunningham, 'The Employment and Unemployment of Children in England, c.1680–1851', *Past and Present*, 126 (1990), tables 3–4, pp. 144–5. Jordan argues that there was a consistent trend of unemployment among young females throughout the second half of the nineteenth century. However, since many more females were employed in the domestic sphere or in casual and part-time work, the census figures are probably simply misleading: E. Jordan, 'Female Unemployment in England and Wales, 1851–1911: An Examination of the Census Figures for 15–19-year-olds', *Social History*, 13 (1988), pp. 175–90.

16. A useful summary of census returns relating to county levels of child employment for the 1851 and 1871 censuses may be found in W. B. Stephens, *Education, Literacy and Society, 1830–70* (Manchester, 1987), app. B, pp. 318–19. Hair estimated that mid-way through the century, the occupied proportion of the five to nine age-group stood at 3.5 per cent and those in the 10–14 age-group at 30 per cent: P. E. H. Hair, 'Children in Society, 1850–1980' in T. Barker and M. Drake (eds) *Population and Society in Britain, 1850–1980* (London, 1982), p. 47. Cunningham suggests 2.04 per cent for the age-group five to nine: Cunningham, 'Employment and Unemployment', table 2, p. 142. Logically, most of the working children in the 10–14 age-group would be concentrated among the 13- and 14-year-olds.

17. Hair, 'Children in Society', p. 47.

18. A. Gritt, 'The Census and the Servant: A Reassessment of the Decline and Distribution of Farm Service in Early Nineteenth-Century England', *Economic History Review*, 2nd ser., 53 (2000), p. 89; Speechley, 'Female and Child Agricultural Labourers', pp. 28–32.

19. A royal commission observed in the 1860s that it was 'not at all uncommon for boys [in agricultural districts] to leave school in the spring and not return again till the late autumn'. *Commission on the Employment of Children, Young Persons and Women in Agriculture*, PP 1867–68, XVII, p. ix.

20. E. Higgs, *Making Sense of the Census* (London, 1989), p. 80; Higgs also notes (pp. 87, 89) that under-enumeration was 'most serious with respect to agricultural employment . . . published tables in the Census reports . . . underestimate the size of the agricultural workforce'.

21. R. Samuel, 'Village Labour', *Village Life and Labour* (London, 1975), p. 3.

22. Hair, 'Children in Society', pp. 49–50. B. Hill, *Servants: English Domestics in the Eighteenth Century* (Oxford, 1996), p. 11.

23. Anderson, 'Households, Families and Individuals', p. 427; E. Higgs, 'Occupational Censuses and the Agricultural Workforce in Victorian England and Wales', *Economic History Review*, 2nd ser., 48 (1995), p. 710. As Tillott remarked, 'it is hard to believe that female servants on farms were necessarily confined to domestic duties': P. M. Tillott, 'Sources of Inaccuracy in the 1851 and 1861 Censuses' in

E. A. Wrigley (ed.) *Nineteenth-Century Society: Essays in the Use of Quantitative Methods for the Study of Social Data* (Cambridge, 1972), p. 119.

24. Gritt, 'Census and the Servant', p. 87.

25. Tillott, 'Sources of Inaccuracy', p. 124. Hill suggests that the term 'domestic servant' may only have been invented in the nineteenth century for the first occupational censuses: B. Hill, *Servants*, p. 13.

26. Kirby, 'How Many Children were "Unemployed"?'

27. B. L. Hutchins and A. Harrison, *A History of Factory Legislation*, 3rd edn (1926; first published 1903), p. 5.

28. G. S. Kenrick, 'Statistics of the Population of the Parish of Trevethin... and... part of the District Recently Disturbed', *Journal of the Statistical Society*, 3 (1841), p. 368.

29. Kirby, 'Children in the British Coalmining Industry', pp. 91–2.

30. Higgs, *Making Sense of the Census*, p. 83.

31. Several useful guides exist to these valuable sources. For more general inquiries, the five-volume index to the Chadwick-Healy fiche collection of the complete nineteenth-century parliamentary papers offers the most comprehensive coverage: P. Cockton, *Subject Catalogue of the House of Commons Parliamentary Papers, 1801–1900*, 5 vols (Cambridge, 1988). The Irish University Press reprint collection of British parliamentary papers is very large (though not complete) and contains a sub-set of volumes containing some of the major state reports on children's employment. This sub-set is complemented by an extremely valuable and detailed *Index*. The factory and mines inspectorate papers survive in the Public Record Office (chiefly in PRO HO45 and HO46).

32. C. S. Paterson, 'From Fever to Digestive Disease: Approaches to the Problem of Factory Ill-Health in Britain, 1784–1833', PhD thesis (British Columbia, 1995), p. 13. The report of the Sadler inquiry, however, was described by Hutchins and Harrison as 'one of the most valuable collections of evidence on industrial conditions that we possess': Hutchins and Harrison, *History of Factory Legislation*, p. 34.

33. Many of the district sub-commissioners working on the 1842 Mines Commission, for example, at the same time collected evidence for the subsequent 1843 report on trades and manufactures.

34. Gatley, *Child Workers in Victorian Warrington*, p. 10; Kirby, 'Children in the British Coalmining Industry', pp. 120–1. Oddly, one of the limitations of the parliamentary reports after 1833 is their sheer size. Hutt warned that there was 'so voluminous a mass of material from the various commissions and committees that it would be possible to make out a case for almost any contention by a judicious selection of passages from them': W. A. Hutt, 'The Factory System of the Early Nineteenth Century' in F. A. Hayek (ed.) *Capitalism and the Historians* (London, 1954), p. 171, n. 26.

35. M. Sanderson, 'Education and the Factory in Industrial Lancashire, 1780–1840', *Economic History Review*, 2nd ser., 20 (1967), p. 278.

36. P. W. J. Bartrip, 'British Government Inspection, 1832–1875: Some Observations', *Historical Journal*, 25 (1982). Some inspectors regarded a mill containing several firms as a single business whilst others treated larger mills as if they comprised separate enterprises: D. T. Jenkins, 'The Validity of the Factory Returns, 1833–1850', *Textile History*, 4 (1973), pp. 28, 31.

37. Jenkins, 'Validity of the Factory Returns', p. 33.

38. P. Kirby, 'The Historic Viability of Child Labour and the Mines Act of 1842' in M. Lavalette (ed.) *A Thing of the Past? Child Labour in Britain in the Nineteenth and Twentieth Centuries* (Liverpool, 1999), p. 113; Bartrip, 'British Government Inspection'.

39. W. Dodd, *The Factory System Illustrated: In a Series of Letters to the Rt Hon. Lord Shaftesbury* (London, 1872), pp. 7–13.

40. F. Keeling, *Child Labour in the United Kingdom: A Study of the Development and Administration of the Law Relating to the Employment of Children* (London, 1914), pp. xi–xii.

41. Keeling, *Child Labour*, p. xii.

42. Hutt, 'Factory System', p. 167.

43. Paterson, 'Problem of Factory Ill-Health', p. 13. Gray cites the case of a medical man who argued that the Almighty would have provided children with stronger bones had He intended them to work in factories: R. Gray, 'The Languages of Factory Reform in Britain, *c.* 1830–1860' in P. Joyce (ed.) *The Historical Meanings of Work* (Cambridge, 1987), p. 148.

44. E. Chadwick, *Report on the Sanitary Condition of the Labouring Population of Great Britain*, ed. M. W. Flinn (Edinburgh, 1965), p. 223.

45. P. Kirby, 'Causes of Short Stature among Coalmining Children, 1823–1850', *Economic History Review*, 2nd ser., 48 (1995); P. Kirby, 'Height, Urbanisation and Living Standards in the North of England, 1822–1837', *Manchester Working Papers in Economic and Social History*, 35 (1996); J. Humphries, 'Short Stature among Coalmining Children: A Comment', *Economic History Review*, 2nd ser., 50 (1997); P. Kirby, 'Short Stature among Coalmining Children: A Rejoinder', *Economic History Review*, 2nd ser., 50 (1997).

46. Speechley has discovered valuable records of child labour in farm wage-books: Speechley, 'Female and Child Agricultural Labourers'.

47. Some attempts have been made to approach such questions: W. Lazonick, 'Industrial Relations and Technical Change: The Case of the Self-Acting Mule', *Cambridge Journal of Economics*, 3 (1979); P. Bolin-Hort, *Work, Family and the State: Child Labour and the Organisation of Production in the British Cotton Industry, 1780–1920* (Lund, 1989); Anderson, *Family Structure*; J. D. Holley, 'The Two Family Economies of Industrialism: Factory Workers in Victorian Scotland', *Journal of Family History*, 6 (1981); O. Saito, 'Labour Supply Behaviour of the Poor in the English Industrial Revolution', *Journal of European Economic History*, 10 (1981); Kirby, 'Viability of Child Labour'. It is extremely difficult to adduce firm evidence about how child labour strategies adopted by households were affected directly by fluctuations in labour-market demand. The author is presently conducting a study (ESRC project no. R000239222) 'Productivity and Household Economy in a Tyneside Mining Community, 1790–1870', which investigates the connections between household strategy and the workplace.

48. R. Mitchison, 'Scotland, 1750–1850' in F. L. Thompson (ed.) *The Cambridge Social History of Britain, 1750–1950* (Cambridge, 1990), vol. 1, p. 176.

49. Kussmaul, *Servants in Husbandry*, p. 37. A Taunton bobbin-net manufacturer told the Factory Commission in 1833 that parents would often ask him to take their children for no pay 'merely to keep them from contracting habits of idleness and mischief': *Factory Commission*, PP 1833, XX, p. 74. Evidence from trade union records is remarkably thin. Union membership (measured by the numbers of payers of union subscriptions) was quite low until the very end of the nineteenth century. Union records do not, therefore, reflect the typical working-class

experience. Where trade unions did resort to action in respect of child labour it was almost always in order to restrict entry to trades.

50. C. Shammas, 'Food Expenditures and Economic Well-Being in Early Modern England', *Journal of Economic History*, 43 (1983), pp. 89–100; S. Horrell and J. Humphries, 'Old Questions, New Data and Alternative Perspectives: Families Living Standards in the Industrial Revolution', *Journal of Economic History*, 52 (1992). Clapham observed that 'estimates of the welfare of the "labouring population" – industrial or agricultural – which are based only upon the earnings of the principal breadwinner are defective': J. H. Clapham, *Economic History of Modern Britain* (2 vols, Cambridge, 1950), vol. 1, p. 565.

51. Horrell and Humphries stress that it is 'not likely that the households sampled are representative of the population': S. Horrell and J. Humphries, '"The Exploitation of Little Children": Child Labor and the Family Economy in the Industrial Revolution', *Explorations in Economic History*, 32 (1995), pp. 488–9. The major sources of household accounts were often unambiguous inquiries into poverty. For example, D. Davies, *The Case of Labourers in Husbandry Stated and Considered* (London, 1795) contains sections on 'their distressed condition' and 'the principal causes of their growing distress and number'; see also Sir F. M. Eden, *The State of the Poor, or a History of the Labouring Classes in England* (3 vols, London, 1797).

52. Saito, 'Labour Supply Behaviour', p. 645; Anderson, 'Married Women's Employment', p. 26.

53. Horrell and Humphries, 'Exploitation of Little Children', p. 501. According to Armstrong, only 47 per cent of the budgets contained in two of the major sources employed (Davies, *Case of Labourers in Husbandry* and Eden, *State of the Poor*) contain evidence of the earnings of children: W. A. Armstrong, 'Rural Population Growth, Systems of Employment and Incomes' in G. E. Mingay (ed.) *The Agrarian History of England and Wales* (Cambridge, 1989), vol. 6, p. 715.

54. It is extremely difficult to derive ages at first participation from such evidence but on this see Horrell and Humphries, 'Exploitation of Little Children', pp. 488–9.

55. Horrell and Humphries, 'Exploitation of Little Children', tab. 4, p. 497. The surviving household accounts are similar in number to the surviving working-class autobiographies whose collectors counsel extreme caution against the assumption that they are representative of the working class as a whole: D. Vincent, *Bread, Knowledge and Freedom: A Study of Nineteenth-Century Working-Class Autobiography* (London, 1981), pp. 1–13. There has also been a failure to integrate the study of household accounts with a broader corpus of literature on child labour.

56. On the use of such sources see Kussmaul, *Servants in Husbandry*, and K. D. M. Snell, *Annals of the Labouring Poor: Social Change and Agrarian England, 1660–1900* (Cambridge, 1985).

57. The registers are most useful for the period before 1760, after which the information recorded became less detailed. For a detailed explanation of the structure of the evidence relating to apprenticeship see J. Lane, *Apprenticeship in England, 1600–1914* (London, 1996) and Snell, *Annals*, pp. 228–319.

58. M. D. George, *London Life in the Eighteenth Century* (Harmondsworth, 1966), app. 4, pp. 415–23.

59. Snell, *Annals*, pp. 270–319; Simonton, 'Training and Gender', pp. 232–4.

60. W. W. Knox, 'British Apprenticeship, 1800–1914', PhD thesis (Edinburgh, 1980), p. 5.
61. Higgs, *Clearer Sense of the Census*, pp. 107–8. Householders were asked to distinguish between apprentices and masters in their returns but the census occupation tables do not report such distinctions.
62. These have been collected and catalogued: J. Burnett, D. Vincent and D. Mayall, *The Autobiography of the Working Class: An Annotated Critical Bibliography, 1790–1945* (3 vols, Brighton, 1986–89); J. Burnett, *Destiny Obscure: Autobiographies of Childhood, Education and Family from the 1820s–1920s* (London, 1994); J. Burnett, *Useful Toil: Autobiographies of Working People from the 1820s to the 1920s* (Harmondsworth, 1977); Vincent, *Bread, Knowledge and Freedom*.
63. Vincent, *Bread, Knowledge and Freedom*, p. 8.
64. R. Wall, 'Leaving Home and the Process of Household Formation in Pre-Industrial England', *Continuity and Change*, 2 (1987), p. 77.
65. W. Neff, *Victorian Working Women* (London, 1929), p. 16.
66. See, for example, I. Kovacevic and S. B. Kanner, 'Blue Book into Novel: The Forgotten Industrial Fiction of Charlotte Elizabeth Tonna', *Nineteenth-Century Fiction*, 25 (1970); W. H. Chaloner, 'Mrs Trollope and the Early Factory System', *Victorian Studies*, 4 (1960) and the critique of Thomas Hardy's novels in Snell, *Annals*, pp. 374–410.

Chapter 2: The Social and Demographic Context of Child Labour

One of the most noticeable features of the social structure of eighteenth- and nineteenth century Britain was the presence of large numbers of children. Laslett remarked of early modern England, 'there were children everywhere; playing in the village street and fields when they were very small, hanging around the farmyards and getting in the way, until they had grown enough to be given child-sized jobs to do'.[1] During the eighteenth and early nineteenth centuries, the child population increased both in absolute numbers and as a proportion of the total population. In 1661, the proportion of the population aged below 15 stood at around 29 per cent, but by 1821 this figure had risen substantially to 39 per cent.[2] By the third decade of the nineteenth century, moreover, half the population was aged below 20.[3] Much of the general increase in population is attributable to a fall in the average age of marriage and an increasing popularity of marriage. The proportion of bachelors and spinsters in the population declined from about 25 per cent in 1701 to about 7 per cent in 1801.[4] This resulted in an increase in the number of families in British society and to a substantial growth in the birth-rate. Over the period 1750–1851 the population of England and Wales increased from 5.8 to 16.7 million and that of Scotland from 1.2 to 2.9 million.[5]

The increasingly youthful population of eighteenth- and early-nineteenth-century Britain was reflected in measurable increases in the burden of child dependency. Historical demographers use the concept of a 'dependency ratio' to describe the changing balance between

Table 2.1   Proportions of the child population by age-group: England and Wales, 1771–1981

	Age groups (%)		
Year	0–4	0–14	5–14
1771	13.06	33.69	20.63
1791	14.60	36.14	21.54
1811	14.98	37.96	22.98
1831	14.39	38.80	24.41
1851	13.53	36.01	22.48
1871	14.05	36.50	22.45
1891	12.25	35.07	22.82
1911	10.69	30.63	19.95
1931	7.48	23.83	16.34
1981	5.99	20.53	14.53

Source: England 1771–1871: E. A. Wrigley and R. S. Schofield, *The Population History of England, 1541–1871* (Cambridge, 1981), app. 3, back-projection results, table A3.1, pp. 528–9; England and Wales 1891–1931: B. R. Mitchell, *British Historical Statistics* (Cambridge, 1988), p. 15; 1981: D. Coleman, 'Population', *British Social Trends Since 1900*, ed. A. H. Halsey (London, 1988), table 2.42, p. 106.

'producers' and 'dependants' in a population. The ratio is expressed conventionally as the number of persons aged below 15 and above 59 (dependent group) against every thousand persons in the age-group 15–59 (producer group). This ratio rose substantially from the early modern period through to the beginning of the nineteenth century. In 1671 there were 624 dependants to every thousand producers whilst in 1826 the ratio had increased to 857 per thousand (in comparison, the dependency ratio at the census of 1981 was 550).[6] The rising burden of child dependency was felt most acutely by married couples with children. This can be demonstrated more clearly if the dependency ratio is expressed as the proportion of dependants in society aged below 15 compared with those aged 25–59 (the presumed 'core' of the married population).

Structured dependency among families with children rose dramatically in the century and a half after 1671, rising from 657 to 1120 dependants per thousand.[7] The steepest increases in dependency occurred during the classic 'Industrial Revolution' period between the 1750s and the

Table 2.2   English dependency ratios, 1671–1826

	Year	
	1671	*1826*
No. of persons below 15 and above 59 years per 1000 persons in age-group 15–59 years	624	857
No. of persons below 15 per 1000 persons in age-group 25–59 years	657	1120

Source: E. A. Wrigley and R. S. Schofield, *The Population History of England, 1541–1871* (Cambridge, 1981), app. 3, table A3.1, pp. 528–9, p. 450.

1820s, a period during which children are thought to have entered the labour market in larger numbers.[8]

Higher child dependency is only one factor encouraging the entry of more children to the labour market. The supply of child workers was also influenced by relative levels of household poverty. Poor families living close to a subsistence wage were often forced to draw on more diverse sources of income and had little choice over whether their children worked. Saito has discovered a strong correlation between high wages for male heads of household and low labour force participation of females and children.[9] As Anderson put it, parents 'who otherwise showed considerable affection for their children ... were yet forced by large families and low wages to send their children to work as soon as possible'.[10] The earnings of children were generally more significant to household income than those of wives and this appears to have been the case in both agriculture and industry. The marginal importance to the household economy of child incomes in two rural counties is demonstrated clearly in Table 2.3.[11]

Children were also more likely to be working if the head of the household was unskilled or if they lived in a family headed by a lone parent. This was especially the case where the head of household was female.[12] In Warrington, in 1841, 17 per cent of children aged five to 14 who lived in households headed by females were working, as against only 10 per cent of children in male-headed households.[13] In the Potteries, in 1861, 23 per cent of the children living with lone mothers worked, against an average figure for all families of 13 per cent.[14] The money earnings of lone-parent families were also much lower than the average. Families composed of widows and children in London in the late 1840s received

Table 2.3   Annual household income by family size, Norfolk and Suffolk, 1839

	No.	£	s.	d.
Single man	36	25	1	4 ½
Couple, no children	64	30	12	10 ½
Couple, two children above ten	92	40	10	1
Couple, three children above ten	44	45	11	9
Couple, four children above ten	17	50	11	10 ½

Source: W. A. Armstrong, 'Rural Population Growth, Systems of Employment and Incomes', *Agrarian History of England and Wales*, vol. 6, ed. G. E. Mingay (Cambridge, 1989), p. 716.

only 40 per cent of the earnings of married households.[15] Parental mortality was a further factor propelling children into work at early ages. About half of the children receiving 'indoor' relief (i.e. in a workhouse) during the nineteenth century had no parents or close relatives, and between the later eighteenth century and the middle of the nineteenth century, between 17 and 20 per cent of all children had lost at least one parent by the age of 15.[16] The balance of parental mortality was also weighted heavily towards fathers. By the mid-nineteenth century, there were two to three times as many widows as there were widowers.[17] Lone-parent households were more likely to be headed by a female and such households were more likely to find themselves in poverty. In Corfe Castle in 1790, 15 per cent of the widowed population were recipients of poor relief compared with only 4 per cent of married couples.[18] The marginal value of children's wages, therefore, was often crucial in raising incomes of such poor households above subsistence level.

Changes in Poor Law policy during the eighteenth and nineteenth centuries (though aimed specifically at removing relief from able-bodied adults) also had far-reaching effects upon the children of poor families.[19] In many southern and eastern parishes in the late eighteenth century, the wages of agricultural labourers with children were often below subsistence level and the 'Speenhamland' system of income support was introduced to stave off severe household poverty.[20] After 1834, however, the Poor Law Commission tried to remove the right of households to claim allowances based upon numbers of children in a family. In the absence of child allowances, the earnings of poor children attained much greater marginal importance in districts where this policy was applied most rigorously.[21] The Poor Law also increased the financial hardships of unmarried mothers by effectively removing their legal ability to obtain child maintenance from a non-resident father.[22] Changes in social policy affecting fatherless children were intensified by a mixture of demographic and labour market changes. A doubling in the ratio of illegitimate births in the six decades after 1750 coincided with a decline in the type of smaller farm that required young live-in servants. Hence, the ability of the rural labour market to absorb fatherless children declined at precisely the time when there were more of them about. It should also be remembered that the residual effects of high import tariffs on foodstuffs between the end of the French Wars and the 1840s had a more general effect of intensifying household poverty and, consequently, increasing the likelihood that children would be put to work.

The different stages of the family life-cycle also influenced the labour force participation of children.[23] The presence in a household of dependent children too young to work increased pressure upon its older children to enter paid employment. The *Report on Unemployed Hand-Loom Weavers* of 1841 described how marriage and the successive births of children intensified household poverty among depressed hand-loom weavers.

[T]he weaver almost invariably marries soon after he is out of his apprenticeship. But the improvement of comfort which marriage brings is of short duration; at the end of the first year, the birth of a child deprives him of his wife's earnings, and at the same time adds to his expenses. During several years his condition is impaired by his increasing family, but he is sustained by the hope, that the labour of his children will in time become productive. There is scarcely any period of the weaver's life where his difficulties are so great as about the ninth or tenth year after his marriage with a family of four, five, or six children, too young to labour; the care of the family occupies the whole of his wife's attention, she cannot possibly contribute a shilling to the income of the family, so that the whole must be fed by his hand alone.[24]

High dependency precluded expensive 'luxuries' such as literacy or schooling. As one mid-nineteenth-century school inspector observed, a lowly paid farm labourer 'supporting his family . . . on 10s. a week cannot be expected to keep the child at school if that child can earn 3s. a week'.[25]

As children grew older, they commanded higher incomes. Earnings remained small among the age-group 10–13 but rose markedly towards the ages of 15–17 when wages might approach 40–50 per cent of the incomes of adult males.[26]

Domestic industry, like small-scale agriculture, relied greatly upon the labour of wives and children, who were often forced to work for long hours and under poor conditions by male heads of household production units.[27] Family labour was widespread in the eighteenth century, especially in 'proto-industrial' districts. Among low-waged Leicestershire framework knitters of the 1840s, 50 per cent of households contained three or more earning members with only 18 per cent of families relying upon a single wage-earner.[28] However, the diversity of domestic production meant that each trade was affected in different ways by wider economic change. The profitability of some rural domestic industries fell during the later eighteenth century as competition from factory-produced goods increased.[29] In other sectors of rural industry, demand for specific products led to increasing concentrations of young children. Children drafted into the straw-plaiting 'schools' of Bedfordshire, Buckinghamshire and Hertfordshire, for example, worked for little or no wages whilst they learned the rudimentary skill of plaiting. Child plaiters aged eight to 13 earned only 18d (pence) per week after deducting the cost of their 'training'. Some young females could earn 3s (shillings) or 4s per week, but were forced to work between 12 and 14 hours per day.[30] These were very low wages compared with the already poor rates of pay for child workers.

Although poverty was a primary cause of children being employed at an early age, it would be unwise to conclude that child labour was always determined by economic distress. Children's employment benefited families doubly in respect of fluctuations in the trade cycle. During depressions, children's wages made up for shortfalls in adult incomes but, when trade was good and local adult labour in short supply, increases in the wage-rate for children might render child labour attractive to parents who might otherwise have objected to their children working. There is some evidence that parents in relatively well-paid working-class occupations often sought to have their children placed in the workplace at early ages to ensure a future continuity of employment. In 1841, the manager of a large Durham colliery noted that the coalminers were 'very anxious, and very dissatisfied if we do not take the children ... constant attempts are made to get the boys engaged to a work to which they are not competent from their years'.[31] The factory inspectors, too, complained frequently about parents' attempts to obtain fraudulent certificates of children's ages from certifying surgeons. Parents in the Potteries were vehemently against attempts to regulate child employment because of the potential loss of income posed by such measures.[32] McKendrick has suggested that opposition to the abolition of child labour was actually greatest in high-wage districts.[33] Employers and workers also seem to have recognised the need for an equitable distribution of work according to family need. In the coalmining districts of Scotland, south Wales and Lancashire, customs existed permitting miners to produce a larger share of output according to the number of children in the miner's household working under him. In order to count for an allowance a child 'was not required to work, only to attend during working hours'.[34] In agriculture, too, *ad hoc* arrangements ensured a fair distribution of work according to family need. The 1843 Poor Law Report on the Employment of Women and Children in Agriculture noted, of the agricultural labourer, 'If his employment be irregular and uncertain, he makes the most of the occasion which offers – and wife and child are called in, to add to the profits of the hour.'[35] Farmers in Suffolk objected 'to employing unmarried females, because it lessens the work for married women and their families'.[36] Such local 'welfare' agreements recognised the increasingly limited nature of Poor Law provision for children during the 1830s and 40s.

Leaving Home and Starting Work

One fundamental difference between the present and the past is the great difference in ages at which children left the parental home. Ages at leaving home cannot be judged with great accuracy for a population that did not have a systematic method of recording children's ages.[37] However, it seems clear that leaving home in eighteenth- and early-nineteenth-century Britain was rarely occasioned by marriage (the average age at marriage between 1750 and 1799 was 26.4 for men and 24.9 for women[38]) and a large majority of children, especially in rural areas, left home to enter work outwith the parental home. Agriculture was the major employer of eighteenth- and nineteenth-century children, and for most rural children their first contractual employment would be on a holding several miles from their home. This precluded them continuing to live with their parents. Between the seventeenth and nineteenth centuries, two-thirds to three-quarters of the population aged between 15 and 24 were engaged in some variety of agricultural service, living and working in the households of others.[39] Many agricultural children commenced work between 12 and 14 and this pattern of early employment is partly reflected in statistics of absence from the parental home. In parts of rural Bedfordshire and Berkshire during the last two decades of the eighteenth century and in Devon in the early 1840s, less than a third of children aged over 14 remained in the parental home.[40] However, the age at leaving home varied enormously: some children left before the age of 10 whilst others stayed on into adulthood.[41] There were also discernable differences in the ages at leaving between children in different social classes and occupation groups. The children of farmers and proto-industrialists remained at home longest whilst those of poor labourers left home earliest. In 1782 and 1841, 46 per cent of the children of skilled tradesmen and craftsmen resided in the parental home at ages over 14 compared with only 36 per cent of the children of proletarians (there was great variation in ages at leaving within the skilled trades, however, with children from households in declining trades such as framework knitting, wool-combing and hand-weaving leaving at ages comparable with those of poor labourers).[42]

There was also considerable variation in respect of regional location and gender. A majority of the seventeenth- and eighteenth-century rural listings examined by Wall show that girls were much more likely than boys to be retained in the parental household after the age of 15.[43] This reflected both the greater employment of females in domestic work and a decline in job opportunities for girls in agriculture. In the agrarian sector, gender differences in ages at leaving were greatest in arable areas and smallest in pastoral districts where the market for female child labour in dairying, domestic service and domestic industry remained relatively buoyant.[44] Estimates based upon a large number of Poor Law settlement examinations show that between 1700 and 1860, boys in arable eastern and midland counties left home at 14.8 years whilst girls left at 16.2 years, whereas in the more pastoral western and south-western agricultural districts boys left at 14.1 and girls at 14.2 years.[45]

The long-term decline of live-in agricultural service also tended to locate children for longer within the household and to increase child dependency. Moreover, a rise in unemployment following the French Wars placed pressure upon the already chronically low living standards of agrarian households.[46] In eastern and midlands arable counties, families placed increasing dependence upon the earning-power of resident children and the increasingly gendered agrarian labour market resulted in a complete reversal of the experiences of boys and girls in terms of the age at leaving home. In the first half of the eighteenth century, agricultural boys and girls left home at 15.1 and 17.8 years respectively but in the 25 years after 1834 boys left at 17.3 and girls at 15.2 years.[47] The tendency to retain male children longer in agrarian families after 1834 was also an effect of government attempts to curtail outdoor relief which forced many dependent families to place greater reliance upon children's earnings as a means of supplementing household incomes.[48] The protracted decline in demand for female labour on the land drove many to join the flow of young unmarried females into domestic service in urban households.[49] This trend was most rapid in the south and east of England and was exacerbated by a decrease in the numbers of small farmers and lesser gentry who had hitherto demanded domestic servants from among local populations.

Children remained at home longest in urban and industrial districts and nineteenth-century urban and industrial households seem to have been first to establish the general custom – later to become nearly universal among the working class until the later twentieth century – of children remaining in the parental home until marriage.[50] In 1861, 98 per cent of Preston children in the age-group 15–19 resided with their parents, compared with only 62 per cent in the rural parish of Colyton in 1841.[51] These differences almost certainly resulted from the relatively higher industrial wages which relieved parents of the pressure to have younger dependent children placed outside the household and by the growing tendency of larger industrial processes to locate in towns, thereby reducing the distance between the parental home and the location of first employment (a matter of prime importance in a society in which almost everybody walked to work). The contrast, statistically, between the rural labour market (in which a majority of adolescents were boarded with masters) and the urban setting (in which older, working, children remained resident in the parental home) is striking.[52] The growing tendency during the mid- to late nineteenth century for employed children in urban and industrial districts to remain in the parental home until their early twenties extended considerably the period during which children could make a contribution to the household income. Hence, household dependency and the effects of life-cycle poverty were ameliorated. The retention of older working children in the household was crucial in curtailing the supply of young child labourers to industry and was an important factor in the decline of child labour in modern industrial society.

The generally protracted process of departure from the parental home during the eighteenth and nineteenth centuries was matched by wide variations in age-specific demand for child workers in the labour market itself.[53] Just as there was no fixed 'age at leaving home', so there was no average 'age at starting work' in eighteenth- and nineteenth-century Britain. The demands of labour-intensity and skill, rather than arbitrary age-regulations, determined the ages at which children commenced work. Snell has observed 'how those entering trades requiring physical strength (blacksmith, bricklayer, cooper, sawyer, mason, millwright) left home rather later than average...watch makers, breeches makers, tailors, or hatmakers left home earlier'.[54] The customary age for apprenticeships to commence was 14 (although there is some evidence that some children went 'on trial', or were employed in menial tasks, or as servants, prior to becoming formally apprenticed). The Children's Employment Commission of 1843 examined a wide variety of occupations and concluded

> Children are in general put to work as soon as the nature of the employment admits of their being of any use, but that this period is different in almost every different occupation, being in some as early as two or three years of age, while in others it is delayed until eight or nine, and in some few even until twelve and upwards.[55]

In agriculture, in particular, the limitations imposed by physical size tended to control ages of entry to 'grown-up' work.[56] Eighteenth-century agricultural servants did not generally commence field work until they had reached about 12 to 14, though there is evidence that the children of farmers, who represented about a third of child labour in agriculture, commenced earlier. However, children were often taken to work before they were capable of productive fieldwork in order that they might become accustomed to the agricultural workplace. The 1843 Poor Law Report on Women and Children in Agriculture noted: 'before a boy is regularly hired by the farmer, he frequently at an early age accompanies his father to work, not to labour, but to wait upon him, as it were, in different ways'.[57] Very young agricultural children might obtain part-time or seasonal work such as bird-scaring, potato-setting, weeding and other menial jobs. Urban and industrial occupations exhibited wide variations in the ages at which children began work. Davin estimates that children in mid-nineteenth-century London commenced work between 10 and 12.[58] In coalmining, boys began to enter at about nine or 10 but did not succeed to adult occupations at the coal-face until the ages of 18 or 19.[59] In the Potteries, the average age at commencement was about nine but even younger children were employed in unskilled ancillary tasks. In the metal-working trades, children began at age nine or 10 but entered the less-skilled functions like pin-making at much younger ages.[60] Figures for Manchester, Salford and Preston in 1851 suggest that 60 per cent of boys were occupied by age 13 and 60 per cent of girls by the age of 14.[61] In the armed forces, youths commenced at later ages, though the vast majority of recruits stated a previous occupation.[62] In 1828, it was observed that army recruits 'rarely enlist in consequence of a deliberate preference of a military life, but commonly on account of some domestic broil, or from a boyish fancy, sometimes from want of work'.[63] A royal commission of 1861 noted that the rate of army recruitment from agricultural districts was greatest during periods of winter unemployment.[64] The minimum age at recruitment for the infantry fluctuated between 16 and 18 from the late eighteenth century to the start of the twentieth, according to the changing demand for fighting men.[65]

It has been argued that the decades leading up to the 1840s saw a peak of child employment and a declining age at first participation, after which ages at starting work increased throughout the rest of the century.[66] Moreover, this supposed decline in the age at first participation is thought to have been greater than might have occurred simply from an increasingly youthful population.[67] This means that a rise in industrial production led to more children working at earlier ages. It is very difficult, however, to confirm or refute such claims since most children were employed in very small-scale enterprises for which very little evidence has survived. In contrast, other studies suggest that the 'classic' Industrial Revolution heralded in a change of form of child labour rather than a rise in its incidence. The Marxist Christopher Hill thought that it was 'absurd to attack the factories as though they introduced child labour: it had long existed in the home. The factories shocked philanthropists by bringing it into the public view, and making brutally clear the dependence of the capitalist's profit on such labour'.[68] Anecdotal evidence suggests that in domestic industry, many children would commence work long before they left home. Again, however, the major difficulty in making general statements about domestic child workers is the fact that each domestic trade was affected in different ways and at different times by the changing fortunes of the economy. Whilst some traditional domestic trades, such as domestic spinning, were in sharp decline by the last quarter of the eighteenth century, others such as hand-weaving, lace-making and straw-plaiting grew enormously in scale.

The increasing diversity of the British economy in the century after 1750, the absence of fixed statutory provisions such as school-leaving ages and the faulty enumeration of children's employment in the censuses render estimates of an average age at starting work extremely difficult. 'Guesstimates' can be misleading. Tranter's observation that eighteenth-century children 'were regularly employed from the ages of five or six', for example, or Hunt's assertion that 'most children in pre-industrial England ... were expected to contribute to their keep long before their tenth birthday' cannot be demonstrated by reference to any reliable body of historical evidence.[69] Poor Law records suggest that the poorest children commenced, on average, no earlier than about 10. In most parishes, the Poor Law operated an upper limit of nine or 10 years for the payment of outdoor relief in respect of the children of widows or other distressed parents.[70] Of 337 Warwickshire parish children recorded as having been apprenticed to husbandry between 1700 and 1834, 75 per cent were aged 11 or younger.[71] Of 424 assignments of Sowerby parish apprentices between 1722 and 1842 (where an age of binding was entered) 76 per cent were aged between seven and 11, and 51 per cent were aged eight, nine or 10.[72] These ages correspond very closely with the prescribed minima for starting work stipulated in the factory and mines legislation of the 1830s and 40s, and might form the closest estimate of a minimum 'official' age at starting work for the children of the poor during the first half of the nineteenth century. It is significant that pauper children who remained resident in workhouses after the age of 10 were not accorded the equal status of indoor adult paupers until they had achieved the age of 15 or 16.[73]

The Parish and the Poor Law

The parish and the Poor Law were undoubtedly the two most important institutional structures affecting entry to work and the training of apprentices and agricultural servants in the eighteenth and early nine-teenth centuries. Serving a properly indentured apprenticeship in a parish conferred a right of settlement which allowed access to a range of benefits such as parish relief and access to common land. Most parish authorities attempted to restrict employment opportunities to their own young parishioners whenever possible because the employment of an outsider might render a settled inhabitant unemployed and thereby tend to increase the burden on the local poor rate. In the pre-industrial economy, therefore, settlement laws acted to promote a degree of security of employment for settled apprentices and servants. The system had obvious benefits to local artisanal households since masters usually wished to apprentice their own children or the children of close relatives or neighbours. This equilibrium was disrupted increasingly from the mid-eighteenth century as a rising rural population prompted growing competition for local places, forcing many time-served apprentices to migrate in search of work. Rural migrants would retain a right of settlement in their parish of origin, however, and whilst rural parishes were deprived of skilled workers they might subsequently become liable for payment of 'non-resident' poor relief for unemployed parishioners living at great distances in urban or semi-urban parishes.[74] As rural-to-urban migration increased from the mid-eighteenth century, the traditional interest of parishes in training skilled workers diminished, as did the institution of apprenticeship itself.

Parish authorities also had a traditional duty towards destitute children. Children who remained in receipt of poor relief were often forced to engage in casual or seasonal work to ease the burden upon local ratepayers.[75] Much of this work was connected with the efficient functioning of the parish. Picking stones from agricultural land for use as road metalling, for example, was among the most common (and most despised) forms of work for children dependent upon the parish.[76] Children were not subject in the same way as adults to the principle of 'less eligibility' which came to dominate Poor Law policy after 1834, though pauper children were expected to contribute to their own subsistence whilst still very young.[77] Orphaned, deserted or illegitimate children in parish care usually found themselves apprenticed at very early ages.[78] The binding of a pauper child almost always resulted in a considerable saving on the poor rate.[79] Where a pauper child might cost four pounds a year to support in a workhouse, the same child might be bound permanently to a master by the provision of a set of clothes and a one-off premium of five pounds.[80] There were distinct differences in the types of trade to which pauper and private apprentices were bound. Simonton found that the four most popular trades for pauper apprentices (agriculture, services, textiles and metal-working) contained very few private apprentices whilst the most popular trades among private apprentices (tailors and cordwainers) contained very few paupers.[81]

The system of parish apprenticeships was also open to abuse by unscrupulous Poor Law overseers. Children sometimes found themselves bound to artisans who were merely in search of cheap labour.[82] An account of London workhouses as early as 1732 noted that parish overseers 'to save Expence, are apt to ruin Children, by putting them out as early as they can, to any sorry Masters that will take them ... on account of the little Money that is given with them'.[83] Some workhouses appropriated the wages of pauper children and hired them out by the day to local industrialists.[84] Others operated an unofficial traffic in pauper children going 'on trial' which never resulted in a legal binding.[85] Many of the early water-powered mills of the north of England and the Lothians of Scotland were established in remote areas and were beset by labour-supply difficulties which prompted some owners to seek child workers from the Poor Law authorities of large towns and cities.[86] By the late eighteenth century, the system of parish apprenticeships had, in some urban parishes, become truly 'a method of transmitting child labour into the low skilled trades, rather than an investment in the human capital of poor children'.[87] Moreover, the binding of pauper children out of parish became more profitable to overseers after a statute of 1757 which afforded apprentices the right of settlement after 40 days' residence in their new parish.[88] Some London parishes bound in excess of 90 per cent of their pauper apprentices out of parish. Rose notes that between the 1760s and 1811, the number of London children apprenticed more than doubled, and the high point of apprenticeship to northern textiles enterprises occurred in the last two decades of the eighteenth century.[89] Aiken reported in 1795 that in Eccles, Royton and Dukinfield 'children of very tender age are employed; many of them collected from the *workhouses* in *London* and *Westminster*, and transported in crowds, as apprentices to masters resident many hundred miles distant, where they serve unknown, unprotected and forgotten by those to whose care nature or the laws had consigned them'.[90] Unsurprisingly, parish apprentices featured prominently in contemporary accounts of ill-treatment and dangerous working conditions.[91] Of the many hundreds of parish apprentices bound over long distances, 'only a few, normally the "elite", who had been trained as mechanics, remained at the mill at the end of their terms'.[92] On completing their apprenticeships, pauper children frequently had to compete for employment with the children of operatives and many would be forced to seek employment elsewhere at the end of their time. Lancashire hand-loom weavers 'who had brought in parish apprentices for their looms during good trade thought nothing of turning them adrift when times were bad'.[93] Farey observed in 1817 that very few girls were kept on when their terms of apprenticeship expired 'but too often, such truly unfortunate young Women, disperse themselves over the Country...and at no distant periods, are passed home to Parishes they were apprenticed in'.[94]

The practice of obtaining groups of parish children to work in factories declined during the first two decades of the nineteenth century. A number of explanations have been offered for this. The locational shift towards urban manufacture occasioned by the spread of steam-powered production led to a reduction in labour-supply problems experienced by isolated water-powered mills.[95] Moreover, in the remote mills, a 'maturation' of the apprentice labour force (where child workers grew older without being replaced by new apprentices) probably also contributed to a decline in demand for pauper apprentices over the early decades of the nineteenth century.[96] Rising living standards and expectations also meant that the costs of keeping apprentices rose considerably. At the Gregs' factory at Styal, the cost of keeping apprentices doubled between the 1820s and 1840s.[97] Significant shifts in social policy also contributed to a decline of the system. An amending Act of 1816 altered the format of parish indentures and compelled magistrates to enquire about the distance over which an apprentice was to be bound and all such bindings were to be restricted to within 40 miles of the home parish.[98] Moreover, from the 1830s, the Poor Law Commission became increasingly hostile to the principle of parish apprenticeships and by the 1840s the system survived only in a few unions.[99]

Production and Reproduction

It has been argued that the greater involvement of children in industrial production and their rising marginal household earnings led to increased demand for new consumer goods. New working-class consumption patterns emerged during the eighteenth century and demand increased for cheap industrially produced goods such as textiles, crockery, cutlery, buckles, buttons, pins, books and toys.[100] The evidence of rising consumer demand is compelling since the value of child labour appears to have increased in industrial communities in the eighteenth century and even the lowest-paid occupation groups, such as agricultural labourers, experienced rises in real incomes in the wake of the Napoleonic Wars.[101] Moreover, it has been argued that the increase in the usefulness of children's labour in domestic production profoundly affected couples' perceptions of their own ability to support larger families. Medick has asserted that the form of production carried out in the 'proto-industrial' family economy was of immense importance to the modern rise of population because it increasingly allowed children to escape from traditional constraints upon marriage.[102] In pre-industrial society, marriages were customarily deferred until people had achieved some measure of economic independence. Most agrarian children left home in their early teens to live a celibate working life for about a decade prior to marriage. Such practices almost certainly helped to restrain population growth and this is borne out by evidence showing that districts harbouring high levels of farm service had a higher unmarried proportion of their populations.[103] In addition, 'inelastic' demand for labour in traditional society often led to children having to wait until the death of a father before they could inherit a farm or workshop.[104] The prohibition upon marriage whilst still apprenticed must also have acted as a brake upon demographic increase since most apprentices did not complete their terms until at least 21 and would subsequently have to spend time finding an opening before marriage.[105] Berg has noted that 'Unlike older peasant and artisan families, where late marriage after a period of service or apprenticeship away from the home prevailed, girls now worked in their parents' home until marriage at an early age. They then set up their own production unit within a new family setting and had more children earlier because of the premium on child labour.'[106] Some contemporaries shared this belief. Arthur Young noted in 1770: 'It is employment that creates population: marriages are early and numerous in proportion to the amount of employment.'[107] Checkland has argued pointedly that the numbers of children born to domestic industrialists may have been related directly to their parents' perceptions of existing labour demand.[108] If the keys to population increase were marriage at earlier ages and an increasing incidence of marriage, then the decline in the importance of live-in agricultural service, the relaxation of entrenched labour customs and the spread of proto-industrial production must have allowed individuals a greater freedom to marry.

However, the relationship between increasing opportunities for child labour, rising household surpluses and rising fertility is not as clear-cut as these historians have claimed. First, the theory that home demand was greatly stimulated by surplus household incomes assumes a high level of industrial and proto-industrial participation by females and children. Yet, recent research has shown that pre-industrial labour practices continued to dominate large areas of the countryside until the mid-nineteenth century and that industrial production was confined to a small number of districts. In other words, in the later eighteenth century, industrial production may not have been widespread enough to have affected the contemporary national population increase. It has also been shown that whilst some early industrial districts did exhibit a low age of marriage, others did not. Goldstone has suggested that earlier marriages after 1750 occurred in the presence of declining real wages and were rather the product of increasing labour opportunities offered by a diversifying economy.[109] Secondly, many other 'traditional' sectors were besides undergoing a parallel shift to wage labour.[110] Even agricultural labourers, though less wealthy than industrial workers, were gaining greater freedom from traditional labour customs and attaining economic independence at earlier ages. Thirdly, it has been argued that rising child dependency has a tendency to increase demand for agricultural products rather than industrial goods. Low, rather than high, dependency conditions tend to favour non-agricultural consumption.[111]

In fact, historians have offered very little reliable statistical evidence relating to the numbers of children involved in domestic production or, indeed, of the practical utility of child labour in such a setting. Studies from modern developing countries have questioned the relationship between demand for child labour and increased fertility. In a domestic industrial setting, children remain economically inactive for at least a decade following birth but continue to demand resources such as food, space and time.[112] Economic returns to having children are further complicated by the fact that there are no rational means of predicting how the labour market might alter between the decision to conceive a child and any point in the future when a child (if it survives to working age) might become capable of contributing to the household economy. The links between industrial growth and fertility are further complicated by studies of variations in nineteenth-century fertility rates which highlight great disparities between the leading industrial occupations. Coalminers, for example, exhibited the highest birth-rate whilst textiles families ranked amongst the lowest.[113] The picture could hardly be less conclusive: the presence of large numbers of children in a household could be both a cause of poverty and the means of its alleviation.

Conclusion

Child labour was not an autonomous or unchanging feature of the economic past but was deeply embedded in the social and demographic fabric of industrialising society. High levels of child dependency coupled with an uncertain adult labour market obliged many working-class families to maximise incomes by putting their children to work. The disproportionately large presence in the child labour market of orphans, illegitimate children and those formerly in the care of Poor Law institutions suggests that child labour at very early ages resulted in a large number of cases from social deprivation and from the failure of formal institutional arrangements to keep pace with a rapidly diversifying economy. The examination of social and demographic influences shows child labour to have been a systemic phenomenon, related largely to relative levels of household poverty. The desire of families to maximise their children's productive capacities, however, was continually moderated by the changing demands and fortunes of local labour markets. Any investigation of the social and demographic factors bearing upon children's employment, therefore, needs to pay close attention to the work that children actually did.[114] The demand for child labour was affected fundamentally by changes in workplace organisation and variations in production technologies. It is to these influences that we now turn.

Notes

1. P. Laslett, *The World We Have Lost* (London, 1965), p. 104.
2. E. A. Wrigley and R. S. Schofield, *The Population History of England, 1541–1871* (Cambridge, 1981), table A3.1, pp. 528–9. By 1911 the proportion had fallen back to about 30 per cent: M. Anderson, 'The Social Implications of Demographic Change' in F. M. L. Thompson (ed.) *The Cambridge Social History of Britain, 1750–1950* (Cambridge, 1990), vol. 2, p. 47.
3. Approximate age-group proportions in 1821 were: age 0–4, 15.36%; 5–9, 13.47%; 10–14, 11.72%; 15–19, 9.89%: B. R. Mitchell, *British Historical Statistics* (Cambridge, 1988), p. 15. Between 1750 and 1871, the proportion of the population aged below 15 ranged between 33 to 40 per cent: Wrigley and Schofield, *Population History*, table A3.1, pp. 528–9.
4. Expressed as the proportion of the population never-married in the age-group 40 to 44 years. Wrigley and Schofield, *Population History*, table 7.28, p. 260.
5. Wrigley and Schofield, *Population History*, table A3.1, pp. 528–9; Anderson, 'Implications of Demographic Change', p. 1.

6. Wrigley and Schofield, *Population History*, table A3.1, pp. 528–9. The 1981 figure includes many more older people than the nineteenth-century ratios: D. Coleman, 'Population' in A. H. Halsey (ed.) *British Social Trends Since 1900* (London, 1988), tab.2.42, p. 106.

7. Wrigley and Schofield, *Population History*, p. 450.

8. N. L. Tranter, 'The Labour Supply, 1780–1860' in R. Floud and D. McCloskey (eds) *The Economic History of Britain Since 1700* (Cambridge, 1981), vol. 1, p. 207.

9. O. Saito, 'Labour Supply Behaviour of the Poor in the English Industrial Revolution', *Journal of European Economic History*, 10 (1981), p. 645. A similar pattern was identified among poor families in early twentieth-century Japan. In Japan, as in Britain, there is evidence of a strong disinclination (even in the most dire household circumstances) to put children younger than 10 into work: O. Saito, 'Children's Work, Industrialism and the Family Economy in Japan, 1872–1926' in H. Cunningham and P. P. Viazzo (eds) *Child Labour in Historical Perspective, 1800–1985: Case Studies from Europe, Japan and Colombia* (Florence, 1996), p. 86.

10. M. Anderson, *Family Structure in Nineteenth-Century Lancashire* (Cambridge, 1971), p. 76; The children of families in depressed trades, in particular, were more likely to be employed: J. S. Lyons, 'Family Response to Economic Decline: Handloom Weavers in Early Nineteenth-Century Lancashire', *Research in Economic History* 12 (1989), p. 56.

11. McKendrick has expressed the ratio of pay between men, women and children in domestic industry as 3:2:1. N. McKendrick, 'Home Demand and Economic Growth: A New View of the Role of Women and Children in the Industrial Revolution' in *idem* (ed.) *Historical Perspectives: Studies in English Thought and Society* (London, 1974), p. 184. The suggestion that the 'husband/father [*sic*] in proto-industrial families may have contributed only one-quarter of total income' probably exaggerates the situation, however: see S. Horrell and J. Humphries, 'Child Labour and British Industrialisation' in M. Lavalette (ed.) *A Thing of the Past? Child Labour in Britain in the Nineteenth and Twentieth Centuries* (Liverpool, 1999), p. 226.

12. J. Humphries, 'Female-Headed Households in Early Industrial Britain: The Vanguard of the Proletariat', *Labour History Review* (Spring 1998), pp. 31–65.

13. D. A. Gatley, *Child Workers in Victorian Warrington: The Report of the Children's Employment Commission into Child Labour* (Stoke, 1996), p. 13.

14. M. W. Dupree, *Family Structure in the Staffordshire Potteries, 1840–1880* (Oxford, 1995), p. 153.

15. R. Wall, 'Some Implications of the Earnings, Income and Expenditure Patterns of Married Women in Populations in the Past' in J. Henderson and R. Wall (eds) *Poor Women and Children in the European Past* (London, 1994), p. 313. Such findings are very close to the situation discovered by Saito in late nineteenth-century Japanese proto-industrial villages. Where both parents were present, the proportion of working children aged five to eleven was as low as 4 per cent whilst in lone-parent families the proportion stood at about 22 per cent. Saito argues that 'factors such as landholding and the mean size of the family workforce ... had some discernable effects, but *no factor had as much influence as the absence of one parent*': Saito, 'Children's Work', p. 86 (emphasis in original).

16. M. A. Crowther, *The Workhouse System, 1834–1929: The History of an English Social Institution* (London, 1981), p. 203; Anderson, 'Implications of Demographic

Change', table 1.5, p. 49. Family breakdown due to formal divorce and separation was infrequent before the mid-nineteenth century, but there is some evidence that when it occurred children were more likely to remain with fathers (in contrast with the modern custom of maternal custody). The greater labour value of children in earlier periods might explain this, especially in proto-industrial districts where children often assisted the head of the household. Mothers had no chance of gaining legal custody of their children prior to the 1839 Custody of Infants Act: K. D. M. Snell and J. Millar, 'Lone-Parent Families and the Welfare State: Past and Present', *Continuity and Change*, 2 (1987), p. 394.

17. During the second half of the eighteenth century, 15–20 per cent of marriage partners were widows or widowers: Mitchell, *British Historical Statistics*, pp. 20–1; Anderson, 'Implications of Demographic Change', pp. 50–1, p. 31.

18. Wall, 'Earnings, Income and Expenditure Patterns', table 15.2, p. 316.

19. As Malthus argued, in a largely agrarian society, dependent children formed a major demand factor in the tendency towards subsistence crises. Policies that increased support for children promoted population growth which placed greater demand upon resources and intensified household poverty: T. R. Malthus, *An Essay on the Principle of Population* (London, 1798).

20. One model of industrial development suggests that economic development precipitates a faster decline in the traditional sectors than the rate of growth of emergent industries: E. Richards, 'Women in the British Economy Since About 1700: An Interpretation', *History*, 59 (1974), p. 337.

21. K. D. M. Snell, *Annals of the Labouring Poor: Social Change and Agrarian England, 1660–1900* (Cambridge, 1985), p. 328. In rural districts, the abandonment of outdoor relief probably acted to force children into low-paid employment in agricultural 'gangs': W. A. Armstrong, *Farmworkers in England and Wales* (Iowa, 1988), p. 67.

22. T. W. Nutt, 'Illegitimacy and the Poor Law in Nineteenth-Century England', MA thesis (Manchester, 2000), pp. 23–9.

23. Charles Booth observed that the well-being derived from a family's income 'will depend upon the entire number who have to be supported by it': Booth, 'Occupations of the People of the United Kingdom, 1801–81', *Journal of the Statistical Society*, 49 (1886), p. 315.

24. *Unemployed Hand-Loom Weavers, Report of the Commissioners*, Parliamentary Papers (PP) 1841, X, p. 45. The model of the life-cycle elucidated is strikingly similar to that developed by Rowntree six decades later.

25. Cited in P. Horn, *Children's Work and Welfare, 1780–1880s* (Basingstoke, 1994), p. 14.

26. Compare the study of rising incomes of children in America in P. H. Lindert, *Fertility and Scarcity in America* (Princeton, NJ), table 4.1, p. 124.

27. L. C. A. Knowles, *Industrial and Commercial Revolutions* (London, 1930), p. 90.

28. D. Levine, 'The Demographic Implications of Rural Industrialisation: A Family Reconstitution Study of Shepshed, Leicestershire, 1600–1851', *Social History*, 1 (1976), pp. 182, 191.

29. W. A. Armstrong, 'Rural Population Growth, Systems of Employment and Incomes' in G. E. Mingay (ed.) *The Agrarian History of England and Wales* (Cambridge, 1989), vol. 6, pp. 716–17.

30. *Children's Employment Commission (Trades and Manufactures)*, PP 1843, XIV, app. to 2nd rep., pt.I, p. A11.

31. P. Kirby, 'The Historic Viability of Child Labour and the Mines Act of 1842' in M. Lavalette (ed.) *A Thing of the Past? Child Labour in Britain in the Nineteenth and Twentieth Centuries* (Liverpool, 1999), pp. 111–12.

32. W. B. Stephens, *Education, Literacy and Society, 1830–70* (Manchester, 1987), p. 135. The weight of such evidence is overwhelmingly at odds with Lavalette's claim that 'For working-class families trying to protect their children from the horrors of work during the Industrial Revolution the removal of children from work (often in the face of opposition from employers) was a victory.' Lavalette, 'Conclusion' in *idem* (ed.) *A Thing of the Past? Child Labour in Britain in the Nineteenth and Twentieth Centuries* (Liverpool, 1999), p. 251; Dupree, *Family Structure*, pp. 231–3, 228.

33. McKendrick, 'Home Demand', p. 201.

34. P. E. H. Hair, 'The Social History of British Coalminers', D. Phil. thesis (Oxford, 1955), p. 178. In the west of Scotland it was said that 'a man who is ambitious of earning more than the sum limited, by taking down a boy at any age, becomes entitled to earn more than if he worked alone. This temptation is too strong for some parents to resist, and instances have been reported . . . of colliers carrying the child too [*sic*] and from the pit on his back': *Children's Employment Commission*, PP 1842, XVI, p. 371. A Lancastrian witness to the 1866 Select Committee on Mines recalled his entry to the pit: 'I began working before I was 5 . . . My father took me down: I did nothing at first for a few months; he took me down to accustom me to the mine; I just knocked about as an errand boy for my father': *Select Committee on Acts for the Regulation and Inspection of Mines*, PP 1866, XIV, p. 33.

35. W. Hasbach, *A History of the English Agricultural Labourer* (London, 1920), p. 225.

36. *Reports of Special Assistant Poor Law Commissioners on the Employment of Women and Children in Agriculture*, PP 1843, XII, p. 231.

37. Civil registration of births only began in England and Wales in 1837 and was not enacted in Scotland until 1854. Estimates for ages at starting work drawn from inscrutable medieval evidence are little more than impressionistic. Shahar notes that apprentices might commence at any age between seven and 20, although most seem to have been bound by the ages of 11–12: S. Shahar, *Childhood in the Middle Ages* (London, 1990) p. 232.

38. Wrigley and Schofield, *Population History*, table 7.26, p. 255.

39. A. Kussmaul, *Servants in Husbandry in Early Modern England* (Cambridge, 1981), p. 3; R. Wall, 'The Age at Leaving home', *Journal of Family History*, 3 (1978), p. 182.

40. Wall, 'Age at Leaving Home', table 1, p. 189.

41. Ibid., p. 200.

42. Snell, *Annals*, p. 330; Wall, 'Age at Leaving Home', table 5, p. 195; J. S. Lyons, 'Family Response to Economic Decline: Handloom Weavers in Early Nineteenth-Century Lancashire', *Research in Economic History*, 12 (1989), p. 56.

43. R. Wall, 'Leaving Home and the Process of Household Formation', table 5, p. 95.

44. Snell, *Annals*, table 7.1, p. 324.

45. Ibid., pp. 322–32.

46. W. A. Armstrong, *Farmworkers*, pp. 79–80.

47. Snell, *Annals*, tab. 7.2, p. 326.

48. Ibid., pp. 326–7. Wall suggests that a tendency to retain sons and daughters over 15 within the household was already developing over the first three decades of the nineteenth century: Wall, 'Process of Household Formation', table 5, p. 95.

49. Towns offered relatively greater employment opportunities for females than did rural districts and almost all eighteenth-century towns contained a surplus of females over males. P. J. Corfield, *The Impact of English Towns, 1700–1800* (Oxford, 1982), p. 99; K. D. M. Snell, 'Agricultural Seasonal Unemployment, the Standard of Living and Women's Work in the South and East, 1690–1860', *Economic History Review*, 2nd ser., 34 (1981), p. 431; H. V. Speechley, 'Female and Child Agricultural Day Labourers in Somerset, c.1685–1870', PhD thesis (Exeter, 1999), p. 155.

50. R. Burr Litchfield, 'The Family and the Mill: Cotton Mill Work, Family Work Patterns, and Fertility in Mid-Victorian Stockport' in A. S. Wohl (ed.) *The Victorian Family: Structure and Stresses* (London, 1978), p. 192.

51. In modern Western societies, the children of more affluent families, almost universally, leave home later than their historic populations: Wall, 'Age at Leaving Home', pp. 190, 193, 197.

52. In 1851, only 10 per cent of Preston children aged 15–19 lived in lodgings. Anderson, *Family Structure*, p. 53.

53. Wall, 'Age at Leaving Home', p. 200.

54. Snell, *Annals*, p. 330.

55. *Children's Employment Commission, Second Report of the Commissioners, Trades and Manufactures*, PP 1843, XIII, p. 7.

56. When a Dorsetshire farmer was asked in the early 1840s at what age children began work on his farm he replied that it depended 'on their size a great deal': *Report on Women and Children in Agriculture*, PP 1843, XII, p. 29.

57. Ibid., p. 30. Speechley notes that male children began work in agriculture at earlier ages than females: Speechley, 'Female and Child Agricultural Labourers', p. 167.

58. A. Davin, *Growing up Poor: Home, School and Street in London, 1870–1914* (London, 1996), p. 157.

59. P. Kirby, 'Aspects of the Employment of Children in the British Coalmining Industry, 1800–1872', PhD thesis (Sheffield, 1995), pp. 53–73.

60. *Children's Employment Commission (Trades and Manufactures)*, PP 1843, XIII, p. 7.

61. Anderson, *Family Structure*, p. 75.

62. R. Floud, K. Wachter and A. Gregory, *Height, Health and History: Nutritional Status in the United Kingdom, 1750–1980* (Cambridge, 1990), p. 107.

63. Ibid., p. 56. Snell suggests that the very high age at leaving home among those enlisting reflected despair over the chances of gaining employment locally. Soldiery was a 'last resort': Snell, *Annals*, pp. 330–1.

64. Floud, Wachter and Gregory, *Height, Health and History*, p. 56.

65. Ibid., p. 60, n. 11.

66. M. Berg and P. Hudson, 'Rehabilitating the Industrial Revolution', *Economic History Review*, 2nd ser., 45 (1992), p. 35; S. Horrell and J. Humphries, '"The Exploitation of Little Children": Child Labour and the Family Economy in the Industrial Revolution', *Journal of Economic History*, 52 (1992), p. 496.

67. Horrell, and Humphries, 'Exploitation of Little Children', p. 498.

68. C. Hill, *Reformation to Industrial Revolution, 1530–1780* (Harmondsworth, 1969), p. 263.

69. Tranter, 'The Labour Supply, 1780–1860', p. 221; E. H. Hunt, *British Labour History, 1815–1914* (1981), p. 9. The literature on the subject is littered with claims that children commenced work 'at early ages' or 'very young' and in 'large numbers'. Apart from a small number of industries which were subject to state inquiry or regulation, however, such statements remain impressionistic.

70. *Children's Employment Commission, Second Report of the Commissioners, Trades and Manufactures*, PP 1843, XIII, p. 104; Hair, 'Social History of British Coalminers', p. 53, n. 1.
71. J. Lane, *Apprenticeship in England, 1600–1914* (London, 1996), table 1.1, p. 14.
72. H. Wright, 'Sowerby Parish Apprentices', *Transactions of the Halifax Antiquarian Society* (1934), pp. 68–9. These figures bear close comparison with late-industrialising Japan where nearly half of the children from poor houses were in employment by the age of 10 (mean age at commencement 10.8) and nearly two-thirds by age 13: Saito, 'Children's Work', fig. 1, p. 81.
73. Crowther, *Workhouse System*, p. 207. One Yorkshire pit-owner noted: 'If they [pauper parents] go to the Union for relief, the Board says, "you must get a job for your children at [the] coal-pits, and let them work; girls as well as boys." ': *Children's Employment Commission*, PP 1842, XVI, p. 234. Simonton argues, however, that most pauper children 'were put out between the ages of seven and nine and only 6 per cent were indentured at fourteen': D. Simonton, 'Apprenticeship: Training and Gender in Eighteenth-Century England' in M. Berg (ed.) *Markets and Manufacture in Early Industrial Europe* (London, 1991), p. 239.
74. K. D. M. Snell, 'The Apprenticeship System in British History: The Fragmentation of a Cultural Institution', *History of Education*, 25 (1996), pp. 308–9, 311, 312.
75. Snell and Millar, 'Lone-Parent Families', p. 407, n. 28.
76. The removal and collection of stones from fields, as Arthur Young suggested, may have been of only marginal agricultural benefit but its utility to the parish economies was great since, prior to the Local Government Act of 1888, parishes were held responsible for the upkeep of roads within their boundaries: G. E. Evans, *Ask the Fellows who Cut the Hay* (London, 1965), pp. 75–6.
77. Crowther, *Workhouse System*, p. 207.
78. Foundlings and illegitimate children, as Dorothy George points out, were 'in a special sense the children of the parish – foundlings being generally given the name of the parish in which they were found': M. D. George, *London Life in the Eighteenth Century* (Harmondsworth, 1966), p. 213. Bastard children were regarded as people who 'could not produce their own subsistence and therefore must reduce the standard of living for all': J. Humphries, ' "... The Most Free from Objection ..." ': The Sexual Division of Labor and Women's Work in Nineteenth-Century England', *Journal of Economic History*, 47 (1987), p. 929.
79. The Committee on Parish Apprentices of 1814–15 found that apprenticeship was 'resorted to of necessity and with a view of getting rid of the burden of supporting so many individuals': *Report of Select Committee on Parish Apprentices*, PP 1814–15, V, p. 6.
80. Lane, *Apprenticeship in England*, p. 165. Poor Law overseers would have approved of the sacrifices made by 'the Lancashire Collier Girl' (the subject of one of Hannah More's Cheap Repository Tracts) who, at the age of about 11, worked in a coal mine in support of her fatherless family, thus relieving local rate-payers of the support of her two brothers and mother: P. E. H. Hair, 'The Lancashire Collier Girl, 1795', *Transactions of the Historic Society of Lancashire and Cheshire*, 120 (1968), pp. 65–6.
81. Simonton, 'Training and Gender', pp. 240–1.
82. Lane, *Apprenticeship in England*, p. 8.
83. Quoted in H. Cunningham, 'The Employment and Unemployment of Children in England, *c.* 1680–1851', *Past and Present*, 126 (1990), p. 119. The Poor Law

commissioners disapproved of the practice of forcing apprentices upon masters, but it survived in some districts long after 1834: Wright, 'Sowerby Parish Apprentices', p. 76.

84. 'Hiring out Paupers from Workhouses', Blackburn Union Letterbook, 28 May 1844, Lancashire Record Office, PUK/10/1; Crowther, *Workhouse System*, p. 204.

85. Kirby, 'Children in the British Coalmining Industry', pp. 273–4.

86. M. B. Rose, *The Gregs of Quarry Bank Mill* (Cambridge, 1986), pp. 26–7; *Report of the Minutes of Evidence on the State of Children Employed in Manufactories*, PP 1816, III, p. 132. Parish children were sometimes advertised in newspapers, frequently in groups.

87. M. B. Rose, 'Social Policy and Business: Parish Apprentices and the Early Factory System, 1750–1834', *Business History*, 31 (1989), p. 9.

88. H. Davey, *Poor Law Settlement and Removal* (1908), p. 104. By 1778, the practice of binding parish children until they were aged 24 was curtailed in favour of a seven-year apprenticeship that should end no later than 21 years of age: Wright, 'Sowerby Parish Apprentices', p. 67.

89. Rose, 'Parish Apprentices and the Early Factory System', pp. 7–9.

90. J. Aiken, *A Description of the Country from Thirty to Forty Miles Round Manchester* (London, 1795), p. 219 (emphasis in original); see also V. Worship, 'Cotton Factory or Workhouse: Poor Law Assisted Migration from Buckinghamshire to Northern England, 1835–7', *Family and Community History*, 3 (2000).

91. Abusive working conditions reported in accounts such as the *Memoir of Robert Blincoe* were found disproportionately among pauper apprentices: see A. E. Musson, 'Robert Blincoe and the Early Factory System', *Trade Union and Social History* (1974).

92. Rose, 'Parish Apprentices and the Early Factory System', p. 19.

93. M. Cruickshank, *Children and Industry: Child Health and Welfare in North-West Textile Towns During the Nineteenth Century* (Manchester, 1981), p. 9.

94. Quoted in I. Pinchbeck, *Women Workers and the Industrial Revolution, 1750–1850* (London, 1930), pp. 183–4.

95. Rose, 'Parish Apprentices and the Early Factory System', p. 21.

96. P. Bolin-Hort, *Work, Family and the State: Child Labour and the Organisation of Production in the British Cotton Industry, 1780–1920* (Lund, 1989), p. 36.

97. Cruickshank, *Children and Industry*, pp. 15–16.

98. Musson, 'Robert Blincoe', p. 200; Rose, 'Parish Apprentices and the Early Factory System', pp. 23–5; Lane, *Apprenticeship in England*, pp. 7–8. However, it was not until 1844 that the right of overseers to make application to justices to bind children was removed and the power given over to boards of guardians: Davey, *Poor Law Settlement and Removal*, p. 115. The Mines Act of 1842 included a restriction upon the time during which boys could legally be bound apprentice and fixed the legal term of binding to between the ages of 10 and 18 years: 5 & 6 Vict., c.99; Kirby, 'Children in the British Coalmining Industry', pp. 286–7.

99. Even by the later nineteenth century, however, acute labour shortages in mill villages sometimes led to requests to boards of guardians for parish children: J. Pressley, 'Childhood, Education and Labour: Moral Pressure and the End of the Half-Time System', PhD thesis (Lancaster, 2000), p. 36.

100. McKendrick, 'Home Demand', pp. 169, 171–2.

101. P. H. Lindert and J. G. Williamson, 'English Workers' Living Standards During the Industrial Revolution: A New Look', *Economic History Review*, 2nd ser., 36 (1983), pp. 1–25.

102. H. Medick, 'The Proto-Industrial Family Economy: The Structural Function of Household and Family During the Transition from Peasant to Industrial Capitalism', *Social History*, 1 (1976).

103. M. Anderson, 'Marriage Patterns in Victorian Britain: An Analysis Based on Registration District Data for England and Wales', *Journal of Family History*, 1 (1976).

104. D. C. Coleman, 'Labour in the English Economy of the Seventeenth Century', *Economic History Review*, 2nd ser., 8 (1955–56), pp. 280–1; Levine, 'Demographic Implications of Rural Industrialisation', p. 178.

105. Knowles, *Industrial and Commercial Revolutions*, p. 67.

106. M. Berg, *The Age of Manufactures* (London, 1985), p. 158; see also L. Stone, *The Family, Sex and Marriage in England, 1500–1800* (1979), pp. 418–19; D. Levine, 'Industrialisation and the Proletarian Family in England', *Past and Present*, 107 (1985).

107. Cited in Levine, 'Demographic Implications of Rural Industrialisation', p. 178.

108. S. G. Checkland, *The Rise of Industrial Society in England, 1815–1885* (London, 1964), p. 131. Though this view was lampooned by one reviewer: 'Such a picture of rational (or feckless) economic men copulating with a crafty eye on the labour market is ludicrous.' E. P. Thompson, 'History's March to the Foot of the Page', *The Times Literary Supplement* (6 May 1965), p. 349.

109. J. A. Goldstone, 'The Demographic Revolution in England: A Re-Examination', *Population Studies*, 45 (1986), p. 145.

110. P. Hudson, *The Industrial Revolution* (London, 1992), pp. 142–3.

111. Lindert, *Fertility and Scarcity*, p. 125; Wrigley and Schofield, *Population History*, p. 450.

112. M. Vlassoff, 'Labour Demand and Economic Utility of Children: A Case Study in Rural India', *Population Studies*, 33 (1979), pp. 415–28. See also the discussion in C. Nardinelli, *Child Labor and the Industrial Revolution* (Bloomington, IN, 1990), pp. 45–57.

113. M. R. Haines, 'Fertility, Nuptiality, and Occupation: A Study of Coal Mining Populations and Regions in England and Wales in the Mid-Nineteenth Century', *Journal of Interdisciplinary History*, 8 (1977). Other studies have highlighted further the differences in demographic behaviour between seemingly analogous communities: T. Hareven, 'Recent Research on the History of the Family' in M. Drake (ed.) *Time, Family and Community: Perspectives on Family and Community History* (Oxford, 1994), pp. 27–8. Hudson argues against a monocausal explanation, suggesting that population growth may have occurred by 'several accepted avenues' converging to the same end: Hudson, *Industrial Revolution*, p. 145.

114. R. Wall, 'Work, Welfare and the Family: An Illustration of the Adaptive Family Economy in L. Bonfield, R. M. Smith and K. Wrightson (eds) *The World We Have Gained* (Oxford, 1986), p. 264.

Chapter 3: Child Labour and the Organisation of Production

Early histories of the Industrial Revolution held that the spread of machine production during the 'factory age' (c.1760 to 1850) led to a rapid transformation in the economic and social life of Britain. Increasingly, however, historians have discovered that the pace of industrial growth was a more gradual process and that 'revolutionary' change in production was confined to a small number of districts (notably, the central belt of Scotland, Lancashire, west Yorkshire, parts of Derbyshire and Cheshire, and the west midlands).[1] Even by the mid-nineteenth century, much of the British labour market remained dominated by 'traditional' forms of labour. At the time of the Great Exhibition, agriculture, horticulture, forestry and fishing employed 1.9 million men and boys and accounted for 29 per cent of the male labour force whilst the 'leading sectors' of the classic 'Industrial Revolution' (cotton, iron and steam) together accounted for less than a quarter of British manufacturing.[2] Even in rapidly industrialising districts, large-scale production continued to rely upon a multiplicity of small domestic manufacturing units.[3] In 1851, the number of workers in domestic textiles production equalled those in factory textiles whilst at the same date the mean size of a British production process was only 20 workers.[4] The diverse workshop and handicraft sector had 1.4 million employees whilst the newer factories accounted only for 567,000 men and boys. Domestic service employed nearly 1.1 million females, agriculture 670,000 and larger factories only 370,000.

A remarkably similar distribution of labour existed among employed children. Although the statistics of the child labour force are affected by a shortage of reliable evidence, Table 3.1 represents the best available estimate of the divisions of child labour in mid-nineteenth-century Britain.

Agriculture, livestock and fisheries formed the numerically largest occupation sector for young males in 1851, accounting for more than a third of the labour force aged 10–14 in England and Wales, with workshops, factories and transport employing further substantial proportions. Domestic service was the largest single occupation among girls in England and Wales with a quarter of occupied females aged 10–14 (19 per cent in Scotland) compared with fewer than 2 per cent of occupied

Table 3.1   Occupations of employed British children aged 10–14 (%), 1851

	England & Wales		Scotland	
	Males	Females	Males	Females
Agriculture, animals and fisheries	34.6	21.6	33.3	28.7
Workshops and handicraft	17.3	23.0	18.3	16.9
Factory	15.4	24.1	21.6	31.5
Transport and communications	11.4	1.1	7.5	1.1
Mines and quarries	8.8	0.8	8.7	0.1
'Indefinite occupation'	3.9	0.3	1.7	0.1
Building	3.1	0.0	1.9	0.0
Retail, foodstuffs and hostelries	2.7	3.5	4.6	2.0
Domestic service	1.8	25.3	1.1	19.2
Professional, clerical and local government	0.9	0.4	1.3	0.3
Armed forces	0.2	n.a.	0.0	n.a.

Source: Census 1851, PP 1852–53, LXXXVIII, tables xxv, xxvi. A large number of occupations given in the census abstracts were classified into the broad groupings given above. The complete listing of groupings and occupations appears in the Appendix. Figures for agriculture include estimates for missing employed kin of farmers. P. Kirby and J. E. Oeppen, 'The Child Labour Market in English and Welsh Agriculture, *c*.1750–1851' (forthcoming). The table assumes that 25 per cent of female general servants worked on farms and that they worked in agriculture 0.5 per cent of their time. M. Anderson, 'Households, Families and Individuals: Some Preliminary Results from the National Sample from the 1851 Census of Great Britain', *Continuity and Change*, 3 (1988), p. 427. Figures for females in armed forces not available.

boys at the same ages. Females in domestic service outnumbered males by about eight to one, whereas males in farm service outnumbered females by two to one.[5] Young unmarried females also featured prominently in the labour forces of textiles factories and small-scale workshops and handicrafts, which together employed about half the recorded female labour force aged 10–14. It is notable that the industry that epitomised the British Industrial Revolution was staffed overwhelmingly by women and children. Only 18 per cent of the cotton labour force in 1816 consisted of adult males.[6] Factory work was largely unaffected by seasonal influences or by periods of inclement weather and, although it was often monotonous and sometimes dangerous, its low labour intensity relative to agriculture made it a popular choice among parents seeking work for children. It would be unwise, however to imagine that factory or mines work was commonly available to children. The best evidence for the British labour market as a whole at the zenith of the Industrial Revolution shows that *concentrations* of child workers were high in both traditional and newer urban-industrial occupations but that the largest *absolute* numbers of child workers remained in agriculture, smaller workshops and domestic production.[7]

It is possible from the surviving census evidence to establish an approximate ranking of the concentrations of children in the major 'child labour' occupations in mid-nineteenth century Britain (Tables 3.2–3.5).

The youngest children were found among errand-runners and porters who, though aggregated in official listings, functioned within and around a variety of different production processes. Forty-four thousand runners and porters below the age of 15 were enumerated in 1851, and London contained more than a quarter of the total of English and Welsh errand-runners aged 10–14.[8] In addition, there existed an extremely diverse mixture of youthful occupations of which live-in agricultural work and textiles production harboured the highest concentrations of 10–14-year-olds. It is also significant that occupations requiring child workers to 'live-in' with their employers (these constituted chiefly the resident working kin of farmers, live-in farm servants and domestic servants) ranked among the most youthful of occupations. The great diversity of children's occupations apparent in official statistics, however, defies generalisation and requires an examination of each of the major employment sectors in turn.

Table 3.2   Concentrations of child workers aged 10–14: males, England and Wales, 1851 (where total employed greater than 2000 and where proportion aged 10–14 above 10 per cent)

	% of occupation aged 10–14	Total employed aged 10–14
Messenger, porter	42.9	38 130
Farmer's, grazier's, son, grandson, etc.	19.8	28 404
Worsted manufacture	17.6	9 061
Earthenware manufacture	17.3	4 078
Cotton manufacture	14.5	25 613
Farm servant (indoor)	13.6	25 667
Silk manufacture	13.5	5 871
Coalminer	12.6	23 038
Woollen cloth manufacture	12.0	9 242
Copper-miner	11.6	2 138
Iron-miner	10.5	2 039

Source: as Table 3.1.

Table 3.3   Concentrations of child workers aged 10–14: females, England and Wales, 1851 (where total employed greater than 2000 and where proportion aged 10–14 above 10 per cent)

	% of occupation aged 10–14	Total employed aged 10–14
Worsted manufacture	20.7	10 586
Farmer's daughter, granddaughter, etc.	20.3	27 689
Earthenware manufacture	20.0	2 137
Domestic servant (nurse)	19.4	6 963
Flax, linen manufacture	19.3	2 552
Straw plait manufacture	18.4	5 041
Lace manufacture	16.5	8 628
Farm servant (indoor)	16.5	16 343
Woollen cloth manufacture	16.1	7 333
Silk manufacture	15.4	10 533
Cotton manufacture	14.9	29 038
Glover (material not stated)	13.3	3 374
Hose, stocking, manufacture	12.4	3 152

Source: as Table 3.1.

Table 3.4   Concentrations of child workers aged 10–14: males, Scotland, 1851 (where total employed greater than 500 and where proportion aged 10–14 above 10 per cent)

	% of occupation aged 10–14	Total employed aged 10–14
Messenger, porter (not govt)	39.4	3 290
Ropemaker	22.2	536
Calico, cotton, printer	21.0	1 862
Farmer's, grazier's, son, grandson	20.7	6 488
Farm servant (indoor)	16.0	7 251
Coalminer	12.0	3 948
Flax, linen manufacture	11.8	3 889
Cotton manufacture	11.8	5 361

Source: as Table 3.1.

Table 3.5   Concentrations of child workers aged 10–14: females, Scotland, 1851 (where total employed greater than 500 and where proportion aged 10–14 above 10 per cent)

	% of occupation aged 10–14	Total employed aged 10–14
Calico, cotton, printer	21.6	1 491
Farmer's daughter, granddaughter, etc.	16.7	6 390
Cotton manufacture	11.9	6 295
Farm servant (indoor)	11.8	3 370
Woollen cloth manufacture	11.7	668
'Other workers in flax, cotton'	11.6	1 484
Flax, linen manufacture	11.5	4 552

Source: as Table 3.1.

The Agrarian Child Labour Market

In spite of the rising urban and industrial populations, most children between 1750 and 1870 lived and worked in rural or semi-rural districts. A great deal of child employment, therefore, was influenced by the changing fortunes of the agrarian economy. Most rural children became accustomed to agricultural work long before they were set to formal occupations, and the tasks they were given at such early ages were usually appropriate to their physical capabilities. The Newcastle Commission reported in 1861 that 'Children begin to have a money value as soon as they can shout loud enough to scare a crow, or can endure exposure to the weather in watching cows in the lane.'[9] Many of the rural autobiographers recall their first work as bird-scaring. This usually involved the patrolling of fields, shouting or operating a rattle or a clacker, to protect newly sown seed. The young Joseph Arch (later to become leader of the agricultural workers' union) started work as a bird-scarer at the age of nine before moving on at the age of 10 to lead a plough, finally driving his first pair of plough horses at the age of 12 or 13.[10] Young children could be found work picking stones from arable land, weeding and planting crops, or performing opportunistic seasonal jobs such as harvesting wild food. The work of young girls tended to be focused upon tasks ancillary to the domestic environment such as pig-keeping and dairying.[11]

Regional variations in the size of farms and in the types of production were crucial determinants of the availability of agricultural work for children. In western and north-western counties, the persistence of pastoral farming and dairy production ensured a continuing market for female and child labour. The greater incidence of domestic industry in this region promoted a mixed market for labour with members of farming families commonly engaged in both agriculture and small-scale manufacture.[12] In contrast, where arable production was most intense, there was less demand for traditional child and female jobs. In the south and east of England, the nucleated villages and strip-farming that had once dominated the rural landscape had given way increasingly since the seventeenth century to larger, consolidated, holdings and to a much more intensive production of crops. The enclosure and cultivation of commons, chases and forests increased in scale from the later eighteenth century in many southern and eastern districts. In Berkshire alone between 1831 and 1866 the amount of cultivated arable land increased by 80 per cent.[13] All of these changes tended to produce a fall in the participation of children and females in agricultural work. Changes in agricultural technologies in grain-growing districts progressively altered the composition of the farming labour force in favour of adult males.[14] The displacement of the sickle (an implement commonly used by females) by the larger scythe raised the productivity of male reapers and may have resulted in a fall in demand for female and child labour.[15] Thus, in a sample of east Suffolk parishes, 73 per cent of girl apprentices in the eighteenth century were bound to

Table 3.6   Child occupations in British agriculture and fisheries, 1851: males aged 10–14

	England and Wales	Scotland
Agricultural labourer (outdoor)	73 054 (8.0)	3575 (3.8)
Employed resident relatives of farmers	28 404 (19.8)	6488 (20.7)
Farm servant (indoor)	25 667 (13.6)	7251 (16.0)
Gardener	1 491 (2.1)	115 (1.4)
Shepherd	1 020 (8.1)	155 (2.4)
Groom, horsekeeper, jockey	770 (2.8)	57 (3.0)
Fisherman	641 (3.8)	363 (1.9)

Source: as Table 3.1.
Note: Figures in parentheses show the proportion of workers aged 10–14 employed as a percentage of total employment by occupation.

agriculture, but by the early nineteenth century that proportion had declined to only 33 per cent.[16]

In British agriculture as a whole, family farm labour remained buoyant throughout the nineteenth and twentieth centuries.[17] In 1851, a third of all farmers did not employ any labourers at all but were, in the words of the census report, 'probably doing the manual labour themselves [or] with the assistance of their children'.[18] The continuing small scale of much agricultural production meant that agriculture remained the largest employer of boy labour in England and Wales, accounting for 35 per cent of the total number of occupied male children aged 10–14. These were concentrated in three main groups: agricultural labourers, the employed children and relatives of farmers and live-in farm servants (see Table 3.6).[19]

Child labour in eighteenth- and nineteenth-century agriculture was deeply embedded in traditional labour customs. Between the early modern period and the later eighteenth century, a majority of rural children and adolescents spent their early careers as 'servants in husbandry', living and working in the households of people other than their parents. Kussmaul has pointed out that such service had three major characteristics: first, it constituted a lengthy transitional stage between living with parents and getting married; second, servants were bound by a contractual agreement (initially, between a parent and a farmer and subsequently between servant and farmer); and, third, servants were maintained within the farmer's household.[20] Live-in farm servants were frequently treated like family members in respect of their day-to-day physical and social needs.

Farmers tended to resort to servants at stages in their household life-cycle when they had insufficient resident kin to provide labour on the farm. Moreover, such servants were not confined to better-off agrarian families but were 'a normal component of all but the poorest households' resulting in 'the near universality of yearly hiring as a life-cycle stage before marriage in the early eighteenth-century agricultural sector'.[21] Farm servants were also highly mobile: though a typical period of service might last 10–12 years, a servant would rarely stay with the same farmer for more than two years.[22] This may have resulted from dissatisfaction on the part of young servants or from the fact that adolescents simply outgrew the original labour requirements of the farmers who employed them. Farm service also offered a great flexibility of labour resources for landless rural families as in the event of the death or incapacity of a breadwinner, a young farm servant could be recalled home at short notice to assume the role of primary earner.[23] In a society with an average marriage age of about 28, service also permitted a lengthy period of saving prior to marriage.

During the eighteenth century, the emergence of larger, more commercial, farms led many farmers to abandon the use of live-in servants in favour of day-labourers, and the institution of service entered a secular decline. The trend was well established at the time of Arthur Young's survey of farming in the early 1770s which discovered that 'great farmers do not keep near the proportion of servants, maids and boys, that smaller ones do'.[24] Agricultural service declined fastest in improving regions, especially those subject to large-scale enclosure, and continued only in areas where it was in farmers' interest to maintain it. It survived longest on farms in areas remote from towns and villages where it was difficult to recruit from the local population.[25] The number of children in farm service in Scotland in 1851, for example, was double that of agricultural day-labourers whereas in England and Wales male outdoor agricultural labourers aged 10–14 outnumbered indoor farm servants by three to one. The decline in live-in service was certainly greatest where the acreage of farms was expanding most rapidly and where the number of farm workers per farm exceeded that which could be accommodated comfortably within a farmer's household.

Whilst demand for child and female labour seems to have declined generally on British farms, the work of the children of farmers and of farm labourers nevertheless remained very important to the rural economy. Scottish farm labourers (or 'hinds') were contractually bound to supply the labour of a wife or daughter as a 'bondager' whilst in England, newspaper advertisements for male farm labourers stipulated that whole families should be prepared to work.[26] In some counties there was an increasing reliance upon the labour of family members during the second half of the nineteenth century.[27] By 1871, 36 per cent of Lancashire males and 73 per cent of females employed in agriculture aged between 15 and 19 worked for their own parents.[28] As late as the 1890s it was remarked of the smaller farmer: 'He and his wife, sons and daughters work from early dawn to late at night with an industry that cannot but excite the admiration of those who witness it'.[29] Indeed, in many parts of Britain, small family farms remained important well into the twentieth century. Moreover, in industrial regions, proximity to markets and to sources of non-agricultural income coupled with diversification of production allowed smaller-scale farmers to continue to benefit from the seasonal labour of their own children whilst they could easily obtain non-agricultural work during the winter slack periods. When further labour was required at times of high seasonal demand it was hired on a casual basis.

The increasing scale of production on larger farms multiplied the amount of menial labour necessary for the general maintenance of the land. By the fourth and fifth decades of the nineteenth century, tasks which required little skill, such as weeding, singling (thinning crops) and spreading manure, were increasingly sub-contracted to gangs of casual child and female labourers under the direction of gang-masters.[30] The rise of the 'gang system' attracted the attention of the Poor Law commissioners who, in 1843, conducted the first state investigation into the employment of women and children in agriculture.[31] The report found that women and children in gangs were subject to higher levels of ill-treatment by gangers and that workers were often forced to walk many miles to their places of work. Children aged between seven and 13 formed 40–50 per cent of the members of agricultural gangs in Lincolnshire, Cambridgeshire and Norfolk, and an estimate based upon 26 Norfolk parishes suggests that 61 per cent of gang members were female; 32 per cent of females employed were aged between seven and 13 and 87 per cent of males in gangs were aged between seven and 18 (though the employment of very young children, i.e. below the age of seven, appears to have been exceptional).[32] The report of 1843 condemned the harsh conditions under which children worked, but no state regulation was forthcoming and the system continued to operate freely in south-eastern counties until 1867 when, following further investigations, the Gangs Act introduced licensing for gangmasters, imposed a minimum age of eight years and sought to ban mixed gangs of males and females.[33] The Gangs Act, however, applied only to public gangs (i.e. those under the hire of a gangmaster) and, immediately the Bill was passed, large numbers of farmers moved to direct payment of privately hired gangs in order to evade prosecution. This 'was done promptly in a number of Lincolnshire towns in the year following the act'.[34] Similarly ineffectual was the Agricultural Children's Act of 1873 which sought to prohibit employment in gangs below the age of ten and to exclude all other children below the age of eight from agricultural employment.[35]

During the period 1750–1870, therefore, the terms of the contract for child labour in agriculture changed fundamentally. In many districts, farms became larger and farming itself became more intensive, and there was a widespread structural shift away from live-in farm service and towards a much greater reliance upon outdoor wage labour. Although the age-structure of the agricultural labour force changed markedly between 1750 and 1870, however, the experiences of England, Wales and Scotland were fundamentally different. By the mid-nineteenth century, most children at work on farms in England and Wales were employed as day-labourers; but 80 per cent of the Scottish agricultural labour force aged 10–14 were either live-in servants or the relatives of farmers, reflecting the continuing importance in Scotland of small-scale farming and crofting.

Workshops, Handicrafts and Apprentices

Though agriculture remained the largest single employer of child labour, its relative importance as a source of child employment declined steadily from the later eighteenth century. The structural changes in the agricultural labour market outlined above were crucial in releasing labour for manufacturing and service industries. Moreover, workshops and factories were not subject to the chronic seasonal labour surpluses that typified the agrarian labour market.[36] Domestic producers found a ready supply of subordinate and compliant labour in their own families and male heads were immune from external scrutiny or legislative controls. The new industrial sectors were also largely unaffected by restrictive practices. They could absorb migratory labour easily and lay off workers with impunity during depressions in trade. At the same time, rapid population growth ensured an abundant and youthful labour force. Under such conditions, small-scale workshop and factory owners preferred the flexibility of cheap hand-labour to the purchase of expensive and often unreliable machinery.[37] The very small scale upon which many industrial processes were carried out was evident as late as 1851 when 58 per cent of employers in silk still employed fewer than 20 workers. So much production was carried out in small workshops (especially in dressing and finishing) that, even by the 1860s, factory returns do not provide accurate levels of children's participation in silk.[38] The Children's Employment Commission of 1843 reported on the structure of the silk industry in Leek: 'it is the general practice to give the silk out in its raw state to *undertakers* who engage to return it full weight, wound, doubled, or twisted, as the case may be: these undertakers again sublet this work to others, hence it is that almost every house becomes a domestic manufactory, the husband, the wife, and their children, or those of their neighbours, being occupied in the upper room, which is devoted to the purposes of winding, doubling, or weaving.'[39] Even in the supposedly 'modern' cotton manufacture, 52 per cent of employers making returns in 1851 employed fewer than 20 persons (in the woollen cloth and worsted industries, the proportions were 74 and 55 per cent respectively). Among the older, traditional, trades small-scale production was even more commonplace with 80 per cent of wheelwrights and 65 per cent of millers employing fewer than four persons. In the boot and shoe industry, only 6 per cent of manufacturers employed more than 10 workers.[40] Most of these trades contained large concentrations of child and family labour.

Domestic production was also sustained by advances in intermediate technologies and by diversification in the demand for goods. From the mid-eighteenth century, the production of woollen and worsted textiles was stimulated by relatively inexpensive hand-powered machinery whilst cottage industries such as lace-making became widespread in a number of southern agricultural counties.[41] In some districts, demand for specific products of domestic manufactures provided much work for children. Bedfordshire and Buckinghamshire, for example, contained 50 per cent of English straw-plaiters and 40 per cent of all pillow-lace makers in 1871 and much of the straw-plaiting labour force was made up of young females.[42] A majority of occupied Bedfordshire girls aged five to nine were straw-plaiters and 40 per cent of the occupied girls aged 10–14 in the same county worked in straw and lace combined.[43]

Bedfordshire also exhibited the highest proportions of employed children of any county in England and Wales in 1851 with 17 per cent of children aged five to nine and 50 per cent of 10–14-year-old children in employment (the comparable within-county figures for industrialising Lancashire were 2.2 per cent and 38.7 per cent respectively).[44] Lace-making in Buckinghamshire and Bedfordshire was boosted by the disruption of imports of finished lace during the French Wars and by the retention of some import duties until 1860.[45] By the middle of the nineteenth century, however, more efficient and reliable lace-making machinery had been developed which rendered hand production increasingly uncompetitive and this led to a decline in reliance upon children in lace 'schools'.[46] Child employment in the straw-plait and hat manufactures of Luton and Dunstable was also stimulated in time of war by disruption of the supply of Italian hats.[47] By the third quarter of the nineteenth century, however, the growing importation of cheap plait from China and Japan reversed the demand for child workers, and the numbers of female straw-plaiters in Bedfordshire declined from a high point of nearly 21,000 in 1871 to only 485 by 1901.[48]

During the later eighteenth and early nineteenth centuries, many domestic manufactures suffered from competition with factory- and foreign-produced goods and from changes in fashion.[49] Leicestershire rural hosiery manufacture was seriously affected by changes in international trade whilst competition from foreign producers increasingly challenged home-produced silks.[50] In silk, the industry responded to competition by reducing labour costs through the employment of still more children.[51] Attempts to cut costs by employing 'half-pay' apprentices in hand-loom factories, however, failed because the high levels of supervision required to keep the children attentive tended to offset savings on the wage bill.[52] The industry most affected by a shift to factory production was domestic spinning. For much of the seventeenth and eighteenth centuries, spinning had provided flexible domestic employment for women, children and servants. It was 'customary for dairy and house maids to sit down and spin when they had no other work to do' and 'schools' of spinning proliferated in many early modern towns where training and production were carried out simultaneously.[53] However, the development of more productive spinning technology between the 1760s and the 1780s (the jenny, water frame and mule) led to fundamental structural changes in the domestic sector. The traditional Jersey and Brunswick spinning wheels were (as Radcliffe described it) 'all thrown into lumber-rooms' and had 'practically ceased' by the end of the century.[54] By the early years of the nineteenth century, the introduction of more labour-intensive spinning machinery and the shift to workshops and factories altered the gender balance of spinners radically in favour of adult males working at piece rates.

In 1851, workshops and handicrafts formed the second most important occupation group for male children in England and Wales after agriculture. Among the larger concentrations of employed males in the 10–14 age-group in England and Wales were shoemakers (9700), silk workers (5871), tailors (4364), hose and stocking manufacturers (3277) and blacksmiths (3150) but these five occupations amounted to only 40 per cent of the total of child labour in workshops and handicrafts. The remainder comprised a wide variety of occupations such as glovers, clog-makers, book-binders, printers, soap-boilers, brush and broom makers, millers, coopers, cabinet makers, rope-makers, sailcloth-makers and nail manufacturers. Among the more important occupations for females were silk workers (10,533), lace-makers (8628), straw-plaiters (5041), glovers (3374), hose and stocking manufacturers (3152). These five accounted for 61 per cent of the female workshop and handicraft labour force aged 10–14 in England and Wales.

The workshop and handicrafts sectors comprised both 'sweated' and skilled child occupations. Differences in labour-intensity and skill requirements across this diverse sector influenced the ages at which children were recruited and this makes it very difficult to derive a generalised picture of child labour in handicrafts. In rural, or semi-rural, settings, production and the labour supply were often closely integrated with the cycles of the agrarian economy, while the frequent requirement for young workers to live-in with employers often rendered distinctions between skilled apprentices and plain 'servants' problematical.[55] It is clear, however, from the distribution of occupations at the mid-nineteenth-century censuses that a great many children worked in skilled, or semi-skilled, trades at ages when they would almost certainly be receiving skilled training of some description (whether indentured as apprentices or otherwise).

In the mid-nineteenth century, males were much more prominent than females in the statistics of skilled occupations (Table 3.7). It has been argued, however, that the striking sexual division of labour was probably less pronounced in the eighteenth century. Much of the decline in girl apprenticeship up to the mid-nineteenth century seems to have been attributable to the increasing tendency among trades to be carried on at sites remote from the domestic environment and to a rise in competition for jobs resulting from rising male unemployment in the wake of the French Wars.[56] In contrast, the concentration of girls within the unskilled textiles sector and in domestic or agricultural service (see Tables 3.3 and 3.5) reflects the growing tendency among mid-nineteenth-century females to concentrate their wage-earning in the period between childhood and marriage. Agricultural and domestic service offered both accommodation and wages for girls, and such 'bridging occupations' between childhood and marriage were increasingly popular among unmarried females.[57] The long period of training and initially poor rates of pay associated with apprenticeship were much less attractive to females seeking to maximise incomes before marriage and child-bearing (see Table 3.7).

The great disparity of fortunes among skilled workshop trades makes it unlikely that the decline in female participation was uniform throughout the skilled occupations. It does seem clear, however, that the range of female workshop and cottage-based occupations became progressively narrower and less skilled during the classic industrial and agricultural revolutions.[58] In metal-working, boys and men predominated in the production of machines and machine parts whilst girls and women dominated the less-skilled areas such as nailmaking, chainmaking and the manufacture of tin toys.[59] In the manufacture of bolts, files, latches, keys and locks in the west midlands, and of cutlery in Sheffield, females were in a minority, but in pin manufactures the low-skilled job of heading pins was 'performed wholly by females'.[60] Such work was poorly paid and regarded as inferior.[61] Apart from factory textiles, therefore, the

Table 3.7 Children and young persons in selected skilled occupations, England and Wales, 1851

	Males		Females	
	10–14	*15–19*	*10–14*	*15–19*
Shoemaker	9 700	27 055	2 197	5 846
Tailor	4 364	14 440	622	3 148
Blacksmith	3 150	15 066	0	14
Engine-, machine-maker	1 292	6 365	111	97
Printer	1 295	4 880	0	0
Miller	1 091	4 494	2	18

Source: As Table 3.1.

female experience of skilled and semi-skilled work from the late eighteenth century was one of increasing exclusion.[62] The very small numbers of female children in the statistics of nineteenth-century skilled trades remains somewhat puzzling, however, since it hardly seems feasible that skilled parents without sons would apprentice unrelated male children in preference to their own daughters.[63]

There are few reliable national quantitative records of the numbers of formal apprenticeships in eighteenth- and nineteenth-century Britain.[64] The census of 1851 required householders to distinguish between masters and apprentices, but the instruction was not universally attended to and the resultant statistics are highly unreliable. It is often impossible to distinguish, even at a local level, between private, charity and parish apprenticeships.[65] Simonton estimates that about 3 per cent of the children in Essex and Staffordshire were serving formal indentured apprenticeships at any one time during the eighteenth century and offers an approximation for the English total of apprentices aged five to 14 at about 56,000 (though many more than this were doubtless employed in an 'informal' capacity).[66]

More is known about the functions and processes of apprenticeship. Here, two major features distinguished an apprentice from a servant. First, an apprentice was bound by written indentures (typically from the age of 14) for a fixed term (the Statute of Artificers of 1563 stipulated seven years' duration for indentured apprentices).[67] Secondly, in contrast with the highly mobile agricultural servants, apprentices would notionally serve the same master until completion of their term. During a term of apprenticeship, a master was expected to teach the 'art and mystery' of his craft, and the apprentice was to reciprocate by keeping such arts and mysteries secret. The long period of apprenticeship transmitted more than simply occupational training. Literacy, numeracy and business-management skills, as well as religious and moral teaching, were all important factors in the socialisation of apprentices. For many children and adolescents, therefore, a formal apprenticeship formed a distinct life-cycle stage as well as a period of craft training.[68] Traditional 'private' craft apprenticeships, moreover, were inherently conservative and were often available only to the kin of established tradesmen (apprentices and masters often share the same name in surviving indentures) or to those on the same social level.[69] The restriction of craft apprenticeships within successive generations of families has been described by one scholar as 'hereditary monopolies'.[70] The statutory regulation of apprenticeship came under increasing strain during the later eighteenth and early nineteenth centuries and concern grew among indentured trades about the entry of non-indentured workers.

As demographic increase contributed further to a surplus of labour, competition for jobs grew in intensity. Impoverished workers in declining trades were increasingly likely to teach the rudiments of their trade to non-indentured labourers in return for cash payments. This prompted many trade societies to strengthen their rules by forbidding the teaching of a trade to people other than family members or properly indentured apprentices.[71] Shipwrights enforced rigorously the production of indentures by intending members, and in framework knitting and silk-weaving the growing number of apprentices was blamed for overstocking the labour market and causing the prices of finished goods to fall.[72] Attempts were also made by carpenters, bricklayers, wheelwrights and croppers to strengthen statutory protection. Silk workshops (traditionally, employers of high levels of child labour) were particularly resistant to the rise in non-indentured labour: the regulation of the industry in Macclesfield was said to be organised 'on quite medieval lines'.[73] By the early nineteenth century, the enforcement of apprenticeship laws was being demanded even by Scottish tradesmen among whom (as Derry observed) 'it had no traditional sanctity'.[74]

Most attempts to bolster apprenticeship by legislation, however, were largely unsuccessful. In the 1770s, alarm about the numbers of parish children apprenticed to London silk-weavers prompted the 'Spitalfields Acts' which limited apprentices to two per weaver.[75] Such legislation, however, though well-intentioned, appeared contrary to prevailing ideas about the freedom of labour.[76] New and expanding trades and manufactures were eager to receive a supply of low-skilled, unregulated and compliant child labour, and the growth of industries not subject to traditional labour regulations allowed greater opportunities for children and adolescents to earn wages on their own account. This resulted in an increase in apprentices 'turning-over' (i.e. leaving before the end of their terms).[77] The decline of many traditional trades also led to apprentices being put out of place due to the masters simply going out of business.[78] By the early nineteenth century, it became clear that many children who were bound to industrial and urban employments were apprentices in little more than name. State inquiries from the 1830s commented that the range of skills acquired by apprentices was becoming progressively smaller. A royal commission of 1843 reported the case of 'a journeyman [builder] who had completed his time [and had] applied for work, but was unable to perform any part of his trade but making stairs, and stated as the reason that the master to whom he had served his apprenticeship had kept him solely to that branch, and that there were many of his fellow-apprentices who could only make window-frames'.[79]

The century after 1750 also witnessed fundamental changes in social relationships between apprentices and their masters. In the seventeenth and eighteenth centuries, it was common for masters to receive payments from parents for board, lodging and instruction. By the nineteenth century, however, traditional 'indoor' apprenticeship was in serious decline and 'outdoor' training (where apprentices remained in the households of their parents whilst receiving a small wage) became more common.[80] The overall rise in incomes in the decades after 1820 would theoretically have made it easier for masters to employ and accommodate 'indoor' apprentices. However, even moderate increases in the size of workshops created severe accommodation problems.[81] Urbanisation further contributed to a decline in live-in training and the highest incidence of 'outdoor' apprenticeship was to be found among urban trades where a greater proportion of children lived within daily walking distance of their masters' workshops.[82] Increasing large-scale migration to urban districts also meant that an increasing number of apprentices would be drawn from families unknown to masters and, from the mid-to-late eighteenth century, a growing social exclusiveness arose among urban masters who became less likely to accept the children of strangers into their households.[83] As Knox put it, 'The prospect of strange "low-bred" boys engaging in social intercourse on equal terms with masters and their families, or interfering with their possessions, did not encourage a continuance of the indoor system'.[84] Traditional apprenticeships suffered further from a growing unwillingness or inability on the part of parents to pay the stamp duty of one pound required to place a binding by indenture on an official footing. This increasingly common omission rendered unsuccessful any attempts to enforce apprenticeship in the courts since, in absence of formal indentures, magistrates were unable to compel apprentices to return to their masters. In the early 1840s, the proportion of stamped apprenticeship indentures in the Staffordshire Potteries was described as '13 to 3000 or more' (i.e. less than a half per cent).[85] Families in poverty also tended to restrict to a minimum their children's period of formal training or schooling in order to benefit from their wages at the earliest opportunity. Such children were more likely to be placed in the first instance in unskilled work which, compared with apprenticeship, would pay an initially higher rate of wages.[86] The decline of indoor apprenticeship, therefore, paralleled in many respects that of farm service. Traditional labour regulations became increasingly unsustainable in the face of a rising population, a growing urban labour force and an increasing size of production processes.

The Urban Labour Market

Large cities harboured a wide range of trades and services and a highly irregular and casualised child labour market.[87] The majority of occupied urban children worked in ancillary and unskilled jobs such as child-minders, delivery boys and workshop assistants.[88] Much of the work of urban children went unrecorded or unspecified in official listings. It is doubtful, for example, that the small number of children returned with the designation 'shopkeeper' in the census reflects accurately the level of child employment in the retail sector. Although less than 1 per cent of 'shopkeepers' were aged 10–14, it is probable that the children of shop-keepers were employed at very early ages and were reported by the census simply as messengers or porters. Fetching and carrying jobs were ubiquitous among urban children and constituted by far the most youthful of occupations. In 1851, London contained 27 per cent of the English and Welsh total of messengers and porters in the age-group 10–14. Children carried domestic fuel, water, household provisions and jugs of beer, and carried work pieces and messages between a variety of small businesses. In some cases, urban child occupations amounted to little more than begging. Often, parents would be the main beneficiaries of children's incomes. A government report noted in 1840: 'A boy is told to follow a gentleman on horseback or in a gig till he stops and requires some one to hold his horse; another has a basket of oranges or nuts put into his hands, or, perhaps, a bundle of children's story books to sell; a third has a besom given him to sweep a crossing'.[89] Informal street trading also employed large numbers of children. Where sufficient capital existed, children bought cat and dog meat from local knackers' yards for sale from their own dog-carts.[90]

The lives of many working-class urban girls were dominated by informal domestic labour and child-care duties. Girls between the ages of nine and 15 would be called upon to care for young children at home or in the homes of relatives, usually in order to allow mothers to perform work outside the home. As a young watercress-seller told Henry Mayhew in the 1850s, 'I had to take care of a baby for my aunt... it was only two months old; but I minded it for ever such a time – till it could walk.'[91] Outside the home, the single most important urban occupation for female children and adolescents was domestic service. In 1851, domestic service accounted for a quarter of the national total of employed females aged 10–14. The age-structure of domestic servants also became more youthful in the second half of the nineteenth century. The proportion of female domestic servants aged below 20 was 36 per cent in 1851, 39 per cent in 1861 and 1871, and 43 per cent in 1881.[92] The metropolis comprised the largest concentrations of domestic servants, with Westminster and the City of London employing between four and five times the national *per capita* average.[93] Many servants were economic migrants from southern rural areas undergoing a decline in labour demand for young, unmarried, females. In 1851, for example, nearly 15 per cent of servants in Rochdale had been born in the southern agrarian counties of England and by 1871 that proportion had reached a remarkable 30 per cent.[94] Young servants were widely dispersed throughout middle-class urban society. The model of the large upper-middle-class household employing a large number of servants (popularised in literature and drama) was, in fact, exceptional in the eighteenth and nineteenth centuries, and a majority of households employing servants had only a solitary 'maid-of-all-work'. [95] Little evidence of the working conditions and pay of such solitary child and adolescent servants has survived, though they were often nicknamed 'slavey' which seems to offer an unambiguous description of their social position. Orphan and workhouse girls were often taken on as drudges in lodging-houses and pubs and would have to 'take up the carpets, scrub the stairs, wash the babies, wait on the boarders, carry the children out for an airing, make the beds, black the grates, and run messages'.[96] Though the true numbers of child domestic servants may never be known, they were undoubtedly far more numerous than the 70,000 aged under 15 enumerated in 1851.[97]

During the nineteenth century, child employment in urban districts became increasingly concentrated in menial occupations. The growing tendency of male school-leavers to enter high-turnover work prior to taking up more permanent jobs or apprenticeships formed the basis of a 'boy labour problem' that preoccupied middle-class social commentators towards the close of the nineteenth century.[98] In London, 54 per cent of school leavers became 'errand boys, shop boys, or van boys', and more than half of a sample of Glaswegian boys leaving elementary school became milk boys or lorry boys whilst a further quarter went into unskilled labouring jobs. Reports by the Poor Law Commission and the Board of Education were unanimous that 'the results of the large employment of boys in occupations which offer no opportunity of promotion to employment as men are disastrous. The boy, thrown out at 16, 17, or 18 or 20 years of age, drifts into the low-skilled labour market or the army of unemployables.'[99] The term 'blind alley labour' was coined to describe children employed in occupations that offered no long-term security.[100]

The rise of urban society and the spread of nineteenth-century notions of 'respectability' also resulted in heightened scrutiny of what children did in public space. Child street entertainers and traders increasingly attracted accusations of destitution and were often depicted as criminal or a threat to the social order.[101] As Davin has pointed out, the middle classes, many of whom relied heavily upon young servants, 'were less shocked by working children than by street children and their independence'.[102] Many of the child-protection charities that emerged during the nineteenth century owed their existence to the public outcry against the apparently increasing public presence of urban 'vagrant' children.[103] Daunton has suggested that urban public space was progressively re-defined as 'connective tissue which was to be traversed rather than used' between the home, the workplace and the school.[104] This major shift in attitudes towards public space was reflected in an increasing number of urban by-laws which sought to classify many types of children's street activity as illegal (although no effective national legislation to regulate child street traders emerged until the very end of the nineteenth century).[105]

Throughout the nineteenth century, a number of charitable institutions resorted to forced emigration as a means of cleansing the streets of the perceived growing numbers of vagrant children. Tens of thousands of children were bound as apprentices to masters in the colonies through schemes operated by 'child savers' such as Dr Barnardo, Annie Macpherson and Maria Rye. Between 1834 and 1837, the Children's Friend Society sent 1300 children to work on South African farms, and between 1868 and 1925, 80,000 children were sent to Canada as agricultural and domestic servants and apprentices.[106] Only about a third of the children sent overseas were actually orphans, and 'philanthropic abduction' and forced emigration of children was often made use of by evangelical groups as a means of separating destitute children from the influence of dissolute parents. Many of the adoptive masters treated the schemes merely as a means of obtaining a cheap servant. As one child émigré observed to a social investigator, ' 'doption, Sir, is when folks get a girl without wages'.[107] To all intents and purposes, the emigration charities operated a system of forced labour migration that was little different from the trade in pauper apprentices that had been practised between urban Poor Law overseers and rural factory owners more than half a century earlier.[108] The long-term aim of such schemes was to settle destitute urban children in colonial rural districts, but this aim was largely unsuccessful and many of the children who were apprenticed (having no familial connections or inheritance rights with the masters to whom they were bound) tended to drift back towards urban or unskilled work during adolescence or early adulthood.[109]

The Industrial Labour Market

Between the 1780s and the 1850s, there was a general shift in the balance of the British population from rural districts towards the industrial towns and trading ports of northern England and central Scotland and this reflected the development of a highly regionalised industrial labour market. By the middle of the nineteenth century half of the inhabitants of Lancashire resided in centres of population greater than 10,000. Much of this growth of population was due to the enormous growth in the production of textiles and the expansion of mineral extraction.[110] Industrial work, where it was available, almost invariably offered higher wages for children. The earnings of child coalminers aged 10–14, for example, were between 54 and 86 per cent higher than the average for working children.[111] However, it is important not to overestimate the significance of large factories and mines to the national child labour market because even at the high point of the classic Industrial Revolution, the new industries employed comparatively small numbers of children in a national context. The number of boys occupied in coal and cotton combined in 1841 was estimated by the census at around 86,000 compared with 187,000 in agriculture and domestic service.[112] The factory did not become commonplace until the late nineteenth century, by which time child employment had fallen to very low levels.[113] The early factories, however, did contain large *concentrations* of child workers and offered new opportunities for children to work.[114]

The technology of textiles production changed very rapidly from the last quarter of the eighteenth century and this had important consequences for the industrial child labour force.[115] In domestic and factory spinning, the roles of child workers were fundamentally different. Traditional spinning (using spinning wheels) had, during the eighteenth century, been dominated by females and girls and was carried out in a domestic setting. Berg points out that children were especially suited to the small treadle-operated traditional jenny having about a dozen spindles.[116] It has also been suggested that some early textiles machinery was designed specifically for use by children (though this argument must be taken to apply chiefly to jennies and water frames rather than to the later adult-dominated and more labour-intensive mules).[117] As Knowles argued, the growing complexity and labour-intensity of spinning machinery ultimately rendered its direct operation unsuitable for young children.[118] Instead, children were employed increasingly in tasks ancillary to the main processes of production, and both workshop and factory spinners employed a variety of young assistants. Andrew Ure described the structure of the small groups of workers attending the common mules in the late eighteenth century.

> In working the common [mule]...various persons are employed...the 'spinner', who directs the general operation of the machine...one or more 'piecers' to join the threads which break during the spinning...a 'creel-filler' to place the 'rovings' from which the yarn is spun, in a part of the machine termed the 'creel' and a 'cleaner', or 'scavenger', to remove the waste cotton...and to clean the machine generally. The 'spinner' being the principal person of the set thus employed, and in most instances, an adult; the others being subordinate to him and always young persons, or children.[119]

It has been argued that the shift to mechanised production 'reduced, and in some cases removed, the differential in strength between the adult and the child' and rendered factory work more amenable to child labour.[120] However, whilst a decline in labour-intensity may have rendered factory production more attractive to children's employment, spinning, weaving and finishing were, to all intents and purposes, separate industrial processes, and it cannot be assumed that machinery always had the effect of displacing adult workers across the textiles sector. The growth of the 'putting-out' system during the eighteenth century, for example, shows how hand-working within one process might be stimulated by centralisation and machine production elsewhere in the same sector. Hence, the complexity of textiles production prevents any general statements about the effects of technology upon factory children.

The relationship between locational, organisational and technological changes and their effects upon the textiles family economy has none the less been one of the most contentious issues in social history. In the 1960s, the sociologist Neil Smelser argued that locational and technological changes in cotton production prior to the 1830s had only a small effect upon the structure of the pre-factory family economy. Smelser argued for a smooth transition of the textiles family economy from domestic to factory production: skilled spinners in factories, it was argued, were permitted by factory owners to retain their traditional control over labour recruitment and continued to hire their own wives and children, or the children of relatives. He claimed that this 'anchor of tradition' only came under threat following organisational changes of the 1820s and 30s, and suggested that much of the agitation for factory reform among operatives during the 1830s and 40s should be attributed to the threat posed to family employment by increases in the use of child labour as a result of the introduction of new spinning technology.[121]

The argument that the movement for factory reform originated in a fear of competition from child labour, however, seems to have no basis in empirical evidence. As Anderson pointed out, a simple increase in the number of assistants required to spinners should not, in principle, have posed a threat to the tradition of family employment; nor should a knowledge of this among operatives have provided the basis of support for factory reform only in the 1830s and 40s.[122] Family incomes were maximised by employing family members, but family labour was necessarily supplemented by employing children from outside the immediate family. Quantitative evidence supports such a view for the first two decades of the nineteenth century. Statistics for Preston in 1816 indicate that only 11.6 per cent of children in 13 factories were employed by their parents, whilst Shuttleworth's pre-1833 study of spinners shows that only 15 per cent of employed piecers were the children of spinners.[123] Moreover, a House of Lords inquiry of 1818–19 showed that only about 25 per cent of piecers in mills had the same name as the spinner for whom they worked.[124] The principal operatives retained the power to restrict the numbers of entrants to the more skilled sectors of the trade. This meant that technical change, rather than initiating a decline in family labour, engendered a two-tier system of child employment in which the children of operatives usually received better jobs and training. This meant that only a minority of piecers could hope to become adult spinners or minders. More importantly, argued Anderson, the age-structure of adult spinners would have rendered it logically impossible for their families to have supplied all the required piecers. For example, in the 1830s and 40s, 88 per cent of the children in Lancashire mule-spinning were recruited directly by spinners and about 50 per cent of the spinners themselves were aged below 32. Only about half of the male spinners, therefore, would have been old enough to have had a child of employable age.[125] Moreover, factory regulation, as enacted in 1833, forced children to remain at home 'perhaps one extra year...and to spend a part of their time from the age of nine to thirteen at home and a part in education'.[126] The Factory Act of 1833, with its limitation upon hours and ages, would almost certainly have been contrary to the wishes of spinners who wished to maximise their own family incomes rather then employing the children of strangers.

Some attempts have been made to reduce the stress upon industrial technology in explaining levels of child employment. Cunningham claims that '[d]ifferences in the composition of the labour force in different places often cannot be explained by the level of technology' and has argued that historians who focus upon the influence of technical changes upon child labour are guilty of 'technological determinism'.[127] In fact, changes in technology in many industries do appear to have been accompanied by substantial and measurable changes in the proportions of employed children. Following initial heavy demand for children in picking and carding in the later eighteenth century, the mechanisation of many preparatory processes resulted by the early 1830s in children becoming concentrated in ancillary work within the mule-spinning process.[128] From the 1830s, progressive improvements to mules meant that each machine could carry a greater number of spindles. This technological shift has been interpreted in different ways. Nardinelli has argued that the gradual transition to the self-acting mule between the 1830s and the 1890s required less piecing work to be performed and resulted in a decline in the employment of children.[129] Bolin-Hort, however, has suggested that the shift to the self-actor required more young piecers to repair broken threads and a greater number of scavengers to clean floors and machinery and that this led to an increase in the numbers of piecers below 13.[130] Unfortunately, the employment statistics that may offer a solution to this question are beset with interpretational problems. The reports of the factory inspectors certainly show an apparent increase in the proportions of children below 13 employed in cotton factories from the late 1850s to the mid-1870s (the picture for worsted is similar, again peaking in the early 1870s).[131]

However, the statistical increase in child labour in cotton may simply result from an increasing reliance upon 'half-time', as against 'full-time', child workers.[132] Children who were employed as 'half-timers' after the Factory Act of 1844 were not recorded separately from full-time workers in the inspectors' reports until 1878. At that time, nearly 100,000 were counted.[133] The mid-Victorian censuses also failed to distinguish between half-time and full-time working. According to the most recent historian of the half-time system, 'the exact number of half-timers on a national level at any given period is extremely difficult to calculate'.[134] Half-time employment was also most common where trade was expanding most rapidly – especially in areas responsible for the textiles boom of the early to mid-1870s.[135] By the mid-1880s, over 90 per cent of half-time child labour was sub-contracted by the operatives, and in some Lancashire districts between 50 and 70 per cent of 'tenting' in weaving processes was undertaken by half-timers.[136] Conclusive statements about national changes in child labour inputs to cotton textiles prior to the 1880s are therefore problematical. It is probable that the failure of the factory inspectors and the census to distinguish between half-timers and full-timers in textiles conceals a stagnation or a relative decline in child participation in the textiles sector throughout the 1850s, 60s and 70s.[137]

The scale of technological change in weaving also had profound implications for employed children. The decline in hand-weaving during the early decades of the nineteenth century was felt most acutely among specialist urban hand-weaving households who sent increasing numbers of their children to work in factories. Rural and semi-rural hand-weaving families suffered less because of the higher incidence of by-employment in agriculture.[138] From about the 1840s, moreover, the balance of child labour in cotton textiles as a whole shifted increasingly from mule-spinning to weaving in line with an increase in the number of power looms that could be operated by a single weaver.[139] An increase from two- to four-loom, and later six-loom, weaving necessitated the employment of more child 'tenters' (general assistants to adult weavers) to prepare shuttles and clean machinery. In Lancashire, the weaving sector

Table 3.8   Proportions (%) of children below 13 in cotton factories, 1835–78

1835	1838	1847	1850	1856	1862	1867	1870	1874	1878
13.2	4.7	5.8	4.6	6.5	8.8	10.4	9.6	14.0	12.8

Source: S. J. Chapman, *The Lancashire Cotton Industry, A Study in Economic Development*, (Manchester, 1904), p. 112.

increased its share of the cotton textiles child labour force from 1 per cent to 43 per cent between the 1850s and 1890s and by the mid-1880s, three-quarters of Lancashire half-timers were employed in the weaving process.[140] Despite the boom in child labour in weaving, however, the prospects for children were among the worst in the textiles industry. As Farnie suggests, they 'needed no strength, knowledge, art, or skill but only manual dexterity ... They had much less hope of promotion than piecers since the weaving shed had no superior caste of employees comparable to the self-actor minders of the mule mill.'[141] Indeed, weaving became increasingly dominated by young females seeking well-paid work prior to marriage. Thus, the continued debate over whether technological advancement in textiles had the effect of increasing or decreasing the proportions of employed children largely depends upon which part of the industry is examined. Although it has been argued that the proportions of children employed in textiles could vary greatly between districts employing similar technologies, the variety of different textiles processes and the complexities of dealing with the frequently faulty statistical evidence does not support such bland generalisations.

The relationship between industrial technology and the composition of the child labour force in the coalmining industry is less controversial. Early twentieth-century historians such as Ashton and Sykes argued that technological advancement in coalmining during the first half of the nineteenth century resulted in an increase in the proportions of employed children, but subsequent research has established that it was, in fact, the coal districts using the most primitive technologies which employed the largest proportions of child workers.[142]

In common with most industries, the nature of coal production was regionally differentiated. The larger coal-producing districts (notably in the north-east and south Wales) expanded their production rapidly to meet increases in demand for the export market and for the industrial and residential markets. Other regions (for example, west Yorkshire and east Lancashire) supplied a larger proportion of 'land-sale' coal (i.e. coal for sale in the immediate locality) and here the scale of production often remained small. Some rural-based coal pits and adits in the smaller coalfields employed only a handful of workers: often one or two men with an equal, or greater, number of children.[143] Child workers in the coalfields of the early 1840s formed about 10–13 per cent of the mining labour force (i.e. approximately 15–20,000 children).[144] Nineteenth-century coal face labour was dominated by adult males and was performed by hand. As late as 1900, only about 1 per cent of total coal output was cut by machine.[145] This meant that increases in output from the end of the eighteenth century were achieved by the employment of more men at the face and by the introduction of more efficient underground haulage technology. Child miners worked in underground haulage operations as 'putters' or 'drivers', pulling carts and sledges or driving horse and pony carriages.

In technologically advanced pits, innovations in haulage technology contributed to a decline in the relative numbers of employed children compared with adults.[146] Haulage operations became increasingly efficient in the early decades of the nineteenth century through the diffusion of rails and horse-drawn carriages and, increasingly, from the 1850s, through the growth of efficient machine haulage. The increased use of ponies in north-east collieries throughout the first half of the century also allowed greater weights of coal to be transported. As Taylor has pointed out, a high proportion of face workers to non-face workers was one of the most important indications of improvement in underground technology in nineteenth-century mining.[147] The effectiveness of haulage technology, however, was constrained by the geology of coal seams. In the narrow seams of west Yorkshire and parts of Lancashire, the use of many forms of underground mechanical conveyance was impractical and haulage technology remained backward and labour-intensive. Moreover, haulage in thin seams was made possible only by the employment of children who would carry or drag coal along the seam to the shaft. Where thicker seams existed, in the north-east of England, coal could be removed from the coal-face more efficiently. A greater roof space allowed access to physically larger workers, and ponies were increasingly substituted for young haulage workers.[148]

Technical innovations and geology, therefore, had a profound effect upon both the physical size and the age-structure of underground workers.[149] This is confirmed by evidence of a lower age of recruitment and a higher incidence of younger workers in coal districts where thin seams and primitive technology predominated. Table 3.9 shows how the age-structure of the labour force was influenced by the prevailing technology in advanced and primitive coal pits.

Larger and more complex coal mines were at greater risk of accidents as a result of accumulations of methane gas (or 'fire-damp') and a mixture of carbon dioxide and nitrogen (or 'choke-damp'), and the dangers of explosion and suffocation were countered by the introduction of increasingly complicated methods of ventilating the workings. During the first four decades of the nineteenth century young children were employed as 'trappers' to operate the underground ventilation doors which maintained the direction of underground air currents. Though this was quite a simple operation, it was also vital to the safety of collieries. Children sometimes caused explosions by leaving doors open or through simple inattention to their duty and, by the 1830s and 40s, an increase in the number of explosions resulting from negligence by child trappers led to calls by employers and managers for their exclusion from pits.[150]

The number of 'trappers' in pits has generally been overestimated by historians. It has been argued that in the 1840s most of the 5000 children between five and 10 working underground in coal mines were employed as 'trappers'.[151] In fact, of the 400 or so child miners aged 10 or under interviewed by the Children's Employment Commission in 1841, only 35 per cent were working in ventilation whilst 55 per cent were in haulage. Only in the north-east coalfield was a majority of under-tens employed in ventilation. Here, the proportion of trappers was highest at 70 per cent. In other, less advanced, coal districts the proportions were much smaller: in south Wales, for example (probably the second most advanced district in ventilation technology in 1841), the proportion of trappers in the under-ten labour force was 44 per cent, in Yorkshire 16 per cent, and in the midlands only 11 per cent.[152] Moreover, few children remained as 'trappers' beyond the age of 11 or 12 and the vast majority of coalmining children aged 10–14 remained concentrated in the haulage sector. Hence, in mining, technological innovation and the geology of coal districts had a profound influence upon the age-structure of the labour force.

Table 3.9 Proportions (%) of coalminers in different coal districts by age-groups, 1841

	Northumberland & North Durham	West Yorkshire	Small pits, West Yorkshire
over 18	68.9	61.4	54.8
13–18	18.3	22.5	21.6
under 13	12.8	16.2	24.7

Source: P. Kirby, 'The Historic Viability of Child Labour and the Mines Act of 1842' in M. Lavalette (ed.) A Thing of the Past? Child Labour in Britain in the Nineteenth and Twentieth Centuries (Liverpool, 1999), table 4.1, p. 105.

The Employment and 'Unemployment' of Children

The work of children, like that of adults, was also sensitive to trade cycles, uncertainties in the supply of raw materials and seasonal fluctuations in demand for labour.[153] An unpredictable labour market resulted in high levels of short-time and part-time working as well as multiple occupations. Such volatile labour-market conditions, together with the problems of analysing census and other listings of child occupations (discussed in Chapter 1) render it extremely difficult to establish how many children were actually at work during the eighteenth and early nineteenth centuries. Hugh Cunningham has suggested that at any point between 1680 and 1851 'there was a large number of children for whom no work was available' and that many children were 'unemployed'.[154] This controversial view is contrary to widespread opinion among economic historians that the Industrial Revolution merely ushered in a change of form in child labour rather than a substantive increase in the numbers of child workers.[155] Cunningham's theory also seems to contradict the view of scholars of proto-industrial development who have argued that one of the most important factors in stimulating the spread of early industrial production was rising consumer demand stimulated by increases in the earnings of children and females during the seventeenth and eighteenth centuries.[156] Cunningham's arguments for the eighteenth and early nineteenth centuries seem to rest partly upon a small number of anecdotes and partly upon flawed replies to a Poor Law questionnaire in the early 1830s.[157] Cunningham calculated his national child 'unemployment' statistics from the 1851 census occupation tables and assumed that children who were recorded as not having a specific occupation and not attending a school were unemployed.[158] However, if Cunningham's definition of 'unemployment' is applied separately to the male and female labour child labour forces, it appears that it was concentrated chiefly among girls. Only one in five of the male population aged 10–14 in England and Wales was 'unemployed' and in Scotland about one in eight. The same criteria show that unemployment was very high among females with 37 per cent of English and Welsh females and 26 per cent of Scottish females in the age-group 10–14 having no recorded occupation.

It is far from clear, however, that large numbers of the female child population were actually 'unemployed'. The census report of 1851 remarked that this substantial group comprised 'large numbers of the population that have hitherto been held to have no occupation; but it requires no argument to prove...that the children are...occupied in filial or household duties'.[159] The wide range of domestic tasks undertaken by young females in the home (cooking, cleaning and child-minding) were not regarded as 'occupations' by census-takers and were not recorded in the census summary tables.[160] Moreover, the detailed summary tables for Britain placed females enumerated without defined occupations under the general heading of 'Persons engaged in the Domestic Offices, or Duties of Wives, Mothers, Mistresses of Families, Children, Relatives'.[161] Home-based work such as child-minding – a role performed predominantly by female children – was especially important because, as Becker has pointed out, such work permitted a reallocation of time within the household, helping other family members to enter the labour market outside the home.[162] The shortfall in the reporting of female occupations in the census, therefore, almost certainly resulted from a contemporary belief by the General Register Office that female work in the domestic sphere did not constitute an 'occupation'. A further problem with Cunningham's theory is that he overlooked an accounting anomaly in the 1851 occupation tables which omitted 62,000 working children aged below 15 from the totals for agriculture alone (this number is greater than the total of children employed in cotton manufacture at the same date).[163]

The problem of estimating the numbers of 'unemployed' children is also complicated by the quinquennial age-groups used in the census which conceal a pattern of cumulative entry to the labour market in which the largest numbers of 'unemployed' in the age-group 10–14 were concentrated at the youngest ages (i.e. 10 and 11). The existence of this pattern is difficult to demonstrate for England and Wales because the mid-nineteenth-century censuses failed to provide statistics of occupations by singulate ages. However, a comparison might be drawn with the pattern of cumulative entry to work in late-industrialising Japan where, in 1879, 35 per cent of children aged 13 had an occupation, 65 per cent at age 14, and 92 per cent at 15. In early twentieth-century England and Wales, fewer children were employed than at earlier dates but the censuses continued to show a pattern of cumulative entry. In 1911, for example, only 2 per cent of the children aged 10–13 were occupied compared with 17 per cent at age 13 and 52 per cent at age 14. Similarly, at the 1921 census, only 5 per cent of children aged 12–14 were at work compared with 52 per cent of children in the age-group 14–16.[164]

Assertions about child 'unemployment' are also crucially dependent upon what is meant by 'employment'. Part-time working and multiple occupations were commonly accepted features of early industrial society and traditional customs such as the keeping of 'St Monday' (abstaining from work on Mondays following pay-day) would cause great disruption in the labour market.[165] The use of the term 'unemployment' to describe the irregular nature of child labour may therefore be regarded as inappropriate.[166] Children in the eighteenth and early nineteenth centuries were certainly affected by widespread job insecurity but there is plenty of evidence demonstrating a similar degree of insecurity in the adult labour market. Moreover, few working-class autobiographers mention unemployment as a feature of their childhoods. The theory that large numbers of eighteenth- and nineteenth-century children were 'unemployed' therefore remains unproven and the question of national levels of child participation awaits more detailed research.[167]

Overall, the secular picture over the period 1750–1870 seems to have been one of increasing exclusion of children from many employment sectors. Such a generalisation, however, must be tempered by an understanding of the enormous diversity of the eighteenth- and nineteenth-century child labour markets. The census occupation abstracts in 1851 reported 332 discrete occupations for males and 197 for females (see Appendix). These designations were themselves derivative of a very much larger number of occupations reported by enumerators in the household schedules. Any attempt to arrive at conclusive answers about the long-term effects of changes in production and technology upon the national child labour market, therefore, will require much further comparative research across sectors as well as an understanding of local causes of changes in demand for child labour within specific occupations.

Notes

1. Theoretical and empirical approaches to comparative regional studies are discussed in S. Pollard, *Peaceful Conquest* (Oxford, 1981); J. Langton, 'The Industrial Revolution and the Regional Geography of England', *Transactions of the Institute of British Geographers*, 9 (1984); P. Hudson, *The Industrial Revolution* (London, 1992).

2. The numbers of males employed in agriculture remained fairly steady over the nineteenth century, though they fell as a proportion of the total of males employed in Great Britain: 1841: 29%, 1851: 29%, 1861: 25%, 1871: 19%, 1881: 18%. B. R. Mitchell, *British Historical Statistics* (Cambridge, 1988), p. 104. C. K. Harley, 'British Industrialization Before 1841: Evidence of Slower Growth During the Industrial Revolution', *Journal of Economic History*, 42 (1982), p. 268.

3. M. Berg, *The Age of Manufactures* (London, 1985), p. 253; P. Hudson, *The Genesis of Industrial Capital: A Study of the West Riding Wool Textile Industry* (Cambridge, 1986), pp. 149–54.

4. S. Pollard, *The Genesis of Modern Management* (London, 1965), p. 163.

5. A. Kussmaul, *Servants in Husbandry in Early Modern England* (Cambridge, 1981), p. 4.

6. S. Pollard, 'Factory Discipline in the Industrial Revolution', *Economic History Review*, 2nd ser., 16 (1963–64), p. 259, n. 3.

7. Numbers of children in traditional rural occupations were doubtless much higher at earlier dates.

8. *Census 1851*, PP 1852–53, LXXXVIII, pt I, tab.54.

9. *Report of the Commissioners Appointed to Inquire into the State of Popular Education in England*, PP (Parliamentary Papers) 1861, XXI, p. 180.

10. J. Arch, *Joseph Arch: The Story of his Life* (1898), reprinted as *From Ploughtail to Parliament: An Autobiography* (London, 1986), pp. 27, 31–2.

11. During autumn, acorns would be picked as soon as they dropped and sold to farmers as pig-food: J. Kitteringham, 'Country Work Girls in Nineteenth-Century England' in R. Samuel (ed.) *Village Life and Labour* (London, 1975), pp. 75–83.

12. As late as 1851, three-quarters of Lancashire farms were smaller than 50 acres: S. Coombs and D. Radburn, 'Children and Young People on the Land' in M. Winstanley (ed.) *Working Children in Nineteenth-Century Lancashire* (Preston, 1995), p. 74; M. Winstanley, 'Industrialization and the Small Farm: Family and Household Economy in Nineteeenth-Century Lancashire', *Past and Present*, 152 (1996), pp. 157–95.

13. D. H. Morgan, 'The Place of Harvesters in Nineteenth-Century Village Life' in R. Samuel (ed.) *Village Life and Labour* (London, 1975), p. 29.

14. E. J. T. Collins, 'Harvest Technology and Labour Supply in Britain, 1790–1870', *Economic History Review*, 2nd ser., 22 (1969).

15. K. D. M. Snell, 'Agricultural Seasonal Unemployment, the Standard of Living and Women's Work in the South and East, 1690–1860 ', *Economic History Review*, 2nd ser., 34 (1981), figs 1–7, pp. 410–16; M. Roberts, 'Sickles and Scythes: Women's Work and Men's Work at Harvest Time,' *History Workshop*, 7 (1979).

16. K. D. M. Snell, 'The Standard of Living, Social Relations, the Family and Labour Mobility in South-Eastern and Western Counties, 1700–1860', PhD thesis (Cambridge, 1979), pp. 165–9. In Suffolk, the binding of apprentices to agriculture *per se* had declined steadily from the late eighteenth century. By the early 1840s, in Suffolk, Norfolk and Lincolnshire, the apprenticing of pauper children to farmers had been 'almost universally abandoned' and the employment of children in gangs more widespread: *Reports of Special Assistant Poor Law Commissioners on the Employment of Women and Children in Agriculture*, PP 1843, XII, pp. 220, 239–40, 250–1, 258–9. Speechley has argued that child labour in agriculture in Somerset averaged about 14 per cent between the late seventeenth and the late nineteenth century: H. V. Speechley, 'Female and Child Agricultural Day Labourers in Somerset, *c*.1685–1870', PhD thesis (Exeter, 1999), p. 198; See also S. Horrell, and J. Humphries, ' "Exploitation of Little Children": Child Labour and the Family Economy in the Industrial Revolution', *Explorations in Economic History*, 32 (1995), pp. 491–5.

17. Winstanley has argued that the censuses 'persistently under-recorded the work of family members, especially women and children': Winstanley, 'Industrialization and the Small Farm', p. 181.

18. *Census 1851*, PP 1852–53, LXXXVIII, p. cclxxxii.

19. *Census 1851*, PP 1852–53, LXXXVIII, tab. xxv. This partly confirms 'the falsity of the belief that manufacturing employment related to distant markets, whether in the home or the factory, was the dominant source of new jobs for the rising generations of young men': E. A. Wrigley, 'Men on the Land and Men in the Countryside: Employment in Agriculture in Early Nineteenth-Century England' in L. Bonfield, R. M. Smith and K. Wrightson (eds) *The World We Have Gained* (Oxford, 1986), p. 302.

20. Kussmaul, *Servants in Husbandry*, p. 31; W. A. Armstrong, 'Rural Population Growth, Systems of Employment and Incomes' in G. E. Mingay (ed.) *The Agrarian History of England and Wales*, vol.6 (Cambridge, 1989), p. 672. The practice of annual binding also existed in some archetypal industrial processes: in the northeast of England, the use of the bond had some transitory success in limiting the migratory habits of coalminers: P. E. H. Hair, 'The Social History of British Coalminers', D. Phil. thesis (Oxford, 1955), p. 314; J. L. and B. Hammond, *The Skilled Labourer, 1760–1832* (London, 1919), p. 12.

21. F. Mendels, 'Family Forms in Historic Europe: A Review Article', *Social History*, 11 (1986), p. 84; B. Hill, *Servants: English Domestics in the Eighteenth Century* (Oxford, 1996), p. 6; K. D. M. Snell, *Annals of the Labouring Poor: Social Change and Agrarian England, 1660–1900* (Cambridge, 1985), pp. 53–4, n. 36.

22. A. Kussmaul, 'The Ambiguous Mobility of Farm Servants', *Economic History Review*, 2nd ser., 34, table 2, p. 224.

23. Kussmaul, *Servants in Husbandry*, pp. 3–10.

24. Cited in Armstrong, 'Rural Population Growth', p. 673.

25. Pollard, 'Factory Discipline', p. 265. The picture is more complex, however, than is allowed for in the scope of the present work. Some of the problems of measuring farm service from census figures are explored in A. Gritt, 'The Census and the Servant: A Reassessment of the Decline and Distribution of Farm Service in Early Nineteenth-Century England', *Economic History Review*, 2nd ser., 53 (2000), pp. 84–106; W. A. Armstrong, *Farmworkers in England and Wales* (Iowa, 1988), p. 96.

26. R. Mitchison, 'Scotland, 1750–1850' in F. M. L. Thompson (ed.) *The Cambridge Social History of Britain*, vol.1 (Cambridge, 1990), pp. 175–6; Kitteringham, 'Country Work Girls', p. 85.

27. Winstanley, 'Industrialization and the Small Farm', p. 182. Although some farmers of small holdings found it difficult to make a living and would sometimes work as day labourers on larger neighbouring farms, leaving their wives and children to do much of the daily farm labour: Coombs and Radburn, 'Children and Young People on the Land', p. 75.

28. Coombs and Radburn, 'Children and Young People on the Land', p. 75.

29. Cited in Winstanley, 'Industrialization and the Small Farm', p. 181.

30. It has been argued by Armstrong that the quantitative importance of such gangs has been exaggerated. Armstrong, *Farmworkers*, p. 97; see also N. Verdon, 'The Employment of Women and Children in Agriculture: A Reassessment of Agricultural Gangs in Nineteenth-Century Norfolk', *Agricultural History Review*, 49 (2001).

The increasing trend towards casual employment of children in agriculture can be said to have resulted in part from changes in Poor Law policy from 1834 which made it more necessary that children work in order to raise household incomes above subsistence.

31. *Reports of Special Assistant Poor Law Commissioners on the Employment of Women and Children in Agriculture*, PP 1843, XII.

32. Armstrong, *Farmworkers*, p. 96; Verdon, 'Employment of Women and Children', p. 50.

33. The Gangs Act of 1867 also allowed JPs to to limit the walking distances of older children. I. Pinchbeck and M. Hewitt, *Children in English Society*, vol.2 (London 1973), p. 394.

34. Armstrong, *Farmworkers*, p. 97. Lord Shaftesbury wanted to abolish all gangs but was thwarted by the profound difficulties of defining a privately employed gang: Tremenheere to Thring, 27 March 1867, Tremenheere Family Papers, packet 11, Morrab Library, Penzance.

35. E. Hopkins, *Childhood Transformed: Working-Class Children in Nineteenth-Century England*, (Manchester, 1994), p. 20; P. Horn, *The Changing Countryside in Victorian and Edwardian England and Wales* (London, 1984), p. 164.

36. McKendrick, 'Home Demand', p. 173; Hudson, *Genesis of Industrial Capital*, p. 57. Most workers experienced a general increase in incomes in the post-Napoleonic War period, but proto-industrial, manufacturing and skilled workers experienced the most substantial increases. P. H. Lindert and J. G. Williamson, 'English Workers' Living Standards During the Industrial Revolution: A New Look', *Economic History Review*, 2nd ser., 36 (1983), pp. 1–25.

37. R. Samuel, 'Mechanisation and Hand Labour in Industrializing Britain' in L. R. Berlanstein (ed.) *The Industrial Revolution and Work in Nineteenth-Century Europe* (London, 1992); D. Levine, 'The Demographic Implications of Rural Industrialisation: A Family Reconstitution Study of Shepshed, Leicestershire, 1600–1851', *Social History*, 1 (1976), p. 179.

38. D. T. Jenkins, 'Factory Returns, 1850–1905', *Textile History*, 9 (1978), p. 64.

39. *Children's Employment Commission (Trades and Manufactures)*, PP 1843, XIV, app. to 2nd rep., pt I, C. 17.

40. J. H. Clapham, *Economic History of Modern Britain: The Early Railway Age, 1820–1850* (Cambridge, 1950), vol. 2, tab., p. 35; Pollard, *Genesis of Modern Management*, p. 163; R. A. Church, 'Labour Supply and Innovation: The Boot and Shoe Industry', *Business History*, 12 (1970), p. 26.

41. C. Hallas, 'The Textile Industry in Wensleydale and Swaledale', *Textile History*, 21 (1990), pp. 204–5; Armstrong, *Farmworkers*, pp. 67–8.

42. P. Horn, 'Child Workers in the Pillow Lace and Straw Plait Trades of Victorian Buckinghamshire and Bedfordshire', *Historical Journal*, 17 (1974), p. 779.

43. W. B. Stephens, *Education, Literacy and Society, 1830–1870* (Manchester, 1987), app. B, p. 319 and table 5.1, p. 171.

44. Stephens, *Education, Literacy and Society*, app. B, pp. 318–19. Industrial counties such as Lancashire did, however, comprise much larger populations and therefore larger *absolute* numbers of child workers. In Meiji Japan in 1900, the proportion of workers of both sexes aged below 14 was greater in handicraft industries such as rug-weaving, rope-braiding and matchmaking than in larger-scale operations such as cotton-spinning and silk-reeling: O. Saito, 'Children's Work,

Industrialism and the Family Economy in Japan, 1872–1926' in H. Cunningham and P. P. Viazzo (eds) *Child Labour in Historical Perspective, 1800–1985: Case Studies from Europe, Japan and Colombia* (Florence, 1996), table 4, p. 78.

45. Horn, 'Pillow Lace and Straw Plait Trades', p. 781.
46. G. F. R. Spenceley, 'The English Pillow Lace Industry, 1840–1880: A Rural Industry in Competition with Machinery', *Business History*, 19 (1977), p. 68.
47. Horn, 'Pillow Lace and Straw Plait Trades', p. 781; D. Bythell, *The Sweated Trades: Outwork in Nineteenth-Century Britain* (London, 1978), p. 119.
48. Horn, 'Pillow Lace and Straw Plait Trades', p. 782 and app. A, p. 796.
49. In the west midlands, the decline of domestic spinning seems to have enlarged the supply of female labour to nail- and chainmaking workshops: *Children's Employment Commission, Second Report of the Commissioners, Trades and Manufactures*, PP 1843, XIII, 2nd rep., p. 16.
50. Levine, 'Demographic Implications of Rural Industrialisation', p. 183. Reductions in import duties on silk in 1824 and 1826 (though causing some short-term optimism about a revival of English silk production) had the effect of exposing English production to foreign competition and the silk trade was transformed into a marginal industry in an international market: S. J. Bush, 'The Technological Development of the English Silk Industry, 1685–1860', M. Phil thesis (Manchester, 1995), p. 66.
51. By 1851 silk had become one of the most youthful trades with 13.5 per cent of its male labour force and 15.4 per cent of females aged 10–14.
52. S. R. H. Jones, 'Technology, Transaction Costs, and the Transition to Factory Production in the British Silk Industry, 1700–1870', *Journal of Economic History*, 47 (1987), p. 86.
53. E. Kerridge, *Textile Manufacturers in Early Modern England* (Manchester, 1985), p. 202.
54. W. Radcliffe, *The Origin of Power-Loom Weaving* (London, 1828), p. 61, cited in M. W. Thomas, *The Early Factory Legislation: A Study in Legislative and Administrative Evolution* (London, 1948), p. 6; I. Pinchbeck, *Women Workers and the Industrial Revolution, 1750–1850* (London, 1930), p. 147.
55. D. Woodward, 'The Background to the Statute of Artificers: The Genesis of Labour Policy, 1558–63', *Economic History Review*, 2nd ser., 33 (1980), table, p. 34. K. D. M Snell, 'The Apprenticeship System in British History: The Fragmentation of a Cultural Institution', *History of Education*, 25 (1996), p. 305.
56. Snell, *Annals*, pp. 270–319. Though many eighteenth-century girls were bound to traditional 'feminine' occupations such as millinery and other textile crafts, a few were still to be found pursuing archetypal masculine occupations such as blacksmith and farrier: Snell, *Annals*, pp. 296–7; M. Berg, 'Women's Work, Mechanisation and the Early Phases of Industrialisation in England' in P. Joyce (ed.) *The Historical Meanings of Work* (Cambridge, 1987), p. 75.
57. E. Roberts, *Women's Work, 1840–1940* (Cambridge, 1988), p. 5. There were some exceptions to the tendency towards 'bridging occupations'. For example, the long (often unpaid) training of apprentice dressmakers and milliners endowed them with skills that could be employed throughout later life: ibid., p. 29; E. Higgs, *Domestic Servants and Households in Rochdale, 1851–1871* (London, 1986), pp. 2, 59.
58. Snell, *Annals*, pp. 309, 318–19; E. Richards, 'Women in the British Economy Since About 1700: An Interpretation', *History*, 59 (1974).

59. *Children's Employment Commission, Second Report of the Commissioners, Trades and Manufactures*, PP 1843, XIII, p. 16.
60. Ibid., p. 17.
61. Hudson, *Industrial Revolution*, p. 125.
62. Richards, 'Women in the British Economy', p. 337.
63. Snell, *Annals*, pp. 270–6.
64. The evidence relating to apprenticeship is discussed in Chapter 1.
65. D. Simonton, 'Apprenticeship: Training and Gender in Eighteenth-Century England', *Journal of Economic History*, 43 (1983), pp. 240–3.
66. Simonton, 'Training and Gender', pp. 238–9.
67. 5 Eliz., c.4, *An Act Touching Divers Orders for Artificers, Labourers, Servants of Husbandry and Apprentices*, 1563, XIX.
68. Simonton, 'Training and Gender', pp. 227–8, 230.
69. Clapham, *Economic History of Modern Britain*, vol. 1, pp. 370–1; see also J. Rule, *The Experience of Labour in Eighteenth-Century English Industry* (New York, 1981), pp. 95–123.
70. I. J. Prothero, *Artisans and Politics in Early Nineteenth-Century London* (Folkestone, 1979), p. 31.
71. T. K. Derry, 'The Repeal of the Apprenticeship Clauses in the Statute of Apprentices', *Economic History Review*, 3 (1931–32), p. 69.
72. Derry, 'Statute of Apprentices', p. 68; J. Lane, *Apprenticeship in England, 1600–1914* (London, 1996), p. 56.
73. Clapham, *Economic History of Modern Britain*, vol. 1, p. 210.
74. Derry, 'Statute of Apprentices', p. 71.
75. M. B. Rose, 'Social Policy and Business: Parish Apprentices and the Early Factory System, 1750–1834', *Business History*, 31 (1989), p. 11; J. H. Clapham, 'The Spitalfields Acts, 1733–1824', *Economic Journal*, 26 (1916), pp. 461–2.
76. Clapham described the Acts as 'state enforcement of a trade agreement in a localised industry': Clapham, *Economic History of Modern Britain*, vol. 1, p. 336.
77. W. W. Knox, 'British Apprenticeship, 1800–1914', PhD thesis (Edinburgh, 1980), p. 21.
78. It is significant that the exclusion of females from skilled training was pronounced among the declining trades: Snell, *Annals*, p. 313.
79. The sub-commissioner thought that such examples demonstrated 'an evil in the apprenticeship system which must increase with every new subdivision of labour', *Children's Employment Commission (Trades and Manufactures)*, PP 1843, XIV, app. to 2nd rep., pt I, B41.
80. Kussmaul, *Servants in Husbandry*, p. 5; S. Shahar, *Childhood in the Middle Ages* (London, 1990), p. 233; Knox, 'British Apprenticeship', p. 11.
81. Knox, 'British Apprenticeship', p. 15.
82. Ibid., pp. 12–13, 17.
83. Ibid., pp. 17–18.
84. Ibid., p. 19.
85. *Children's Employment Commission (Trades and Manufactures)*, PP 1843, XIV, app. to 2nd rep., pt I, C7.
86. M. MacKinnon, 'Living Standards, 1870–1914' in R. Floud and D. N. McCloskey (eds) *The Economic History of Britain Since 1700* (Cambridge, 1994), vol.2, pp. 275–6.
87. G. S. Jones, *Outcast London* (Harmondsworth, 1984), p. 31.

88. A. Davin, *Growing up Poor: Home, School and Street in London, 1870–1914* (London, 1996), pp. 159, 256.

89. *Report on the Condition of the Hand-Loom Weavers*, PP 1840, XXIV (Report of W. E. Hickson), p. 52.

90. *Report on the Condition of the Hand-Loom Weavers*, PP 1840, XXIV (Report of W. E. Hickson), p. 52. Many of the poorest children were simply left to scavenge what they could from the urban environment. Jack Lanigan recalled his childhood in Salford: 'Besides the heartbreaking cry, '"Ave yer any bread left master?" there was another common cry at all the "Fish and Chips" shops, "Can you spare any scrapings, Sir?" . . . The kids, myself included, travelled from shop to shop to ensure we had collected sufficient for the family . . . These scrapings with some bread made a meal.' J. Lanigan, 'Incidents in the Life of a Citizen', quoted in J. Burnett, *Destiny Obscure: Autobiographies of Childhood, Education and Family from the 1820s to the 1920s* (Harmondsworth, 1977), p. 86.

91. Cited in Davin, *Growing up Poor*, p. 158.

92. Higgs, *Domestic Servants and Households*, table 32, p. 331.

93. L. Schwarz, 'English Servants and their Employers During the Eighteenth and Nineteenth Centuries', *Economic History Review*, 2nd ser., 52 (1999), table 2, p. 242; B. Hill, *Servants*, p. 4.

94. Higgs, *Domestic Servants and Households*, table 40, pp. 340–1.

95. In mid-nineteenth-century Rochdale more than 60 per cent of servants were in households containing a single servant: Higgs, *Domestic Servants and Households*, p. 57. By 1871 the proportion remained high at 57 per cent.

96. Davin, *Growing up Poor*, pp. 159–60.

97. *Census 1851*, PP 1852–53, LXXXVIII, pt I, tab.54, p. cxli. The careful use of settlement examinations has produced some insights into the lives of agricultural servants. Settlement examinations were judicial examinations (carried out under the Settlement Act of 1662) to determine the parish of settlement of applicants for poor relief: Snell, *Annals*, esp. pp. 17–37; Kussmaul, 'Ambiguous Mobility'; Kussmaul, *Servants in Husbandry*, pp. 150–65.

98. On this see H. Hendrick, *Images of Youth: Age, Class and the Male Youth Problem* (Oxford, 1990); D. Fowler, *First Teenagers: The Lifestyle of Young Wage-Earners in Interwar Britain* (London, 1995), pp. 21–4; E. J. Urwick (ed.) *Studies of Boy Life in Our Cities* (London, 1904).

99. R. H. Tawney, 'The Economics of Boy Labour', *Economic Journal*, 19 (1909), pp. 524, 520, 517.

100. A. Greenwood, 'Blind-Alley Labour', *Economic Journal*, 22 (1912), p. 309.

101. See, for example, J. E. Zucchi, *The Little Slaves of the Harp: Italian Child Street Musicians in Nineteenth-Century Paris, London and New York*, (Montreal, 1992); F. Keeling, *Child Labour in the United Kingdom: A Study of the Development and Administration of the Law Relating to the Employment of Children* (London, 1914), pp. 11–16.

102. Davin, *Growing up Poor*, p. 160.

103. A. Kidd, *State, Society and the Poor in Nineteenth-Century England* (Basingstoke, 1999), p. 88.

104. M. J. Daunton, *House and Home in the Victorian City* (London, 1983), p. 12.

105. Keeling, *Child Labour*, p. 16. The fears of the respectable middle classes were probably exaggerated. The Honorary Secretary of the Ragged School Union argued that children visible on the London streets were 'not paupers or criminals;

they are the children of costermongers, who sell in the streets . . . or of those who go with barrows about the street . . . of pig-feeders, persons earning a good deal of money, but altogether careless about the education of their children; the children of rag-dealers and Spitalfields weavers out of employment, and many others of uncertain occupations . . . Sometimes the children of labourers, who are out of work in frost or bad weather, or who are thrown out of work at the docks frequently by ships not arriving; the children of knackers and cat's-meat men; of slop-tailors, who form a large number, who earn a bare subsistence, and who yet will not condescend to accept parochial relief.' *Returns Made to the Poor Law Board on the Education of Pauper Children. Reports of Poor Law Inspectors*, PP 1862, XLIX, pt I, p. 100.

106. Kidd, *State, Society and the Poor*, p. 87; J. Parr, *Labouring Children: British Immigrant Apprentices to Canada, 1869–1924* (London, 1980), p. 11.

107. G. Wagner, *Children of the Empire* (London, 1982), p. 84.

108. In 1814, the Select Committee on Parish Apprentices observed that many pauper children bound at great distances from the London parishes were not orphan children but the offsping of destitute parents: *Report of Select Committee on Parish Apprentices*, PP 1814–15, V, pp. 5–6.

109. Parr, *Labouring Children*, pp. 130–9.

110. A. H. Robson, *The Education of Children Engaged in Industry in England, 1833–1876*, (London, 1931), p. 3; J. S. Lyons, 'Family Response to Economic Decline: Hand-loom Weavers in Early Nineteenth-Century Lancashire', *Research in Economic History*, 12 (1989), p. 55.

111. C. Nardinelli, 'Corporal Punishment and Children's Wages in Nineteenth-Century Britain', *Explorations in Economic History*, 19 (1982), pp. 283–95; C. Nardinelli, *Child Labor and the Industrial Revolution* (Bloomington, IN, 1990), table 4.3, p. 93.

112. *Census 1841*, PP 1841, II, pp. 43–56.

113. Clapham pointed out that the cotton-mill population of Great Britain in 1830 stood at about 'one-eightieth of the total population': Clapham, *Economic History of Modern Britain*, vol. 1, p. 54, n. 6.

114. In 1816, for example, the average size of the labour force at 41 Glasgow mills was 244 and in a collection of Manchester mills in 1832 the average was 401: Clapham, *Economic History of Modern Britain*, vol. 1, pp. 184–5.

115. R. V. Jackson, 'Rates of Industrial Growth During the Industrial Revolution', *Economic History Review*, 2nd ser., 45 (1992), table 8, p. 18.

116. One contemporary noted: 'The awkward posture required to spin on them was discouraging to grown up people, while they saw, with a degree of surprise, children from nine to twelve years of age, manage them with dexterity, which brought plenty into families that were before overburthened with children.' J. Ogden, *A Description of Manchester by a Native of the Town*, reprinted as *Manchester a Hundred Years Ago*, ed. W. E. Axon (London, 1887), p. 87.

117. M. Berg and P. Hudson, 'Rehabilitating the Industrial Revolution', *Economic History Review*, 2nd ser., 45 (1992), p. 36; Berg, 'Women's Work', p. 79. Honeyman suggests that machines 'were often invented specifically for this workforce, on whom they were initially tested': K. Honeyman, *Women, Gender and Industrialisation in England, 1700–1870* (Basingstoke, 2000), p. 44.

118. L. C. A. Knowles, *Industrial and Commercial Revolutions* (London, 1930), p. 50.

119. Cited in W. Lazonick, 'Industrial Relations and Technical Change: The Case of the Self-Acting Mule', *Cambridge Journal of Economics*, 3 (1979), pp. 231–62.

120. McKendrick, 'Home Demand', p. 158. The type and incidence of child labour in industrial occupations, however, were hardly ever determined solely by technology.

121. N. J. Smelser, 'Sociological History: The Industrial Revolution and the British Working-Class Family', *Journal of Social History*, 1 (1967–68), pp. 26–9.

122. M. Anderson, 'Sociological History and the Working-Class Family: Smelser Revisited', *Social History*, 1 (1976), p. 323.

123. M. M. Edwards and R. Lloyd-Jones, 'N. J. Smelser and the Cotton Factory Family: A Reassessment' in N. B. Harte and K. G. Ponting (eds) *Textile History and Economic History: Essays in Honour of Miss Julia de Lacy Mann* (Manchester, 1973), table 12.2, p. 313; Anderson, 'Smelser Revisited', p. 324. It has been suggested more recently that in 1843 only 15 per cent of Manchester factory children were employed by a parent: P. Bolin-Hort, *Work, Family and the State: Child Labour and the Organisation of Production in the British Cotton Industry, 1780–1920* (Lund, 1989), pp. 52–3.

124. Anderson, 'Smelser Revisited', p. 325.

125. Anderson assumes an average age at marriage among spinners of 21 years: M. Anderson, *Family Structure in Nineteenth-Century Lancashire* (Cambridge, 1971), p. 115.

126. Anderson, 'Smelser Revisited', p. 323.

127. H. Cunningham, 'Decline of Child Labour: Labour Markets and Family Economies in Europe and North America Since 1830', *Economic History Review*, 2nd ser., 53 (2000), p. 417. Cunningham does not provide any primary research findings of his own to substantiate this view.

128. Bolin-Hort, *Work, Family and the State*, pp. 45–7.

129. C. Nardinelli, 'Child Labor and the Factory Acts', *Journal of Economic History*, 40 (1980), pp. 743–4.

130. Bolin-Hort, *Work, Family and the State*, pp. 102–6.

131. S. J. Chapman, *The Lancashire Cotton Industry: A Study in Economic Development* (Manchester, 1904), p. 112.

132. Nardinelli, 'Child Labor and the Factory Acts', p. 748.

133. Ibid.

134. J. Pressley, 'Childhood, Education and Labour: Moral Pressure and the End of the Half-Time System', PhD thesis (Lancaster, 2000), p. 50. Moreover, as Bolin-Hort has suggested, employment agreements 'were often made on an informal or tacit level, and are not to be found overtly stated in historical records': Bolin-Hort, *Work, Family and the State*, p. 149.

135. Bolin-Hort, *Work, Family and the State*, pp. 151–2. It has also been argued that the numbers of half-timers would have risen even more rapidly had the minimum age of entry not been raised in 1874: M. Winstanley, 'The Factory Workforce' in M. B. Rose (ed.) *The Lancashire Cotton Industry: A History Since 1700* (Preston, 1996), p. 134.

136. Bolin-Hort, *Work, Family and the State*, pp. 118, 156.

137. The use of 'full-time equivalent' inputs might offer a better basis for studying children in cotton textiles. The generally poor quality of much of the surviving evidence, however, probably prevents the extension of such a model to national labour markets.

138. Lyons, 'Family Response to Economic Decline', pp. 49–50

139. Bolin-Hort, *Work, Family and the State*, pp. 116–17.

140. Winstanley, 'The Factory Workforce', p. 132. Again, however, the statistics may be affected by the failure to count half-timers separately: Bolin-Hort, *Work, Family and the State*, p. 118.

141. D. A. Farnie, *The English Cotton Industry and the World Market, 1815–1896* (Oxford, 1979), p. 297.

142. T. S. Ashton and J. Sykes, *The Coal Industry of the Eighteenth Century* (Manchester, 1929), pp. 172–3; Hair, 'Social History of British Coalminers', pp. 166–9; P. Kirby, 'Aspects of the Employment of Children in the British Coalmining Industry, 1800–1872' PhD thesis (Sheffield, 1995), pp. 165–215; P. Kirby, 'The Viability of Child Labour and the Mines Act of 1842' in M. Lavalette (ed.) *A Thing of the Past? Child Labour in Britain in the Nineteenth and Twentieth Centuries* (Liverpool, 1999), pp. 101–17.

143. Kirby, 'Children in the British Coalmining Industry', p. 170.

144. Hair, 'Social History of British Coalminers', pp. 3–4; P. E. H. Hair, 'Children in Society, 1850–1980' in T. Barker and M. Drake (eds) *Population and Society in Britain, 1850–1980* (London, 1982), p. 49.

145. Mitchell, *British Historical Statistics*, p. 262; D. Greasley, 'The Diffusion of Machine Cutting in the British Coal Industry, 1900–1938', *Explorations in Economic History*, 19 (1982), pp. 246–68.

146. Kirby, 'Viability of Child Labour', p. 103.

147. A. J. Taylor, 'Labour Productivity and Technological Innovation in the British Coal Industry, 1850–1914', *Economic History Review*, 2nd ser., 14 (1961–62), p. 57.

148. Kirby, 'Children in the British Coalmining Industry', p. 170.

149. Kirby, 'Viability of Child Labour', pp. 103–6; P. Kirby, 'Causes of Short Stature Among Coalmining Children, 1823–1850', *Economic History Review*, 2nd ser., 48 (1995); J. Humphries, 'Stature Among Coalmining Children: A Comment', *Economic History Review*, 2nd ser., 50 (1997); P. Kirby, 'Short Stature Among Coalmining Children: A Rejoinder', *Economic History Review*, 2nd ser., 50 (1997).

150. Kirby, 'Viability of Child Labour', pp. 106–11.

151. J. Benson, *British Coalminers in the Nineteenth Century: A Social History* (Dublin, 1980), p. 48.

152. Kirby, 'Viability of Child Labour', pp. 106–7.

153. Hopkins, *Childhood Transformed*, p. 24.

154. H. Cunningham, 'The Employment and Unemployment of Children in England, c.1680–1851', *Past and Present*, 126 (1990), pp. 120–1, 115.

155. Cunningham's theory of child 'unemployment' has been widely cited. See H. Cunningham, *Children and Childhood in Western Society Since 1500* (Harlow, 1995), pp. 82–3; H. Cunningham and P. P. Viazzo, 'Some Issues in the Historical Study of Child Labour' in *idem* (eds) *Child Labour in Historical Perspective, 1800–1985: Case Studies from Europe, Japan and Colombia* (Florence, 1996), p. 16; H. Cunningham, 'Combating Child Labour: The British Experience', *ibid.*, p. 41; Cunningham, 'The Decline of Child Labour', pp. 415, 419; S. Horrell and J. Humphries, 'Old Questions, New Data and Alternative Perspectives: Families' Living Standards in the Industrial Revolution', *Journal of Economic History*, 52 (1992), pp. 850–1; Horrell and Humphries, 'Exploitation of Little Children',

p. 486; M. Lavalette, 'The Changing Form of Child Labour *circa* 1880–1918: The Growth of "Out of School" Work' in *idem* (ed.) *A Thing of the Past? Child Labour in Britain in the Nineteenth and Twentieth Centuries* (Liverpool, 1999), p. 120; P. Horn, *Children's Work and Welfare, 1780–1880s* (Basingstoke, 1994), p. 14.

156. D. Levine, 'Industrialisation and the Proletarian Family in England', *Past and Present*, 107 (1985). See also F. Mendels, 'Proto-Industrialisation: The First Phase of the Process of Industrialisation', *Journal of Economic History*, 32 (1972); H. Medick, 'The Proto-Industrial Family Economy: The Structural Function of Household and Family During the Transition from Peasant to Industrial Capitalism', *Social History*, 1 (1976); L. A. Clarkson, *Proto-Industrialization: The First Phase of Industrialization?* (London, 1985); McKendrick, 'Home Demand'; J. de Vries, 'Between Purchasing Power and the World of Goods: Understanding the Household Economy in Early Modern Europe' in J. Brewer and R. Porter (eds) *Consumption and the World of Goods* (London, 1993).

157. The most recent historian of female and child labour in agriculture has doubted the accuracy of this last source, arguing that it contained 'poorly worded questions'. This led to the questionnaire returns being used 'as supporting evidence only': Speechley, 'Female and Child Agricultural Labourers', p. 33.

158. P. Kirby, 'How Many Children were "Unemployed" in Eighteenth- and Nineteenth-Century England?', *Past and Present* (forthcoming).

159. *Census 1851*, PP 1852–53, LXXXVIII, pt I, p. lxxxviii.

160. A. Davin, 'Working or Helping? London Working-Class Children in the Domestic Economy' in J. Smith, I. Wallerstein and H. Evers (eds) *Households in the World Economy* (London, 1984); E. Higgs, 'Occupational Censuses and the Agricultural Workforce in Victorian England and Wales' *Economic History Review*, 2nd ser., 48 (1995). See also H. Hendrick, *Child Welfare: England, 1872–1989* (London, 1994), p. 30.

161. *Census 1851*, PP 1852–53, LXXXVIII, pt I, table 54, Great Britain and the Islands in the British Seas. Classified Arrangement of the Occupations of the People, p. cxli.

162. G. S. Becker, 'A Theory of the Allocation of Time', *Economic Journal*, 75 (Sept. 1965), pp. 493–517.

163. Kirby, 'How Many Children were "Unemployed"?' The number of agricultural children omitted from the census in England is also roughly equal to the English total of 'official' apprenticeships below 15 estimated by Simonton at 56,000: Simonton, 'Training and Gender', pp. 238–9.

164. Saito, 'Children's Work', fig 1, p. 81; Hair, 'Children in Society', p. 47.

165. Even some large-scale industrial employers could lose 90 per cent of their labour force on 'St Monday': E. Hopkins, 'Working Hours and Conditions During the Industrial Revolution: A Reappraisal', *Economic History Review*, 2nd ser., 35 (1982), p. 56.

166. Though references to a 'want of employment' may be found during the nineteenth century, the concept of unemployment itself did not become widely used by economic theorists until the 1890s: J. Harris, *Unemployment and Politics: A Study in English Social Policy* (Oxford, 1972), p. 4.

167. For implicit and explicit objections to the 'unemployment' thesis, see J. Styles, 'Manufacturing, Consumption and Design in Eighteenth-Century England' in J. Brewer and R. Porter (eds) *Consumption and the World of Goods* (London, 1993),

p. 552, n. 51; Hopkins, *Childhood Transformed*, pp. 316–17; Berg and Hudson, 'Rehabilitating the Industrial Revolution', p. 35; Saito, 'Children's Work', p. 87; C. Tuttle, *Hard at Work in Factories and Mines: The Economics of Child Labour During the British Industrial Revolution* (Boulder, CO, 1999), pp. 11–12, 184; Speechley, 'Female and Child Agricultural Labourers', p. 198; Schwarz, 'English Servants', p. 255.

Chapter 4: Child Labour and the State

The secular decline of child labour during the nineteenth century has traditionally been explained as a result of a struggle for factory reform and the introduction of education laws. This form of analysis dominated the detailed studies of state legislation produced during the first half of the twentieth century by historians such as Hutchins and Harrison, Robson and Thomas.[1] Many of the early social historians overtly couched their discussions of child labour in terms of a political struggle for the achievement of industrial regulation. The Hammonds concentrated almost exclusively upon children in factories and mines, and placed great stress upon the campaigns of humanitarians such as Robert Owen, John Fielden, Michael Sadler and Lord Shaftesbury.[2] Contemporary economists such as Alfred Marshall also encouraged the belief that state legislation had been instrumental in the decline of child labour.[3] The stress upon legislative progress was continued by historians in the second half of the twentieth century. MacDonagh argued for a nineteenth-century 'revolution' in government in which a variety of social 'evils' were identified by a widening scope of parliamentary inquiries and remedied by state legislation and the establishment of inspectorates.[4] Walvin suggested that a 'growing sensitivity to the industrial conditions of... children ... led to early parliamentary control of labour' and, more recently, Seccombe has argued that children were 'withdrawn from factories and sent to school in the face of mass campaigns against their exploitation in industry'.[5]

Others, however, have questioned such uncomplicated explanations of social improvement and have argued that the traditional stress upon the role of humanitarians and government intervention has exaggerated the power of the early Victorian state to exercise effective change in the labour market. Coleman has warned that the historian 'too often ascribes to state policy or to short term forces a potency which neither possesses'.[6] Moreover, it has been argued further that rising wages coupled with technological and organisational changes in the workplace were much more important influences upon child employment than state intervention.[7]

An examination of the chronology and scope of the major child labour legislation certainly supports a less 'state-centred' explanation of child labour decline. The much celebrated Factory Act of 1833, for example, delayed the entry of children to the factory labour force by only about a year, and as late as 1874 children as young as eight were permitted to work as half-timers in factories. The Mines Act of 1842, often regarded as a major landmark in the regulation of industrial child labour, excluded less than 1 per cent of the national child labour force below 10 from employment (10-year-old children continued to work legally in coalmines until the 1870s).[8] Domestic service and workshops largely escaped regulation, and child labourers in agriculture did not become subject to state restrictions until the late 1860s. Even chimney-sweeps' apprentices, despite their high public profile and a century of vigorous campaigning from the 1770s, did not become subject to effective prohibitive regulation until 1875.[9] Improvements in children's working conditions were equally unsystematic. Successive factory acts contained provisions to force employers to fence off dangerous machinery, and inspectors sought to prevent the cleaning of machinery by children whilst it was in motion, but the majority of workplaces remained uninspected and working conditions remained largely unchanged until the twentieth century.[10] Thus, state legislation aimed at regulating ages and conditions of children in specific industries were of little practical application outside a small number of child occupations between 1750 and 1870. Most child occupations remained entirely unregulated. As Keeling pointed out, the most intractable cases of child labour were those in which children were employed 'not in large aggregations, but in scattered units, and very largely in occupations which do not involve continuous employment in a single workplace'.[11]

In fact, state policies with a more widespread application almost certainly had a greater effect upon the incidence of children's employment than specific child labour laws. In the wake of the Poor Law Amendment Act of 1834, for example, alarm over the high cost of maintaining the offspring of paupers led to the imposition of punitive sanctions which sought to abolish outdoor relief to able-bodied adults and cut allowances based upon family size. The effect of such policies upon poor households was to increase dependence upon the earnings of children and to push more children into employment.[12] As J. P. Kay argued before a Lords' Committee of 1837–38, 'The extent of employment for women and children has most wonderfully increased since the Poor Law came into operation. It has had that effect by rendering it necessary that the children should be so employed in order to adjust the wages to the wants of the family.'[13] It would be a serious mistake, therefore, for the historian of child labour to focus exclusively upon the development of specific child labour laws at the expense of other reforms that had an equal or greater effect upon levels of child employment.

The early nineteenth-century state was also active in deregulating large areas of the child and adolescent labour market. Perhaps the most important state action in this respect was the repeal in 1814 of the apprenticeship clauses of the Statute of Artificers of 1563.[14] The traditional apprenticeship laws prevented people from practising trades unless they had served at least seven years as an apprentice to a skilled master. The statute had formed part of an attempt by the Elizabethan state to restrict labour mobility and to maintain the supply of labour during a time of demographic stagnation and rising wage-rates.[15] Throughout the eighteenth century, however, the emergence of new industries and trades together with a rising child and juvenile population rendered the law increasingly anachronistic in the eyes of contemporaries. Violations of apprenticeship law became increasingly common and by the end of the century the statute had been 'much whittled away by narrowing decisions of the judges, who disapproved of it on principle'.[16] The will of Parliament was also inclined against labour market regulations. In 1810–11, cotton weavers presented petitions in an effort to restrict the entry of unskilled children and juveniles to their trade, but the report on the petitions concluded that the campaign had been 'calculated . . . to restrict the number of hands when manufactures are flourishing . . . and to infringe on personal liberty in . . . the free exercise of Industry, of Skill, and of Talent'.[17]

The drive to abolish statutory protection for skilled apprenticeships was underpinned by a political economy that revered the freedom of labour. Political economists and jurists applied the same logic to apprenticeship regulations as they did to the law of settlement, believing that such restrictions were irrational and tended to inhibit the occupational and spatial mobility of workers. Adam Smith argued consistently that traditional seven-year apprenticeships were unnecessarily long and that a majority of trades might be learned in a much shorter period.[18] It was certainly questionable whether trades such as basket-weaving or fellmongering should be regarded as crafts requiring seven years' training. In contrast, the supporters of statutory apprenticeship argued that the institution formed a distinct life-cycle stage and had a wider social value than simple training for work.[19] The pro-apprenticeship pamphleteer William Playfair, for example, argued that parents in towns preferred to bind their sons to trades, even where a trade was quite unskilled, 'to keep them from becoming vagabonds and blackguards'.[20] The repeal of the statute in 1814 had the effect of liberalising the child and adolescent labour market to the extent that subsequent efforts by craft guilds to enforce apprenticeship regulations succeeded only among the elite trades.[21] It is significant in this respect that industrial growth during the later eighteenth and early nineteenth centuries appears to have been most rapid in factory sectors that had been largely free of statutory regulation (notably the textiles and metal trades).[22]

Political economists justified de-regulation of apprenticeship on the grounds that the statutes had been detrimental to the free operation of labour in the market. Laws aimed specifically at regulating child employment, however, posed more difficult intellectual problems. There was an obvious tension between the desirability of protecting children and the danger that such intervention might lead to unwarranted interference in the adult labour market.[23] The presumption among historians has been that political economists would always support a *laissez-faire* approach to the labour market and this has led to a belief that they would therefore always oppose state intervention on behalf of children. There is, however, a good deal of evidence that by the 1830s many political economists had recognised industrial child labour as a growing social problem and gave at least their passive support to the limited forms of regulation proposed at the time.[24] As a leading supporter of the short-time movement observed, 'as men, they could not longer screw up their minds and hearts so far as to sacrifice any more limbs and lives of infants [but] the science would not suffer them to invade the "freedom of industry" by involving the adults in that protection which they were obliged to give the child.'[25] At root, many political economists supported the regulation of child labour because they blamed the protectionist Corn Laws for creating the poverty that forced poor children to work in industry.[26] By the 1830s and 40s political economists had become a major force on many state inquiries and they played a crucial role in framing early Poor Law and factory legislation.[27]

A growing political will to intervene in specific child occupations was matched in the 1830s and '40s by a much greater public awareness of social conditions. The earliest social inquiries into child employment had been hampered by a lack of funds as well as by simple logistical problems such as difficulties in travelling around the country to collect evidence. Improvements in communications, widening literacy and a growing rail network, however, were bringing under the public gaze for the first time evidence of living conditions and working practices from distant parts of the country.[28] Government commissions and committees of inquiry also became much larger and more methodical. A pattern of systematic inquiry into the child labour market was set by the large-scale Factory Commission of 1833. Thereafter, parliamentary inquiries into child labour employed larger numbers of investigators who worked in different districts or regions and reported back to a central administrative body. The mode of inquiry became increasingly standardised and the practice of publishing substantial reports and minutes of evidence became established.

Humanitarianism

The widening scope of state inquiries also bore an intimate relationship with the public campaigns of social reformers. Indeed, the first major investigations into industrial child employment were embarked upon at the behest of leading philanthropists such as Lord Shaftesbury.[29] Humanitarians like Shaftesbury, in common with the political economists, portrayed children as 'unfree' labourers and argued that their economic position was little different from that of slaves. Like slaves, children lacked the legal status to negotiate their own working conditions.[30] Unlike the political economists, however, humanitarian campaigners believed that the root of the problem lay in the system of industrial production itself and its inherently disruptive effect upon established social and political relationships. They pointed to the misery of urban and industrial life and to the poverty of groups such as the domestic hand-loom weavers. Evangelical reformers also believed that large-scale industrial production reduced parental supervision of children and undermined the scriptural principles stressing the primacy of the family unit.[31] Shaftesbury described the traditional system of domestic industry as 'one of the first ordinances of God' and argued that '[d]omestic life and domestic discipline must soon be at an end; society will consist of individuals no longer grouped into families; so early is the separation of husband and wife, of parents and children.'[32] As well as attempting to counter the exploitation and abuse of children, therefore, philanthropists and religious reformers wished to promote a spiritual ideal of middle- and upper-class family life. Other humanitarian reformers supposed that the rightness of their cause justified an aggressive stance towards obstinate employers of children. Richard Oastler (the 'King of the Factory Children'), for example, argued that factory legislation should allow for the imprisonment, flogging and pillorying of recalcitrant factory owners.[33] As Hartwell put it, the reformers were 'moral rather than analytical, passionate rather than sober, abusive rather than conciliatory'.[34]

The ostensibly moral platform of wealthy philanthropists was also linked with more deeply held fears that the rapid increase in factory production would come to threaten traditional privilege by creating a class of rich and powerful industrialists. Factory owners were often of humble origin and harboured little respect for landed aristocrats. Industrialists also clamoured for greater political representation, and the debate over factory reform was carried out against the backdrop of fierce disagreements between the landed interest and the emergent industrial classes over the protectionist Corn Laws, the Poor Law and reform of the franchise. It would be a mistake, therefore, to view the campaigns against child factory labour in the early 1830s as a matter solely of humanitarian concern. As Henriques pointed out, Tories 'still smarting under their defeat on the reform question...[were]... endeavouring with delight to bring to the surface everything likely to damage in the eyes of the public, the industrial middle class'.[35] Indeed, many of the supporters of ardent reformers such as Sadler and Shaftesbury actually cared little for the plight of child workers but would vote for factory reform 'as a means of putting a spoke in the manufacturers' wheel'.[36] More importantly, although philanthropists and humanitarians condemned child labour on moral grounds, they exhibited much less interest in the economic consequences of their proposals upon poor families. The enactment of laws to regulate the employment of children almost always had a depressive effect upon the incomes of poor families but child labour laws never contained provisions to compensate parents for the loss of their children's earnings.[37]

The perceived decline in the integrity of the family was further reflected in widespread middle-class alarm about moral degeneracy. The placing together in the workplace of large numbers of children and adults of both sexes was thought to provide occasions for illicit sexual activity. Factories separated family members during the working day and the exposure of children in the industrial workplace to 'adult' conversation was held to be inherently corrupting. To contemporaries, the child was 'the father of the man' and immoral and brutalising habits acquired in childhood would result in an unruly and dangerous adult.[38] A greater number of young females in the industrial workforce, in particular, was thought to lead to rising economic independence, a weakening of parental controls and greater sexual freedom.[39] Hudson has argued that one of the major reasons why small workshops and domestic workplaces were overlooked by legislators was because the decline in parental moral authority was thought to be more advanced in the larger manufactories.[40]

Evidence published by the Children's Employment Commission in 1842 and 1843 seemed to confirm such fears. Staffordshire potteries were portrayed as 'emporiums of profligacy'. The sub-commissioner observed that 'sexual intercourse ... is of very common occurrence ... bastardy, the natural result, is thought *very lightly* of'.[41] In the Kidderminster carpet industry the Commission found 'frequent instances of seduction on the part of married men and *fathers of families* ... afforded by the solitary night-working with their draw girls [and] the frequent occasion of girls becoming mothers almost as *soon as nature will allow them to become so*'.[42] In coalmining, the secluded nature of the underground levels gave rise to similar accusations. The commissioners voiced their concern that children were working in close proximity to naked and semi-naked adult miners and their report contained several drawings illustrating the conditions of such child workers. The most famous image depicted a 14-year-old boy and a girl of about 15 being wound up a mine shaft 'cross-lapped' (see Fig. 4.1). The girl is clearly naked from the waist up, and has her legs around the body of the boy.[43] However, the original drawing was almost certainly much more explicit and it is clear that breeches had been drawn on to the two naked figures prior to publication.[44]

The dissemination of such images in periodicals and provincial newspapers scandalised early Victorian society and was met by fierce denials by colliery owners and miners. Lord Londonderry, the leader of the powerful north-east coal owners, described them as having an 'obscene

Figure 4.1.   Child miners being drawn up a pit
Source: *Children's Employment Commission*, PP 1842, XVII, p. 61.

character . . . more calculated to excite the feelings than to enlighten the judgement'.[45] Londonderry argued that a 'mania' had arisen concerning women and children in coal mines as a direct result of 'the exaggerated report of the commissioners, and the disgusting pictorial woodcuts with which they had embellished their report. These prints were seen in the *salons* of the capital [and] the ladies were all enlisted in the cause of their own sex, thus represented in so brutal a manner'.[46] In spite of the protestations of employers, many opponents of factory and mines employment argued freely that industrial working life harboured numerous opportunities for illicit sexual relations. Mrs Tonna wrote of the manufacturing system in 1843–44, 'our women are changed into men, and our men into devils'.[47] Fears of moral collapse were not confined to philanthropists and evangelicals. Both the radical Francis Place and the communist Friedrich Engels believed that the working

class and factory workers in particular had no chastity.[48] Allegations of
moral decline also extended to parts of the agrarian economy where the
'gang system' of casual, sub-contracted, labour had led to a decline in
parental supervision of children. When working at too great a distance
from their homes, gangs of men, women and children would sometimes
sleep overnight in barns and this was supposed to have given rise to illegitimacy among young girls.[49] Traditional 'live-in' agricultural servants
were widely regarded as more respectable than 'outdoor' wage labourers
because the behaviour of servants was subject to greater scrutiny by
employers.[50] As Humphries has suggested, 'the employing farmer and
his wife took their supervision seriously because they too could be
adversely affected by any sexual lapse'.[51]

Working-Class Organisations and Child Labour

The issue of child welfare was also taken up by working-class labour
organisations. By the end of the eighteenth century, many traditional
trades had entered a serious decline in the face of competition from
factory-produced goods. Children were cast increasingly as victims of
the new technology and were frequently exploited in campaigns by
workers' representatives.[52] Felkin noted that following the French Wars
the distressed framework-knitters of Nottingham placed children and
women at the head of their protests against the effects of new machinery.[53]
Factory operatives, too, used the issue of child employment in their
agitation for a shorter working day. In the early 1830s, the Ten Hours
campaign focused upon alleged examples of cruelty and ill-treatment
towards factory-employed children. The leader of the Lancashire cotton
textiles operatives, John Doherty, published the *Memoir of Robert Blincoe*,
an horrific account of the experiences of an illegitimate orphan apprenticed more than three decades earlier by London Poor Law officers to
silk mills in Nottinghamshire and Derbyshire.[54] During his apprenticeship, Blincoe had been subjected to frequent beatings, deprived of food
and clothes, forbidden to wash, and worked for an average of 16 hours
per day. His overseers delighted in devising ever more sadistic and
degrading punishments, and Blincoe's life became 'one continued
round of cruel and arbitrary punishments'.[55] Blincoe's story of ill-
treatment, though anachronistic in the 1830s, became an important focus
in mobilising public support for the Ten Hours Movement.[56] Allegations of
ill-treatment and exploitation of children in factories prompted the

appointment of Michael Sadler, Tory MP and leader of the Ten Hours Movement, as chairman of a select committee of 1831–32 which was charged with investigating the treatment of children in factories.[57] Sadler's Committee, however, was grossly biased against the manufacturing interest. It took evidence from individuals and groups who were opposed to the factory system and published its report before the manufacturers' lobby had been called to give its own views on the matter.[58] Even Friedrich Engels, a strong opponent of child labour, noted that Sadler's report 'was emphatically partisan, composed by strong enemies of the factory system, for party ends... [containing] the most distorted and erroneous statements'.[59]

Dissatisfaction with the conduct of the Sadler Committee prompted the more extensive and detailed Factory Commission Report of 1833 and the first major Factory Act of the same year. The Report of the Commission, however, was highly controversial. The short-time committees had campaigned for a reduction in the hours during which factory engines could operate, largely because this would have resulted in a shortening of hours for the entire labour force – both adults and children.[60] However, the Commission recommended that legislation should avoid interference in the adult labour market and that it should apply solely to employed children. The resulting Act of 1833 was immediately condemned by operatives as a capitulation to the factory owners.[61] The Bradford Short Time Committee claimed that the factory commissioners 'had a Committee of large Factory Proprietors at their elbows. These Gentlemen suggested to the Central Board much of what had been passed into an Act.'[62] Although such claims were probably true, it is difficult to escape the conclusion that the welfare of children had not been the primary concern of the short-time committees and that they had, as Nardinelli pointed out, 'judged measures of reform not by their direct effects on the labor of children but by their indirect effects on the labor of adults'.[63] Indeed, it is significant that after 1833 the emphasis of the Short Time Movement shifted away from child labour and towards attempts to limit the numbers of females in the factory labour force.

The workers' opposition to child labour regulation varied according to their perceptions of changing levels of competition in the labour market. Rostow examined the chronology of major factory legislation during the first half of the nineteenth century and noticed that each major Act was passed at or near to a low point in the trade cycle at a time when workers might be most likely to promote the exclusion of women

Table 4.1 Origin, by region, of petitions to the House of Lords on the Mines Bill, 1842

West Riding of Yorkshire	105
Lancashire	19
South Staffordshire	11
Northumberland and Durham	2
East Scotland	14
South Wales	1
Shropshire	2
London	6
Total:	160

Source: P. Kirby, 'Aspects of the Employment of Children in the British Coalmining Industry, 1800–1872', PhD thesis (Sheffield, 1995), table 17, p. 118.

and children from the workplace and thereby reduce labour competition.[64] Humphries too has argued for much greater attention to be paid to the exclusionary tactics of working-class adult males.[65] In most industries, however, opinion among workers and employers towards proposals to regulate child employment ranged from indifference to outright opposition. During the debate of 1842 over the Mines Bill, nearly three-quarters of the petitions to the House of Lords on the Bill were against the proposed regulation. The most implacable objections emanated from coal districts in which the work of children remained a viable part of the work process. As many as 86 per cent of petitions came from the technologically backward districts of the West Riding, Lancashire and east Scotland where higher levels of child labour existed, and less than 2 per cent from the technologically advanced coal fields of Northumberland and Durham where the usefulness of child labour had declined at a much faster rate (see Table 4.1).[66]

Regional variations in support for mines regulation show how attitudes to child labour laws depended largely upon the extent to which children continued to represent a viable factor of production.

The Regulation of Child Occupations

Most early attempts to place restrictions on child labour were unsuccessful. Perhaps the most glaring example of failed legislation was the case of the climbing boys. An Act of 1788 set at eight years the minimum age at which chimney-sweeps' apprentices could be employed, but amendments put forward by the Lords ensured that the law remained inoperable and it was not until 1875 that the use of child sweeps was finally abolished.[67] The earliest regulation of industrial child employment emerged in Manchester in the 1780s where the confinement of pauper apprentices in factories was thought to have caused outbreaks of fever among operatives. Local magistrates prohibited the employment of apprentices at night or in mills for longer than 10 hours per day.[68] Continuing concern for the health of apprentices led to the first national legislation to regulate textile mills.[69] The Health and Morals of Apprentices Act of 1802 sought to limit the employment of pauper apprentices in woollen and cotton mills to 12 hours per day and to prohibit night working.[70] In common with much of the early nineteenth-century legislation, however, the law relied for its operation upon inspection by local magistrates who often held a financial interest in mills and, hence, many employers were never visited.[71] Witnesses at the 1816 committee of inquiry into mills and factories declared that they were unaware of the existence of the Act.[72] Moreover, the 1802 Act applied solely to pauper apprentices and sometimes caused a displacement effect by bringing into the factories the unapprenticed children of poor families.[73] Further legislation relating to parish apprentices was enacted in 1816, and a subsequent Factory Act of 1819 prohibited the employment in cotton factories of any child below nine, whilst limiting to 12 hours per day the employment of those aged nine to 16. The latter Act applied only to cotton textiles and led to only two convictions whilst it was operable.[74] Other lesser Acts were passed in 1825 and 1831 but these too were very limited in their scope and implementation, and it was not until 1833 that the first workable intervention on the part of factory children was achieved.

The principal provisions of the Factory Act of 1833 prohibited the employment of children aged below nine and prevented employment between the ages of nine and 13 unless a schoolmaster had provided certification that the child had attended school for at least two hours each day during the previous week. The Act stipulated a nine-hour day for children aged 10 to 12 in textiles factories (except for silk mills, where the limit was 10 hours).[75] The silk industry was afforded special treatment under the 1833 Act after successful lobbying by throwsters and their agents, who claimed that the industry would perish without the employment of very young children. Silk was 'dependent almost exclusively on child labour' and in some workshops and mills nearly

80 per cent of the labour force was aged below 16.[76] The second major Factory Act of 1844 contained mixed benefits for factory-employed children. The age at which children could be employed was lowered from nine to eight years, but children aged between eight and 12 were required to attend school each day for three hours and their hours of work were reduced to six and a half.[77] The 1844 Act also set a minimum age for employment in silk mills of eight years with 8–11-year-olds limited to a maximum of seven hours' work per day.[78]

In coal mines, the picture of hard and unremitting labour painted by the Children's Employment Commission of 1842 led in the same year to a Mines Act which prohibited the employment underground of boys below the age of 10 and excluded females altogether from underground work.[79] The age limit for the employment of boys remained unchanged until 1861 when a further Act extended the prohibition to boys aged below 12 (employment between 10 and 12 was still permitted if boys could produce a certificate from a schoolmaster indicating that they could read and write).[80] From 1872, boys below the age of 12 were excluded from underground employment (although with a clause that permitted the Secretary of State to grant exemptions to mines working very thin seams).[81]

Inspection and Enforcement

Although the terms of the major child labour laws have been well documented by historians, the effects and implementation of such laws have received comparatively little attention. Clearly, the ancillary and connective nature of child occupations posed practical problems of inspection and often rendered well-meaning reforms impotent. Even where children were employed in large groups and subject to statutory inspection, the implementation of child labour laws was extremely difficult. Bartrip, among others, has argued that the importance of government inspectors in applying such laws has been greatly exaggerated.[82] There can be no doubt that the inspectorates set up in the wake of the major government inquiries were subject to stringent financial constraints. In 1854, more than 20 years after the first Factory Act was passed, the annual budget for British mines and factory inspection together stood at £15,000 at a time when the Home Secretary's annual salary alone amounted to £5,000.[83] Moreover, the early child labour legislation allowed inspectors to decide for themselves how best to apply the law in their own districts.[84] Inspectors did not visit all factory premises and it was 'left to their discretion to exclude such of the places that may appear to them when in the district, to be least important'.[85] Since smaller factories tended to rely more heavily upon the work of children, evasion of the law almost certainly went unreported in many instances. Inspectors also tended to rely upon questionnaire returns rather than visiting factories themselves. In mines inspection, the commissioner usually provided coal owners with written notice of his visits.[86]

Much of the difficulty in implementing child labour regulations stemmed from unworkable enforcement provisions in the statutes. The Factory and Mines Acts gave inspectors few powers of enforcement other than fines. Since children's wages were often paid directly to parents or other operatives, there was often great difficulty in deciding who was the legally responsible employer of children. Fines arising from evasion of the law limiting to eight hours the employment of piecers aged nine to 12, for example, might be levied not against a factory proprietor but against the spinner who actually employed the child.[87] Indeed, most of those prosecuted in 1846 for disobeying the Factory Acts were themselves the parents of the children concerned.[88] Similarly, the penalty for violating the Mines Act, as an inspector pointed out in 1866, would often fall 'not upon the colliery owner, but upon the father or the guardian of the boy'. Some mines inspectors explained that they would enforce the Act only where a child had been killed in an underground accident.[89]

The age limitations imposed by the Factory and Mines Acts presented particular problems for inspectors. The 1833 Factory Act sought to exclude children below the age of nine and regulate the hours of work of 10–12-year-olds, but these age limitations were imposed at a time when there was no official means of recording dates of birth. Parish records of baptisms did not contain a record of birth dates, and civil registration of births was not introduced in England until four years after the Act was passed. This meant that the earliest date at which a nine-year-old applicant for factory work could provide reliable documentary proof of a date of birth was 1846. In Scotland, formal registration of births was not enacted until 1854 and the age-limitations imposed by factory legislation could not practically be enforced until the 1860s.[90] This posed huge problems for the inspectors who were frequently presented with unofficial and often falsified forms of evidence by parents. The lack of certificated evidence of births required the appointment of a large number of certifying factory surgeons who were required to examine applicants and make empirical judgements about their ages. The surgeons were given powers to reject children whom they believed did not possess the 'ordinary strength and appearance' of a child aged nine or over.[91] The subjectivity of such judgements prompted inspectors to devise their own methods of estimating the ages of children. Some suggested the examination of children's teeth as a guide to the ages of applicants, whereas others urged the use of statistical evidence of average heights.[92] Nothing, however, could prevent the frequent practice of parents fraudulently presenting older siblings in order to obtain certificates for their younger offspring.[93] In the absence of official means of proving the ages of child applicants, the age regulations were practically unenforceable. Indeed, the frequent failure of the factory surgeons to provide accurate certificates of age was a common complaint among factory owners who regarded the expense of age certificates as an unnecessary tax upon their operations.[94]

The question of the effectiveness of the early Factory Acts has prompted considerable debate about the role of magistrates in enforcing regulations. Peacock has argued that the Factory Acts were successfully prosecuted and that magistrates cooperated with inspectors to bring breaches of regulations before the courts. He argued that the proportion of successfully prosecuted charges brought against factory owners was very high.[95] Bartrip, however, has questioned Peacock's interpretation, arguing that the real level of convictions was actually very low. Bartrip suggested that a steady decline in convictions under the 1833 Act (in spite of the introduction of new offences in the Acts of 1844 and 1847) did not indicate a decline in violations of the law but raised the possibility that the perceived difficulties in using the courts, together with a recognition of the low levels at which fines would be levied, had forced inspectors to seek 'compliance through alternative channels'.[96] The conciliatory tone adopted by many of the factory inspectors towards the larger and more powerful manufacturers would seem to support Bartrip's contention. Leonard Horner almost certainly had such employers in mind when he referred to the 'men of warm temperament and of a proud spirit who wish to have their own way of doing good, and who kick against any attempt to do good in any other way'.[97] Both Nardinelli and Marvel suggest that the Factory Act of 1833 was passed to 'benefit the class of mill-owners from which the magistrates were drawn'.[98] The larger owners supported the 1833 Factory Act because they employed a smaller proportion of children compared with marginal water-powered rural mills. Indeed, Marvel argues that the Factory Act was designed specifically to restrict output, raise prices and to place heavier labour costs upon the smaller, marginal, employers.[99] Urban mills did not suffer the labour-supply problems associated with rural mills and in many cases children below 13 whose work was restricted by the Act were simply dismissed in favour of older workers. The educational provisions of Factory Acts have also been regarded as an implicit tax upon rural producers who, in the absence of local schools, would be compelled to make their own educational provision at considerable expense. Sanderson has shown how cases of neglect of education under the Factory Act were most prevalent among smaller employers who 'could least afford this diversion of their child-labourers' time'.[100]

In the wake of the 1833 Factory Act, some proprietors sought to get around the limitation on hours of children aged nine to 12 by employing them in 'relays' where one shift of children took over from another during the working day. Factory inspectors were initially supportive of the relay system on the grounds that working hours were lessened and that at least some education was being received.[101] Leonard Horner enthusiastically advocated its extension in his reports of 1841 and 1842 and a 'half-time system' of child factory labour became embodied in the second Factory Act of 1844.[102] The inspectors encountered great difficulty, however, in checking how many hours children were actually working in any one day. It was quite easy for children to end a shift in one part of a factory and to be assigned to start in another, or to move to a different factory altogether. When cases of violation of the hours limitation were brought before magistrates they were often dismissed in consequence of the difficulty in adducing evidence of there having been a breach of the law.[103]

Whilst large factories provided the most visible concentrations of child workers, the dispersed nature of ancillary processes such as bleaching and dyeing works made regulation almost impossible. Bleaching and dyeing works and lace factories escaped legislation until 1860. Even then, such laws applied only to larger industrial processes and encountered the same difficulties of enforcement associated with the Factory Acts proper. The employment of children in trades that might be injurious to health, such as potteries, matchmaking and the construction of explosive devices, moreover, remained entirely unregulated until 1864 and several newer industrial processes such as steel mills escaped regulation until 1867 when the first comprehensive industrial regulations were achieved in the form of a further Factory Act and a Workshops Regulation Act. The latter Act applied to workshops employing fewer than 50 persons and prohibited the employment of any child aged below eight. The legislation was for the first time applicable to home-workers but this clause was mostly symbolic since domestic workshops continued to present insurmountable problems of inspection.[104] In 1878, the Factory and Workshop Act consolidated the major regulatory child labour laws.

The inspection of coal mines was performed on a much smaller scale than factories. The Mines Act empowered the Home Secretary to appoint inspectors 'to visit and inspect any Mine or Colliery ... to enter and examine such Mine or Colliery'. Coal owners and agents, moreover, were 'required to furnish the means necessary for such Person or Persons so appointed to visit and inspect such Mines'.[105] However, widespread – and often violent – opposition among employers and miners made underground inspection very difficult.[106] Lord Shaftesbury noted that underground inspection was 'altogether impossible, and, indeed, if it were possible it would not be safe ... I, for one, should be very loth to go down the shaft for the purpose of doing some act that was likely to be distasteful to the colliers below'.[107] In his report of 1854, the mines commissioner, H. S. Tremenheere, reported 'two instances where persons attempted [inspection] of their own accord, [and] were maltreated, and very nearly lost their lives'.[108]

The Mines Act appeared to be coercive but was actually, to all intents and purposes, permissive legislation. Only a single commissioner was appointed to inspect all British mines and, seven years after the Act was passed, the commissioner was forced to admit under questioning by a Lords' Committee that he had 'never been in a mine at all'.[109] The operation of the Act was, therefore, dependent largely upon attitudes of local owners, and the small number of cases that were brought before the courts resulted from evidence gathered by local watchmen and constables whom the commissioner instructed to spy on the mouths of pits.[110] In districts such as the north-east of England, where strong competition existed among parents to get their children employed, parents often knew the ages of other miners' children and would inform employers if any were admitted below the legal age.[111] In the north-east, however, the rising complexity of coal production had, by the 1840s, rendered child labour an increasingly inefficient factor of production. Employers and mining engineers openly recognised the inefficiencies and dangers of employing young children. In the complicated ventilation systems of larger pits (as discussed above), young and inexperienced 'trappers' were often held responsible for causing explosions by leaving open their ventilation doors, and the exclusion of the very young children from complex ventilation systems, where it was applied, had a tangible effect in reducing accidents from explosions.[112] As the commissioner reflected in 1858, 'the tendency of the more scientific working of the collieries, which was becoming more general even before the Act passed ... is to make the labour of very young boys far less necessary underground than it used to be'.[113] In less advanced colliery districts where pits were small or where haulage in narrow seams was necessary and demand for child workers relatively higher, colliery owners were afforded virtual immunity from inspection and prosecution under the Act.[114] Hence, the Mines Act tended to be applied only where it was in the interests of colliery owners.

Child Labour Laws and the Labour Market

For all their imperfections, the early child labour laws were socially important since they served for the first time to focus a range of political opinions upon the welfare of children in large industries. As Bolin-Hort has argued, the earliest legislation should 'not be judged primarily against alternatives which were politically impossible to realize, but rather in the light of the effects it actually had'.[115] The very limited effect of state intervention upon the wider child labour market, however, cannot simply be overlooked. Indeed, the framers of the legislation themselves were often pragmatic in their assessment of what could be achieved. The factory commissioners of 1833 noted that children in textiles factories were probably no worse off than children in other industries and concluded that 'regulation must be applied first, not necessarily to the worst conducted trades, but to those best known'.[116] Hence, most child occupations escaped regulation until the later nineteenth century and the general consolidation of industrial child labour law with its subsequent extension to workshop production during the 1860s and 70s came about at a time when child employment in British society had fallen to unprecedentedly low levels. Although humanitarians and other reformers provided a focus for debate over the conditions of child labourers, the regulations that emerged tended to follow a pattern governed largely by fundamental changes in workplace organisation, technological factors and the interests of the leading employers.[117] In contrast, the state showed little inclination prior to the 1870s to act on behalf of the largest numbers of children employed in agriculture, services and workshops. This almost certainly resulted in the former case from the dominance of the landed interest in the legislature and from a practical realisation that the level of adult wages in agriculture was pitched so low that the exclusion of children would, in many cases, lead to abject poverty among many rural families. Parliament obviously had no way of controlling wage-rates in the economy at large.[118] In the case of services and domestic workshops, the problems of inspection and implementation were insurmountable. In contrast, the higher wages paid to parents in industrial districts together with greater numbers of older resident working children almost certainly supported increasing levels of compliance with child labour legislation.[119]

Schooling and Child Labour

It has frequently been assumed that the increasing complexity of the labour market and workplace during the nineteenth century led to a need for a more highly educated labour force and that the spread of formal education prompted a decline in the use of child labour in British society. Several historians and scholars of social policy have claimed that schooling 'rescued' children 'from factory work and from the farms so that they could be trained to meet the demand for increasingly specialized jobs' or that education 'effectively ended widespread child labour in Britain'. Walvin argues more pointedly that 'it was schooling, and not industrial or agricultural legislation, which effectively ended the nation's commitment to widespread child labour'.[120] The assumption that schooling eradicated the historic problem of child labour has also influenced modern social policy towards children in developing economies. Weiner's study of child labour in India, for example, suggests that 'compulsory primary education is the policy instrument by which the state effectively removes children from the labour force'.[121]

The supposed link between increasing education provision and the decline of child labour, however, is less simple than might be imagined. Indeed, the chronology of state education law suggests that formal state action had only a minimal effect upon children's employment in Britain. The Education Act of 1870 contained provisions to allow school boards to compel attendance but a decade after it was passed only a quarter of boards had introduced the necessary by-laws to permit enforcement.[122] Compulsory elementary education was only introduced nationally in 1880 (and only applied to children aged between five and 11). By that time, the incidence of employment among very young children had already fallen to extremely low levels (Table 4.2).[123] In 1881, the proportion of occupied children in the five to nine age-group had fallen so low that the census had ceased to record them on the ground that they had become insignificant to general employment statistics.[124] Schooling, meanwhile, remained an uncompensated expense upon working-class families until 1891 when attendance was made free.[125]

Formal and informal educational provision was concentrated chiefly among children aged 10 or below who were mostly too young to embark upon independent labour. The Newcastle Commission of 1861 discovered that 81 per cent of attenders at publicly sponsored 'day-schools' and 87 per cent in private-venture schools were below the age of eleven.[126] The proportions of older children of working age in formal education only increased significantly during the last couple of decades of the nineteenth century. Even then, however, the increase in school attendance among children of working age was only gradual. The proportion of 14-year-old children in full-time schooling rose from 2 per cent in 1870 to 9 per cent in 1902 and 38 per cent in 1938.[127]

Prior to the 1870s, most working-class parents thought that schooling should be provided only for the youngest children, and they tended to choose a form of schooling that best fitted their economic household needs. The pattern of attendance at Sunday schools from the late eighteenth century suggests that the nature of working-class parents' demands for schooling were consistently of a fundamentally different nature to that prescribed by middle-class educationists. Children who worked during the week could obtain the rudiments of literacy and numeracy at Sunday schools without losing income.[128] Sunday school attendance seems to have been highest in the industrial districts of Lancashire and the West Riding as well as in counties such as Bedfordshire and Buckinghamshire where child employment in cottage industries remained high. Indeed, detailed regional research by Snell has shown

Table 4.2   Employed British children aged five to nine, 1851–71

Census date	Total employed	Proportion of age-group 'occupied'
1851	41 926	1.72
1861	36 515	1.34
1871	21 836	0.70

Source: B. R. Mitchell, *British Historical Statistics* (Cambridge, 1988), pp. 16–17, 103.

that Sunday school attendance had a stronger correlation with levels of child labour than with more general cultural influences such as religious attendance. Snell has argued that the emergence of the Sunday school movement from the 1780s may have been largely a response to a more disciplined routine for children during the working week.[129]

Census figures for the numbers of 'scholars' certainly suggest that, by the mid-century, working-class parents were already seeking to place their children in some kind of school during the adult working day. In 1851, 58 per cent of English and Welsh children aged five to nine and 41 per cent of those aged 10–14 were returned by the census as 'scholar' and by 1871 these proportions had risen to 68 and 53 per cent.[130] It would be a mistake, however, to conclude that children who were returned as 'scholars' in the mid-nineteenth-century censuses were attending formal educational establishments, since the term denoted a very wide variety of schooling experiences.

For many nineteenth-century working parents, 'private venture' or 'dame' schools offered a flexible, informal, source of child care in return for modest fees.[131] Many private working-class schools did impart some skills of reading and writing but their chief appeal lay in the fact that they were usually within walking distance of the home and provided of a safe environment for young children during their parents' absence during the working day. Gardner has argued that such schools offered 'a true extension of the domestic environment'.[132] The majority of keepers of private schools received no formal training and were often themselves only partly literate.[133] The factory inspector Leonard Horner found numerous examples of teachers who were unable to read and who signed pupils' school vouchers with a mark.[134] Many such teachers were disabled, elderly or widowed, and took to keeping a school mainly as a source of extra income. Records of attendance were not usually kept and children tended to drift between school and various forms of domestic or casual work that might be available. An inquiry for the Statistical Society in 1838 found that children in working-class private schools attended 'for a fortnight, or a week, and often only for a few days'.[135] Part-time and seasonal school attendance was also commonplace in many agricultural districts. Children were often taken out of school at planting and harvest seasons. One schoolmaster claimed that 'In summer months (April to Michaelmas) one-third are absent'.[136] In agrarian society, the main harvest months of August and September stood above all other considerations, and rural school log-books show copious evidence of widespread seasonal absences during the harvest.[137] In parts of Scotland it was the tradition that 'children would bring handfuls of the near ripening corn and place them on the teacher's desk as a reminder that holiday time was near'.[138] Schooling in agricultural districts, therefore, was compelled to fit in with the traditional patterns of rural life. The modern pattern of school holidays remains the most tangible survival of the historic seasonal demand for agricultural child labour.[139]

'Social Control'

Historians have sometimes linked the provision of schooling with the interests of employers in maintaining discipline among their workers. Indeed, many nineteenth-century industrialists and educationists themselves believed that the roots of working-class social unrest lay in ignorance. Schooling, it was thought, would make clear to those who wished to threaten the social order the unreasonableness of their cause and would inculcate respect and deference for their supposed social superiors. Such assumptions were evident in the many emphatic calls for 'moral education' of the working class that underpinned the early nineteenth-century campaigns against child labour.[140] Johnson has argued that the early Victorian 'obsession' with education 'is best understood as a concern about authority' and that a decline in parental supervision of children during the working day led to a perceived need 'for some substitute for the abrogated functions of the working-class parent'.[141] Colls has extended this model of 'social control' to schools provided by employers and has suggested that the motive of colliery owners in building schools was an attempt to shape the attitudes of future employees so that they would be less inclined to engage in actions hostile to their masters. He argued that the leading north-east coal owner, Lord Londonderry, had been opposed to the idea of education for mining children but had been converted to its usefulness as a means of social control following a damaging miners' strike in 1844.[142]

In contrast, Heesom has argued that although the idea of social control may well have been evident in the educational writings of some coal owners and government reporters, it is not at all clear that the north-east owners had built schools simply in response to industrial unrest.[143] Indeed, many owners had adopted educational schemes before the 1840s and Duffy points also to a 'remarkable effort by the established church to provide a school place for every miner's child'.[144] Hence, Colls's model of social control in mining districts seems to have been strongly influenced by the popular stereotype of the coal owner rather than by attention to broader historical evidence.[145] In factory districts, too, employers provided schools and, where these were conducted on factory premises, it was undoubtedly to an employers' advantage that classroom discipline could be transferred to the shop floor.[146] However, whether such provision can be described as 'social control' remains open to question. Early nineteenth-century employers frequently assumed responsibility for the provision of numerous public amenities that are today provided by local or national government. The building of schools by employers, therefore, might be regarded as no more of a means of control than the building of a new road, hospital or public library.[147] Indeed, it might be concluded that there is a sense of triviality about the finding that employers' schools would teach subjects of which an employer approved. As Crowther has argued, it may be impossible 'to discover *any* system of formal education which does not inculcate a respect for the values of the social leaders'.[148] 'Social control' models of schooling (in which children and parents are cast as passive recipients of employers' dogma) may also be interpreted as inherently demeaning to working-class children and parents who often had little choice about the type of schooling that was open to them. Much of the surviving evidence of working-class attitudes suggests that parents were a great deal more pragmatic in their approaches to the limited educational alternatives on offer to them.

Literacy and Labour

There is little evidence that working-class parents in the eighteenth or early nineteenth centuries regarded the acquisition of formal learning as an advantage to their families. Indeed, many parents objected to formal education on the ground that the traditional curriculum imparted to their children little in the way of training for the life of labour that lay ahead. Many industrially employed parents were themselves poorly educated yet had managed to command high wages. They could not, therefore, logically, accept the arguments of educationists about the necessity of schooling.[149] Such parents found an ally in William Cobbett who observed in 1831 that 'great numbers of people are very clever at their different trades, and earn a great deal of money, and bring up their families very well, without even knowing how to read'.[150] Working-class parents measured the utility of schooling by its effect upon family earning-power. Vincent has suggested that even during the last quarter of the nineteenth century, 'formal schooling represented trouble and expense. It disrupted the intricate relationship between learning and practice within the household, prevented a child from contributing to the family economy or looking after younger siblings while parents worked, and caused the diversion of always scarce resources'.[151] The usefulness of literacy to child workers was discussed in a government report of 1840 which noted, 'a tradesman who wants an apprentice will not take one who has not been taught to read and write, because a lad would be of little use to him, even for an errand boy, if unable to read the direction of a parcel [but in] the factory districts, a boy who can read and write is seldom of more value to a mill-owner than one who cannot. His ignorance is no obstacle to his employment.'[152] Indeed, the 'classic' Industrial Revolution period seems not to have been accompanied by a revolution in literacy. In late eighteenth-century Britain 'barely half of [the] adult population could sign their names' and by the 1840s that proportion had altered little.[153]

Literacy among historic populations is usually calculated from the frequency of signatures in marriage registers. In the 1780s, only about 60 per cent of grooms and 40 per cent of brides could sign their names. By 1830, these proportions had risen only slightly to 65 and 50 per cent respectively and in 1844 the Registrar General noted that 67 per cent of men and 51 per cent of women could sign their names.[154] Evidence of regional literacy rates, moreover, suggests that literacy and industrialisation often stood in an inverse relationship. Literacy was generally highest in the shires and lower in industrial areas.[155] Among domestic industrialists of Leicestershire, for example, only a third of grooms could sign their names whilst in colliery districts the percentage of people signing with a mark was commonly twice the national level (in nearly all cases, the level of literacy among brides was much lower than that of bridegrooms).[156] The antipathy of miners to formal skills of literacy was evident as late as the 1870s when literacy stood at about half that of traditional artisans.[157] Schemes offering cash inducements to mid-nineteenth-century mining children in return for educational attendance were spectacularly unsuccessful.[158]

Much of the poor literacy in industrial areas resulted from the social dislocations caused by rapid urbanisation and by the relative absence of provision by church organisations. A growing secularism among the urban poor also tended to reduce formal contacts with church authorities (in particular, with the established church which was the chief recipient of government aid and the main provider of public education).[159] Sanderson has suggested that literacy may have declined in Lancashire between 1750 and 1830 and attributed this to an increase in the use of child labour in factory work coupled with the swamping of established school provision by large numbers of migrants.[160] It is unclear, however, to what extent factory work alone was responsible for poor literacy since any fall might equally be attributed to an intensification of production among domestic producers such as hand-weavers in the decades up to the 1830s. Evidence relating to the literacy of specific occupation groups prior to the 1830s is extremely difficult to interpret and the influence of occupations upon literacy is probably too complex to allow for general conclusions.[161] Moreover, evidence of adult illiteracy may not reflect urban childhood experiences. The simple enlargement of migrant groups alone probably depressed general literacy rates among urban-industrial populations since industrial employment tended to recruit from among less-literate migrants rather than among local skilled domestic workers.[162] There is also little evidence of an increase in literacy in factory districts in the wake of the educational provisions of the 1833 Factory Act.[163] Moreover, the educational clauses of the Factory Acts only applied in a small number of industrial regions. For example, 80 per cent of children attending factory schools lived in the counties of Lancashire, Cheshire, the West Riding of Yorkshire and Monmouthshire.[164] Perhaps the major stumbling-block in enforcing school attendance for factory children was the scarcity of schools.[165] Although inspectors were authorised to enforce attendance, the chief problem was identifying who was to be responsible for the provision of schools. The education clauses of the early Factory Acts did not specify how schools were to be made available, and provision was often dependent upon the size and wealth of employers. In the larger industrial districts schooling was often provided in factories, whilst in rural districts children were more likely to attend regular village schools.[166] Vincent has shown that variations in literacy levels between industrial and commercial occupations were commonly greater than those between urban and rural districts. In the mid-nineteenth century, textiles workers' literacy (at 70 per cent) was more than twice that of miners (30 per cent). Postal workers exhibited the highest levels of literacy (98–100 per cent) whilst only a minority of unskilled labourers were literate before the mid-nineteenth century (between 27 and 41 per cent).[167]

It is likely that the rise of near-universal literacy by the start of the twentieth century stemmed less from a desire of parents to improve the economic prospects for their children than from a recognition of the growing importance of literate working-class culture as reflected in the greater availability and declining costs of books, newspapers and periodicals.[168] Stephens has argued that the 'expansion of school attendance cannot... be explained solely in terms of increased supply by the better-off classes... the rising school attendance figures over the two generations before [1870] must reflect a growing demand from working-class parents for formal schooling, however, minimal'.[169] The conclusion that state education and higher levels of literacy emerged in response to a need for a trained labour force, therefore, is misleading. Most occupations required a significant degree of learning, but there was a substantial gap between formal 'education' and occupational training. The latter, for much of the nineteenth century, remained embedded in the workplace in the form of skilled apprenticeships and other 'trainee' positions rather than in schools.[170]

Education reforms were also largely powerless to prevent the employment of children out of school hours.[171] As Robert Roberts observed, even in the early twentieth century, 'before they left school, most boys from the undermass had been working part-time in shops or as street traders of some sort... Round all the city termini "station boys" gathered in great numbers daily... to... earn coppers by doing odd jobs... errand boys, telegraph boys, van boys swarmed like summer flies.'[172] The employment of young girls in child-minding or in cooking and cleaning also contributed to poor attendance. An attendance officer observed that 'a girl of eight or nine is often wanted at home "to mind the baby", so as to leave the mother free to go out and do a day's work, and the ultimate meaning of that child having to be sent to school is that the mother's work and wages must cease, and the family in consequence go short of a loaf.'[173] The attendance of girls at school was consistently worse than that of boys. In industrial districts, moreover, as living standards rose and more mothers entered the labour market, the burden upon girls tended to increase.[174] About a quarter of children aged below ten in mid-nineteenth-century Preston had working mothers and in half of those cases the mother worked outside the home.[175] Enforcement of educational legislation in agricultural districts was also very difficult. The sheer size and remoteness of many of the areas under inspection, the appointment of part-time attendance officers, and the constant attempts by local school boards, employers and poor parents to get around the law conspired to keep rural school attendance low.[176] Rate payers in Norfolk in the late 1870s actually campaigned to lower the school-leaving qualification on the grounds that education to a higher level was unnecessary in a predominantly agricultural district.[177] The Newcastle Commission of 1861 noted that 'if the wages of the child's labour are necessary, either to keep the parents from the poor rates, or to relieve the pressure of a severe and bitter poverty, it is far better that it should go to work at the earliest age at which it can bear the physical exertion than that it should remain at school.'[178] In districts dominated by absentee landowners and a high proportion of tenant farmers, support for schooling was often very low.[179] Joseph Arch, born in Warwickshire in the 1820s, noted that 'teaching in most of the village schools was bad almost beyond belief'.[180] Much rural opposition to schooling stemmed from a 'considerable if inarticulate resistance' to popular education among farmers.[181] Farmers in the 1840s complained that rural children ought to 'learn most things by "rule of thumb," i.e. observation, shrewdness, and practical sagacity [and] should have their wits sharpened, and their general faculties stirred, rather than their memories stored with knowledge sometimes obsolete, sometimes useless for any of the purposes of practical life'.[182]

Until the closing decades of the nineteenth century, demand for formal schooling remained low because its economic benefits did not outweigh its costs. Between the 1870s and 1890s, however, the continuing fall in demand for child workers and the introduction of free schooling tended to remove the problem of lost earnings. As Mitch suggests, the supply of state education was only fully accepted by parents when its costs fell below that of private venture schools.[183] Over the same period, the child-minding and educative functions of schooling were subsumed beneath an increasing state provision. Increasingly, working-class parents regarded having a child at school as an indication of social status, and by the early twentieth century child labour came to be seen as a symptom of household poverty. Cunningham has argued that the move to universal education for children may be 'explained by a concern to structure the time of the idle rather than to rescue the poor factory child from labour'.[184] It might be further speculated that the continued increases in the school-leaving age since the late nineteenth century (11 in 1893, 12 in 1899, 14 in 1918, 15 in 1947, and 16 in 1972) occurred not primarily as a result of state efforts to eradicate child labour but from a progressive decline in the ability of the British economy to absorb large numbers of child workers.

Notes

1. B. L. Hutchins and A. Harrison, *History of Factory Legislation*, 3rd edn (London, 1926); A. H. Robson, *The Education of Children Engaged in Industry in England, 1833–1876* (London, 1931); M. W. Thomas, *The Early Factory Legislation: A Study in Legislative and Administrative Evolution* (London, 1948).

2. J. L. Hammond and B. Hammond, *The Town Labourer, 1760–1832: The New Civilisation* (London, 1966), pp. 145–91.

3. C. Nardinelli, 'Child Labor and the Factory Acts', *Journal of Economic History*, 40 (1980), p. 741.

4. O. MacDonagh, *Early Victorian Government* (London, 1977). The approach has been characterised as 'administrative momentum': E. Hopkins, *Childhood Transformed: Working-Class Children in Nineteenth-Century England* (Manchester, 1994), p. 6.

5. J. Walvin, *A Child's World: A Social History of English Childhood, 1800–1914* (Harmondsworth, 1982), p. 61; W. Seccombe, *Weathering the Storm: Working-Class Families from the Industrial Revolution to the Fertility Decline* (London, 1993), p. 182.

6. D. C. Coleman, 'Labour in the English Economy of the Seventeenth Century', *Economic History Review*, 2nd ser., 8 (1955–56), p. 287.

7. Nardinelli, 'Child Labor and the Factory Acts', pp. 739, 755; P. Kirby, 'The Historic Viability of Child Labour and the Mines Act of 1842' in M. Lavalette (ed.) *A Thing of the Past? Child Labour in Britain in the Nineteenth and Twentieth Centuries* (Liverpool, 1999).

8. M. Anderson, 'Sociological History and the Working-Class Family: Smelser Revisited', *Social History*, 1 (1976), p. 323; P. E. H. Hair, 'Children in Society, 1850–1980' in T. Barker and M. Drake (eds) *Population and Society in Britain, 1850–1980* (London, 1982), p. 53.

9. K. H. Strange, *The Climbing Boys: A Study of Sweeps' Apprentices, 1773–1875* (London, 1982), pp. 38–9. Keeling noted 'the spectacle, at once tragic and ridiculous, of the Legislature spending ninety years in unsuccessful attempts to protect a few thousand boys from the daily risk of being suffocated, burnt or crippled': F. Keeling, *Child Labour in the United Kingdom: A Study of the Development and Administration of the Law Relating to the Employment of Children* (London, 1914), p. 9.

10. For example, the use of leather harnesses and chains for dragging sledges of coal along thin coal seams (described as 'a wretched and slave-like mode of labour' by the commissioners of the 1840s) remained in use in some British coalmines in the 1920s: Kirby, 'Viability of Child Labour', p. 116.

11. Keeling, *Child Labour*, p. viii.

12. K. D. M. Snell, *Annals of the Labouring Poor: Social Change and Agrarian England, 1660–1900* (Cambridge, 1985), pp. 125, 328.

13. W. Hasbach, *The History of the English Agricultural Labourer* (London, 1920), p. 225.

14. Eliz.5, c.4., *An Act Touching Divers Orders for Artificers, Labourers, Servants of Husbandry and Apprentices*, 1563, xxiv. The statute was commonly known as the Statute of Artificers.

15. F. J. Fisher, 'Influenza and Inflation in Tudor England', *Economic History Review*, 2nd ser., 18 (1965), pp. 120–9; D. Woodward, 'The Background to the Statute of Artificers: The Genesis of Labour Policy, 1558–63', *Economic History Review*, 2nd ser., 33 (1980), p. 32. There is some evidence from earlier periods that farmers

and other masters sought to secure a less-mobile labour force by increasing the numbers of live-in servants and apprentices: P. J. P. Goldberg, *Women, Work and Life Cycle in a Medieval Economy: Women in York and Yorkshire, 1300–1520* (Oxford, 1992); B. A. Hanawalt, *Growing up in Medieval London: The Experience of Childhood in History* (Oxford, 1993). M. Bailey offers an alternative view in 'Demographic Decline in Late Medieval England: Some Thoughts on Recent Research', *Economic History Review*, 2nd ser., 49 (1996), pp. 1–19.

16. D. C. Coleman, 'Labour in the English Economy', p. 291; A. Kussmaul, *Servants in Husbandry in Early Modern England* (Cambridge, 1981), p. 148; T. K. Derry, 'The Repeal of the Apprenticeship Clauses in the Statute of Apprentices' *Economic History Review*, 3 (1931–32), p. 7.

17. O. J. Dunlop and R. D. Denman, *English Apprenticeship and Child Labour* (London, 1912), p. 240; Derry, 'Statute of Apprentices', p. 75. Indentured service at sea was maintained throughout the legislative changes affecting apprenticeship. The Merchant Vessels Apprenticeship Bill passed in 1823 on the grounds that a sufficient number of good seamen could only be found and trained by obtaining parish apprentices. Political economists like Ricardo objected to the Bill claiming it to be an unwarranted interference in the labour market: W. Smart, *Economic Annals of the Nineteenth Century* (London, 1917), p. 168.

18. D. Simonton, 'Apprenticeship: Training and Gender in Eighteenth-Century England' in M. Berg (ed.) *Markets and Manufacture in Early Industrial Europe* (London, 1991), pp. 235–6, 229–30.

19. Dunlop and Denman, *English Apprenticeship*, p. 172.

20. Derry, 'Statute of Apprentices', p. 81.

21. J. Lane, *Apprenticeship in England, 1600–1914* (London, 1996), p. 247; Snell, *Annals*, p. 264.

22. Snell, *Annals*, pp. 268–9.

23. M. Blaug, 'The Classical Economists and the Factory Acts – A Re-examination', *Quarterly Journal of Economics*, 72 (1958).

24. K. O. Walker, 'The Classical Economists and the Factory Acts', *Journal of Economic History*, 1 (1941), p. 171.

25. C. Wing, *Evils of the Factory System Exposed* (London, 1836), p. 17.

26. Blaug, 'Classical Economists and the Factory Acts', p. 215.

27. J. B. Brebner, 'Laissez-Faire and State Intervention in Nineteenth-Century Britain', *Journal of Economic History Supplement*, 8 (1948), p. 64; U. R. Q. Henriques, *The Early Factory Acts and their Enforcement* (London, 1971), p. 20.

28. F. A. Hayek, *Capitalism and the Historians* (London, 1954), p. 18.

29. Shaftesbury had emerged as the parliamentary leader of the Ten Hours Movement following Michael Sadler's failure in 1832 to win a seat in the newly reformed House of Commons.

30. The analogy between slavery and the employment of young children in British factories was a recurrent theme in the writings of humanitarian reformers. In a famous letter of 1830, entitled 'Yorkshire Slavery', the radical Richard Oastler claimed that factory children endured worse conditions than colonial slaves: R. M. Hartwell, *The Industrial Revolution and Economic Growth* (London, 1971), pp. 398–9.

31. W. R. Greg, 'Protection of Children in Mines and Collieries', *Westminster Review*, 38 (July 1842), p. 138.

32. Cited in H. Perkin, *The Origins of Modern English Society, 1780–1880* (London, 1969), p. 150.
33. P. Bolin-Hort, *Work, Family and the State: Child Labour and the Organisation of Production in the British Cotton Industry, 1780–1920* (Lund, 1989), p. 60.
34. Hartwell, *Industrial Revolution*, p. 391.
35. U. R. Q. Henriques, *Before the Welfare State: Social Administration in Early Industrial Britain* (London, 1979), p. 73.
36. Hutchins and Harrison, *History of Factory Legislation*, p. 87.
37. The general disregard for the financial effects of child labour and educational reform was later evident in the imposition of compulsory education from 1880 which placed an uncompensated expenditure upon working-class families. As a pamphleteer argued in 1818, the regulation of child labour 'sets the child against the parent, by telling the former that his bodily and mental welfare have been saved from the grasp of his parent's avarice only by the strong hand of an act of parliament . . . On the other hand, it teaches the parent to look upon the child as one who is only a burden, when he might have been an aid.' *An Inquiry into the Principle and Tendency of the Bill now Pending in Parliament for Imposing Certain Restrictions on Cotton Factories*, p. 45.
38. See William Wordsworth, *My Heart Leaps Up* (1807).
39. J. F. C. Harrison, *The Early Victorians, 1832–51* (London, 1971), p. 74; N. McKendrick, 'Home Demand and Economic Growth: A New View of the Role of Women and Children in the Industrial Revolution' in *idem* (ed.) *Historical Perspectives: Studies in English Thought and Society* (London, 1974), p. 167.
40. P. Hudson, *The Industrial Revolution* (London, 1992), pp. 124–5.
41. *Children's Employment Commission (Trades and Manufactures)*, PP 1843, XIV, app. to 2nd rep., pt I, app. III, p. C6–7 (emphasis in the original).
42. Ibid., p. C24 (emphasis in the original).
43. *Children's Employment Commission*, PP 1842, XVII, p. 61.
44. P. Kirby, 'Children in the British Coalmining Industry', pp. 138–64.
45. *Hansard* (Lords), 24 June 1842, vol. LXIV, col. 539.
46. Quoted in A. J. Heesom, 'The Coal Mines Act of 1842, Social Reform and Social Control', *Historical Journal*, 24 (1981), p. 71.
47. I. Kovacevic and S. B. Kanner, 'Blue Book into Novel: The Forgotten Industrial Fiction of Charlotte Elizabeth Tonna', *Nineteenth-Century Fiction*, 25 (1970), p. 171.
48. McKendrick, 'Home Demand', p. 166.
49. One gang overseer observed to the 1843 Poor Law Report that 70 per cent of girls affected by the gang system were 'prostitutes': *Reports of Special Assistant Poor Law Commissioners on the Employment of Women and Children in Agriculture*, PP 1843, XII, p. 231.
50. J. Kitteringham, 'Country Work Girls in Nineteenth-Century England' in R. Samuel (ed.) *Village Life and Labour* (London, 1975), p. 97.
51. J. Humphries, ' . . . "The Most Free from Objection . . . ": The Sexual Division of Labor and Women's Work in Nineteenth-Century England', *Journal of Economic History*, 47 (1987), pp. 930, 936; Kussmaul, *Servants in Husbandry*, pp. 7–8. Verdon argues that the early reports exaggerated the scale of gang labour: N. Verdon, 'The Employment of Women and Children in Agriculture: A Reassessment of Agricultural Gangs in Nineteenth-Century Norfolk', *Agricultural History Review*, 49 (2001).

52. The radical view in the 1790s was that the factory was little more than 'a common prison-house, in which a hapless multitude are sentenced to profligacy and hard labour': E. P. Thompson, *The Making of the English Working Class* (Harmondsworth, 1968), pp. 378–9. It has been argued that one reason why the early mills had recruitment problems was that they resembled workhouses or houses of correction: J. S. Heywood, *Children in Care* (London, 1965), p. 20.

53. W. Felkin, *History of the Machine-Wrought Hosiery and Lace Manufacture* (London, 1967), p. 441.

54. In being bound to a silk manufacturer, Blincoe was untypical even among the London apprentices of whom only 7 per cent were bound into silk; the vast majority (74 per cent) being bound to cotton, fustian and calico manufacturers: *Select Committee on Parish Apprentices*, PP 1814–15, p. 5.

55. A. E. Musson, 'Robert Blincoe and the Early Factory System' in *Trade Union and Social History* (London, 1974), p. 197.

56. The short-time campaign had sought a restriction on the hours that machinery could be used: H. P. Marvel, 'Factory Regulation: A Reinterpretation of Early English Experience', *Journal of Law and Economics*, 20 (1977), p. 381. Doherty later collaborated with Mrs Trollope in her 1839–40 fictionalised account of Blincoe's *Memoir (The Life and Adventures of Michael Armstrong, the Factory Boy)*, was a central figure in the Ten Hours Movement and had connections with Lord Shaftesbury (who arranged the meeting between Doherty and Trollope): W. H. Chaloner, 'Mrs Trollope and the Early Factory System', *Victorian Studies*, 4 (1960), p. 160. Chapman wrote 'the *Memoir of Robert Blincoe* was written by a gullible sensationalist, whose statements must be treated with the utmost caution': cited in Musson, 'Robert Blincoe', pp. 202–3. For a more lengthy debate see S. D. Chapman, *The Early Factory Masters: The Transition to the Factory System in the Midlands Textile Industry* (Newton Abbot, 1967); M. H. Mackenzie, 'Cressbrook and Litton Mills, 1779–1835', *Derbyshire Archaeological Journal*, 88 (1968); S. D. Chapman, 'Cressbrook and Litton Mills: An Alternative View', *Derbyshire Archaeological Journal*, 89 (1969); M. H. Mackenzie, 'Cressbrook and Litton Mills: A Reply', *Derbyshire Archaeological Journal*, 90 (1970); *idem*, 'Cressbrook Mill, 1810–1835', *Derbyshire Archaeological Journal*, 90 (1970).

57. Marvel, 'Factory Regulation', p. 381–2.

58. W. H. Hutt, 'The Factory System of the Early Nineteenth Century' in F. A. Hayek (ed.) *Capitalism and the Historians* (London, 1954), pp. 161–2.

59. F. Engels, *The Condition of the Working Class in England in 1844* (Oxford, 1993), p. 179. The Hammonds, however, believed that the report of Sadler's Committee formed 'one of the main sources of knowledge of the conditions of factory life at the time. Its pages bring before the reader . . . the kind of life that was led by the victims of the new system.' J. L. Hammond and B. Hammond, *Lord Shaftesbury* (London, 1923), p. 16.

60. Blaug, 'The Classical Economists', p. 214. The rationale of the campaign was noted by J. P. Kay: 'Whilst the engine runs the people must work – men, women, and children are yoked together with iron and steam.' Quoted in G. Clark, 'Factory Discipline', *Journal of Economic History*, 54 (1994), p. 129.

61. Marvel, 'Factory Regulation', p. 386.

62. Marvel, 'Factory Regulation', p. 383. Indeed, by the time the Act was passed, many of the larger Manchester employers had lent their support to the legislation because they were already employing fewer young children.

63. C. Nardinelli, *Child Labor and the Industrial Revolution* (Bloomington, IN, 1990), p. 11.
64. W. W. Rostow, 'Business Cycles, Harvests and Politics', *Journal of Economic History*, 1 (1941), pp. 214–16.
65. J. Humphries, 'Protective Legislation, the Capitalist State and Working Class Men: The Case of the 1842 Mines Regulation Act', *Feminist Review*, 8 (1981).
66. Kirby, 'Children in the British Coalmining Industry', table 17, p. 117.
67. G. L. Phillips, *England's Climbing-Boys: A History of the Long Struggle to Abolish Child Labour in Chimney Sweeping* (Boston, MA, 1949), pp. 5, 56.
68. *Select Committee on Parish Apprentices*, PP 1814–15, V, app. B, p. 8; Hutchins and Harrison, *History of Factory Legislation*, p. 7. As an anonymous physician observed in 1784, 'Youth is the time [during which] the foundations of health must be laid, and strength of constitution acquired . . . nothing can more powerfully tend to prevent either, than the want of pure air, and loss of proper sleep': C. S. Paterson, 'From Fever to Digestive Disease: Approaches to the Problem of Factory Ill-Health in Britain, 1784–1833', PhD thesis (British Columbia, 1995), p. 55.
69. M. B. Rose, 'Social Policy and Business: Parish Apprentices and the Early Factory System, 1750–1834', *Business History*, 31 (1989), pp. 14–15; *An Act for the Preservation of the Health and Morals of Apprentices and others employed in Cotton and other Mills, and Cotton and other Factories*, 42 Geo. III, c. 73.
70. Blaug points out that the 1802 Act was not a factory act at all but an extension of the Poor Law since it applied solely to the conditions of pauper apprentices: Blaug, 'The Classical Economists', p. 212.
71. Rose, 'Parish Apprentices and the Early Factory System', p. 22; J. Lane, 'Apprenticeship in Warwickshire Cotton Mills, 1790–1830', *Textile History*, 10 (1979), p. 161.
72. J. Fielden, *The Curse of the Factory System*, ed. J. T. Ward (London, 1969), p. 10.
73. Ibid., p. 10.
74. L. C. A. Knowles, *Industrial and Commercial Revolutions* (London, 1930), p. 93; C. Driver, *Tory Radical: The Life of Richard Oastler* (Oxford, 1946), p. 59, n. 1; Marvel, 'Factory Regulation', p. 381.
75. Hutchins and Harrison, *History of Factory Legislation*, pp. 40–2.
76. S. Pollard, 'Factory Discipline in the Industrial Revolution', *Economic History Review*, 2nd ser., 16 (1963–64), p. 259; 3 & 4 Will., c. 103; S. J. Bush, 'The Technological Development of the English Silk Industry, 1685–1860', M. Phil. thesis (Manchester, 1995), p. 74.
77. *Factories Regulation Act, 1844*, 7 & 8 Vict., c. 15; Bolin-Hort, *Work, Family and the State*, pp. 138–42.
78. Bush, 'Technological Development of the Silk Industry', p. 75.
79. Kirby, 'Viability of Child Labour', p. 101.
80. Boys could also be employed if it could be proved that they had attended school for three hours during two days of each week during the month prior to their employment: 23 & 24 Vict., c. 151.
81. Keeling, *Child Labour*, p. xiv.
82. P. W. J. Bartrip, 'British Government Inspection, 1832–1875: Some Observations', *Historical Journal*, 25 (1982), p. 605; see also P. W. J. Bartrip and P. T. Fenn, 'The Administration of Safety: The Enforcement of the Early Factory Inspectorate, 1844–1864' *Public Administration*, 58 (1980) ; *idem*, 'Conventionalization of Factory Crime: A Reassessment', *International Journal of the Sociology of Law*, 8 (1980); *idem*,

'The Evolution of Regulatory Style in the Nineteenth-Century British Factory Inspectorate', *Journal of Law and Society*, 10 (1983).

83. Bartrip, 'British Government Inspection', pp. 615–16. The budget for mines inspection in 1844 was less than 10 per cent of that provided for factory inspection. Ten years later, with the appointment of a further six inspectors, the share of the budget given over to mines inspection had risen to 41 per cent (but by that time, the emphasis of the inspectorate had shifted to underground safety rather than social issues): PRO HO87/1, Factory and Mines Entry Books, 14 Dec. 1843: Bartrip, 'British Government Inspection', pp. 613–16. The Mines Act failed to give powers to magistrates to summon witnesses in prosecutions.

84. W. C. R. Hicks, 'The Education of the Half-Timer', *Economic History: A Supplement of the Economic Journal*, 3 (1939), p. 224.

85. D. T. Jenkins, 'The Validity of the Factory Returns, 1833–1850', *Textile History*, 4 (1973), p. 26.

86. Kirby, 'Children in the British Coalmining Industry', pp. 202–3.

87. Hutchins and Harrison, *History of Factory Legislation*, pp. 74–5, n. 4.

88. J. Pressley, 'Childhood, Education and Labour: Moral Pressure and the End of the Half-Time System', PhD thesis (Lancaster, 2000), p. 68.

89. Kirby, 'Viability of Child Labour', p. 115.

90. 6 & 7 Will. IV, c. 86; 17 & 18 Vict., c. 80.

91. Keeling, *Child Labour*, p. xi.

92. E. Saunders, *The Teeth, a Test of Age, Considered with Reference to the Factory Children* (London, 1837); P. Kirby, 'Height, Urbanisation and Living Standards in the North of England, 1822–1837', *Manchester Working Papers in Economic and Social History*, 35 (1996). Horner ruled subsequently that no child below 3 foot 10 inches should be taken as aged nine and that no child below 4 foot $3\frac{1}{2}$ inches should be regarded as 13 years of age: Hicks, 'Education of the Half-Timer', p. 223. However, this system would have permitted the employment of 48 per cent of eight-year-old children as if they were aged nine and 57 per cent of 12-year-olds as if they were 13 or over. As Roberts was later to point out, 'there are no physical qualities sufficiently distinct and constant to indicate the age of a child within two, and often three years, of its actual birthday': C. Roberts, 'The Physical Requirements of Factory Children' *Journal of the Statistical Society*, 39, p. 682.

93. Hutchins and Harrison, *History of Factory Legislation*, pp. 72–3, 74.

94. C. Roberts, 'Physical Requirements of Factory Children', p. 682.

95. A. E. Peacock, 'The Successful Prosecution of the Factory Acts, 1833–55', *Economic History Review*, 2nd ser., 37 (1984), pp. 197–210.

96. P. W. J. Bartrip, 'Success or Failure? The Prosecution of the Early Factory Acts', *Economic History Review*, 2nd ser., 38 (1985), p. 427.

97. Cited in M. Sanderson, 'Education and the Factory in Industrial Lancashire, 1780–1840' *Economic History Review*, 2nd ser., 20 (1967), p. 278.

98. C. Nardinelli, 'Successful Prosecution of the Factory Acts: A Suggested Explanation', *Economic History Review*, 2nd ser., 38 (1985), p. 428; Marvel, 'Factory Regulation'.

99. Marvel, 'Factory Regulation', p. 380.

100. Sanderson, 'Education and the Factory', pp. 276–7.

101. According to the Children's Employment Commission, the most common relay system in Lancashire was to swap shifts at twelve noon and twelve midnight so as

to allow an equal share of daylight between shifts: *Children's Employment Commission (Trades and Manufactures)*, PP 1843, XIV, app. to 2nd rep., pt I, B14.

102. Hutchins and Harrison, *History of Factory Legislation*, p. 77. The half-time system survived into the twentieth century and was finally ended in 1921: Pressley, 'Childhood, Education and Labour', p. 1.

103. Hutchins and Harrison, *History of Factory Legislation*, pp. 102–4.

104. For detailed surveys of legisation relating to non-textiles industries refer to Keeling, *Child Labour* and Hutchins and Harrison, *History of Factory Legislation*, pp. 150–72.

105. 5 & 6 Vict. c. 99.

106. Lord Londonderry, one of the largest coal owners, declared in the House of Lords that he would say to any inspector: 'You may go down the pit how you can, and when you are down you may remain there': *Hansard* (Lords), vol. LXV, 1 Aug. 1842, col. 891; R. N. Boyd, *Coal Pits and Pitmen: A Short History of the Coal Trade and the Legislation Affecting it* (1892), p. 73.

107. Quoted in Boyd, *Coal Pits and Pitmen*, p. 66.

108. *Report of the Commissioner on the Population in Mining Districts*, PP 1854, XIX, p. 6. Similar threats of violence had earlier been levelled at the factory commissioners. An operatives' pamphlet of 1833 warned: 'When your Honours arrive at, or near any large Manufacturing Town, give the postillion an extra half-crown... to drive you in the back way, and not to tell where you come from... By the by, have you all made your Wills?' Quoted in Marvel, 'Factory Regulation', p. 382, n. 14.

109. Kirby, 'Viability of Child Labour', p. 114.

110. 5 & 6 Vict., c. 99; *Report of the Commissioner on the Population in Mining Districts*, PP 1846 XXIV, p. 5; Heesom, 'Coal Mines Act', p. 78; Kirby, 'Viability of Child Labour', p. 114.

111. Kirby, 'Viability of Child Labour', p. 115.

112. Kirby, 'Viability of Child Labour', pp. 106–11.

113. *Report of the Commissioner on the Population in Mining Districts*, PP 1857–8, XXXII, p. 8.

114. N. K. Buxton, *The Economic Development of the British Coal Industry from the Industrial Revolution to the Present Day* (London, 1978), p. 132. As the commissioner reported from the West Riding in 1845, 'in the portions of the district where the thin seams of coal are worked, varying in thickness from 18 to 30 inches only, considerable laxity prevailed as to the employment of boys under age': *Report of the Commissioner on the Population in Mining Districts*, PP 1845 XXVII, p. 19. Engels noted in 1845 that 'evasion of the law is very easy in the country districts in which the mines are situated': Engels, *Condition of the Working Class*, p. 255. Attempts by reformers to regulate child labour in mining showed a remarkable level of misunderstanding of the structure of the industry. Shaftesbury's original proposal for a Mines Bill to exclude boys below 13 from working underground, for example, would (given the very young age structure of the underground haulage labour force) almost certainly have put a halt to much of British coal production.

115. Bolin-Hort, *Work, Family and the State*, p. 66.

116. Hutchins and Harrison, *History of Factory Legislation*, p. 120.

117. Nardinelli has compared the British situation with that of Japan. 'By the time the first Factory Act was passed in 1911, 98 per cent of the children between the ages

of six and thirteen were in school, as were a high proportion of older children. The battle to get young children out of factories and into schools ... was already over by the time factory legislation appeared in Japan.' Nardinelli, *Child Labor and the Industrial Revolution*, p. 147.

118. Hasbach, *English Agricultural Labourer*, pp. 232–3.

119. This is one of the major arguments put forward by Nardinelli, *Child Labor and the Industrial Revolution*.

120. W. Minge-Kalman, 'The Industrial Revolution and the European Family: The Institutionalization of "Childhood" as a Market for Family Labour', *Comparative Studies in Society and History*, 20 (1978), p. 454; A. Fyfe, *Child Labour* (Cambridge, 1989), p. 33. Walvin, *Child's World*, p. 77.

121. M. Weiner, *The Child and the State in India* (London, 1981), p. 3, quoted in O. Saito, 'Children's Work, Industrialism and the Family Economy in Japan, 1872–1926' in H. Cunningham and P. P. Viazzo (eds) *Child Labour in Historical Perspective, 1800–1985: Case Studies from Europe, Japan and Colombia* (Florence, 1996), p. 74.

122. J. Lawson and H. Silver, *A Social History of Education in England* (1973), p. 321.

123. Compulsory schooling did help in eradicating a small but stubborn residuum of young child workers from poor families.

124. Hair, 'Children in Society, 1850–1980', p. 47.

125. During the 1880s, prosecutions for violations of the Education Acts numbered 83,000 per annum. However, these figures fell substantially following the introduction of free education. W. A. Armstrong, *Farmworkers in England and Wales* (Iowa, 1988), p. 124.

126. P. Gardner, *The Lost Elementary Schools of Victorian England* (London, 1984), p. 41, n. 41.

127. Hair, 'Children in Society', p. 51, n. 19.

128. W. B. Stephens, *Education in Britain, 1750–1914* (Basingstoke, 1998), p. 4; K. D. M. Snell, 'The Sunday-School Movement in England and Wales: Child Labour, Denominational Control and Working-Class Culture', *Past and Present*, 164 (1999), p. 139.

129. Snell, 'Sunday-School Movement', pp. 140, 144. Not all children could avail themselves of Sunday schools. A strict dress code was often imposed which led to very poor children being excluded: *Children's Employment Commission (Trades and Manufactures)*, PP 1843, XIV, app. to 2nd rep., pt I, p. D7.

130. Hair, 'Children in Society', p. 52.

131. In the 1830s, weekly fees amounted to between 31/2d and 9d, dependent upon the quality of care and instruction. Gardner, *Lost Elementary Schools*, p. 22.

132. Gardner, *Lost Elementary Schools*, p. 179. The Children's Employment Commission noted that 'in Manchester during the year 1840 alone, there were 5,475 lost children found by the police and restored to their parents': *Children's Employment Commission (Trades and Manufactures)*, PP 1843, XIV, app. to 2nd rep., pt I, p. B17.

133. R. Johnson, 'Educational Policy and Social Control in Early Victorian England' *Past and Present*, 49 (1970), p. 114. The position was little better in many public day-schools (where funding was derived from sources other than children's fees). In Liverpool in 1836, for example, 65 per cent of children at common day-schools were following what amounted to a dame's school curriculum: Gardner, *Lost Elementary Schools*, p. 23.

134. Hutchins and Harrison, *History of Factory Legislation*, pp. 77–8.
135. W. Cargill, 'Educational, Criminal, and Social Statistics of Newcastle-upon-Tyne', *Journal of the Statistical Society*, 1 (1838), p. 358.
136. *Reports of Special Assistant Poor Law Commissioners on the Employment of Women and Children in Agriculture*, PP 1843, XII, p. 248.
137. The seasonality of attendance was often dependent upon the type of agriculture carried out locally: H. V. Speechley, 'Female and Child Agricultural Day Labourers in Somerset, c.1685–1870', PhD thesis (Exeter, 1999), p. 164; *Kitteringham*, 'Country Work Girls', pp. 82–5.
138. Kitteringham, 'Country Work Girls', pp. 86–7.
139. Among poorer families, children's harvest incomes were used 'to pay off past bills (e.g. for the pig or the doctor), or to buy shoes and other necessities for the coming winter'. Many agricultural gangs were disbanded during the busy harvest months so that their members could return to their own townships and villages to bring in the harvest: Kitteringham, 'Country Work Girls', pp. 82, 100–1.
140. I. Pinchbeck and M. Hewitt, *Children in English Society*, vol. 2 (London, 1973), pp. 412–13.
141. Middle-class educationists were driven 'by their picture of what the [bourgeois] family should be': Johnson, 'Educational Policy and Social Control', pp. 119, 100, 107.
142. R. Colls, ' "Oh Happy English Children!": Coal, Class and Education in the North-East', *Past and Present*, 73 (1976), pp. 75–99.
143. A. J. Heesom, 'Coal, Class and Education in the North-East', *Past and Present*, 90 (1981), pp. 136–7. The mining engineer Nicholas Wood thought that education 'would not benefit the men and boys as work-people': PP 1842, XVI, p. 588.
144. B. Duffy, 'Coal, Class and Education in the North-East', *Past and Present*, 90 (1981), pp. 142–5.
145. Differences in opinion between owners and pitmen over the utility of education seem to have been confined to the 1830s and 40s. From the mid-nineteenth century, colliery managers, mines inspectors and union leaders had largely come to an agreement over the urgent need for education in technical and safety matters: R. Colls, 'Coal, Class and Education in the North-East: A Rejoinder', *Past and Present*, 90 (1981), p. 153, n. 8.
146. Sanderson, 'Education and the Factory', p. 273.
147. On this see Pollard, 'Factory Discipline', p. 268.
148. M. A. Crowther, *The Workhouse System, 1834–1929: The History of an English Social Institution* (London, 1981), p. 202.
149. Stephens, *Education in Britain*, p. 16.
150. D. Vincent, *Literacy and Popular Culture: England, 1750–1914* (Cambridge, 1989), p. 56.
151. Ibid., p. 72.
152. *Report by Mr Hickson on Conditions in the Weaving Districts*, PP 1840, XXIV, p. 45.
153. D. F. Mitch, 'The Role of Human Capital in the First Industrial Revolution' in J. Mokyr (ed.) *The British Industrial Revolution: An Economic Perspective* (Boulder, CO, 1993), p. 267.
154. R. S. Schofield, 'Dimensions of Illiteracy, 1750–1850', *Explorations in Economic History*, 10 (1973); Lawson and Silver, *Social History of Education*, p. 278. However, it was noted of the Newcastle miners that in signing their annual bond: 'very few sign their names; but it would not be fair to infer from that circumstance that

they are unable to write. They usually make their marks in order to save time, and because, from their hands being stiff with work, writing is rendered a slow process.' Cargill, 'Educational, Criminal, and Social Statistics', p. 357.

155. B. I. Coleman, 'The Incidence of Education in Mid-Century' in E. A. Wrigley (ed.) *Nineteenth-Century Society: Essays in the Use of Quantitative Methods for the Study of Social Data* (Cambridge, 1972), pp. 399–400.

156. D. Levine, 'The Demographic Implications of Rural Industrialisation: A Family Reconstitution Study of Shepshed, Leicestershire, 1600–1851', *Social History*, 1 (1976), p. 182; W. B. Stephens, *Education, Literacy and Society, 1830–70* (Manchester, 1987), app. F, pp. 325–38.

157. Miners were less literate than even unskilled labourers. In the early 1840s, four out five grooms who were miners signed the marriage register with a mark: Vincent, *Literacy and Popular Culture*, pp. 96–7 and table 4.1, p. 97.

158. E. Hopkins, 'Tremenheere's Prize Schemes in the Mining Districts, 1851–1859', *History of Education Society Bulletin*, 15 (1975).

159. Stephens, *Education in Britain*, p. 32, app. P, p. 363.

160. Sanderson, 'Education and the Factory'.

161. D. Vincent, *Bread, Knowledge and Freedom: A Study of Nineteenth-Century Working-Class Autobiography* (London, 1981), pp. 97–8.

162. Vincent, *Literacy and Popular Culture*, p. 100.

163. Nardinelli, 'Child Labor and the Factory Acts', p. 742.

164. Stephens, *Education, Literacy and Society*, p. 28.

165. Hutchins and Harrison, *History of Factory Legislation*, p. 77.

166. Hicks, 'Education of the Half-Timer', pp. 225–6.

167. Vincent, *Literacy and Popular Culture*, p. 97.

168. This a major finding of D. F. Mitch, *The Rise of Popular Literacy in Victorian England: The Influence of Private Choice and Public Policy* (Philadelphia, PA, 1992).

169. Stephens, *Education, Literacy and Society*, pp. 48–9; This view is shared by Gardner, *Lost Elementary Schools*, and E. G. West, *Education and the Industrial Revolution* (London, 1975). As Hair put it, 'parents preceded reformers in deciding for more schooling': Hair, 'Children in Society', p. 51.

170. Vincent, *Literacy and Popular Culture*, pp. 14–15.

171. Keeling, *Child Labour*, pp. xx–xxii.

172. R. Roberts, *The Classic Slum: Salford Life in the First Quarter of the Century* (London, 1973), pp. 157–8.

173. Cited in A. Davin, 'Child Labour, the Working-Class Family, and Domestic Ideology in Nineteenth-Century Britain', *Development and Change*, 13 (1982), pp. 643–4.

174. Davin, 'Child Labour', p. 647.

175. M. Anderson, *Family Structure in Nineteenth-Century Lancashire* (Cambridge, 1971), p. 74.

176. Armstrong, *Farmworkers*, p. 124.

177. A. Digby, *Pauper Palaces* (London, 1978), p. 195.

178. Cited in Davin, 'Child Labour', p. 638.

179. Stephens, *Education in Britain*, p. 32.

180. J. Arch, *Joseph Arch: The Story of his Life*, reprinted as *From Ploughtail to Parliament: An Autobiography* (London, 1986), p. 25.

181. Johnson, 'Educational Policy and Social Control', p. 98.

182. *Reports of Special Assistant Poor Law Commissioners on the Employment of Women and Children in Agriculture*, PP 1843, XII, p. 218.
183. Mitch, *Rise of Popular Literacy*.
184. H. Cunningham, 'The Employment and Unemployment of Children in England, *c*.1680–1851', *Past and Present*, 126 (1990), p. 121.

Conclusion

Despite the severe limitations of the surviving evidence of child labour, some general conclusions may be drawn. First, the employment of very young children was never widespread in British society. Child labour below the age of 10 invariably formed part of the survival strategies of the poor. The demographic structure of eighteenth- and nineteenth-century Britain led to an increased burden of dependency among poor families and early employment might be explained as a rational response by households to structural dependency and endemic poverty. Child labour at abnormally young ages was associated especially with lone-parent households, orphans, and children formally in the care of parish authorities. Such children were often victims of a failure of local welfare arrangements to provide adequate care to the destitute.

Second, for the vast majority of people in history, the period between the ages 10 and 14 marked a major transition from childhood dependency to remunerative labour. This near-universal transition was important for children in establishing an identity within local communities and formed a major life-cycle stage comparable with the attainment of educational qualifications among children today.[1] The characteristics of this transition changed over time. Many mid-eighteenth-century children made the transition to work by leaving home and entering a formal apprenticeship or farm service and the highest concentrations of child workers existed in occupations where children were required to live-in with their masters. Concentrations of children aged 10–14 in farm service, for example, were commonly twice as high as among the agricultural day-labour force. Increases in the size of agricultural holdings and workshops, however, resulted in severe accommodation problems among farm servants and apprentices. From the late eighteenth century, traditional labour contracts declined in many parts of Britain in trades and agriculture and were replaced by an increased reliance upon older day-labourers. By the mid-nineteenth century, most working children commenced employment whilst still resident in the parental home.

Third, for almost all of the period encompassed by this study, the child labour force remained concentrated predominantly in 'traditional' sectors such as agriculture, small-scale workshop manufacture and a variety of services. The archetypal model of child labour in large factories and mines was never the predominant mode of child labour. Indeed, even at the zenith of the Industrial Revolution, child workers remained quite evenly distributed across traditional occupation groups. As late as 1851, more than a third of male child workers were employed in agriculture (the largest single employer of boy labour) whilst female child workers were divided evenly between agriculture, handicrafts, factories and domestic service. The spread of child workers throughout the 'informal' economy, moreover, is evident in the ubiquity of children in jobs such as 'messenger' and 'porter'. The greatest diversity of experience among child workers existed in the workshop and handicraft sectors where a great deal of production was conducted in a rural or semi-rural setting. In the small workshop sector, children's employment was often integrated with the seasonal patterns of agrarian employment or with home-based tasks such as child-minding. The flexibility of child labour was also an advantage in ancillary work in early textile mills or in coal mines. However, although some industrial processes offered new and lucrative opportunities for some working children, such advantages were short lived. Rapid changes in the location of industries, increasing complexity in production and a growing requirement for workplace safety led to falling demand for child labour in large-scale industrial production. Industrial child labour was, as Mathias has argued, a clear example of 'straight transfers from a "pre-industrial" context and a "pre-industrial" tradition'.[2]

Finally, the traditional role of state legislation and education in regulating or eradicating child labour (which has long occupied a central position in the historiography of children's employment) has been grossly overstated. Between 1750 and 1870, the vast majority of employed children remained beyond the reach of state regulation which was confined to a very small number of industrial occupations and which was frequently unenforceable. More widely applicable state legislation such as the repeal of statutory apprenticeship or the increasingly punitive Poor Law almost certainly had a greater effect upon levels of child employment. Humanitarian campaigns against child labour, therefore, should be viewed realistically as the product of a convergence of political interests rather than an attempt to improve the long-term welfare of most working children.[3] By the second half of the nineteenth century, legislation to regulate child labour had become largely unnecessary. Rising real wages and an increasing tendency for older working children to remain in the parental home until marriage had reduced reliance upon the employment of younger children. Moreover, the influence of state education in reducing child employment has been more implied than real. There was no sense in which the spread of industrialisation required an increase in formal educational provision. Nor did industrialisation result in increases in working-class literacy prior to the mid-nineteenth century. Education laws were probably successful in eradicating a small residuum of poor working children by the late nineteenth century. Compulsory schooling, however, had no appreciable effect upon overall levels of child employment which, by the time it was introduced, had declined to statistically insignificant levels. The view that a shift in ethical standards on the part of the ruling class resulted in major changes in the child labour market is, therefore, clearly untenable.

Ultimately, most of the problems associated with the study of British child labour prior to the mid-nineteenth century stem from the scarcity of reliable national statistics. As this study has suggested, this shortage of evidence has given rise to widely differing estimates of the numbers of employed children. Consequently, accounts that seek to offer definitive statements about the national market for child labour market prior to the mid-nineteenth century should be approached with great caution.[4] Child labour in the eighteenth and early nineteenth centuries existed within a highly complex set of relationships between households and local labour markets. The lack of national labour market statistics may eventually be circumvented by the continuing growth of local demographic, regional and sectoral studies of child and family labour. Such studies may provide the basis for a future integrated approach to children's employment in the context of the overall development of the British economy between 1750 and 1870.

Notes

1. The importance of occupational status in the past is attested to by the widespread occurrence of occupation designations as surnames.

2. P. Mathias, 'Labour and the Process of Industrialization in the First Phases of British Industrialization' in P. Mathias and J. A. Davis (eds) *The Nature of Industrialization, Vol. 3. Enterprise and Labour: From the Eighteenth Century to the Present* (Oxford, 1996), p. 42.

3. Hutt found it 'hard to believe that rich philanthropists felt more strongly than parents about the welfare of their children': W. H. Hutt, 'The Factory System of the Early Nineteenth Century' in F. A. Hayek (ed.) *Capitalism and the Historians* (London, 1954), p. 183.

4. Hutchins and Harrison observed a century ago, 'no materials exist for anything like a statistical or accurate study of child labour in the eighteenth century'. B. L. Hutchins and A. Harrison, *A History of Factory Legislation* (3rd edn, London, 1926), p. 5.

Appendix: Classification of Occupations Used in Tables 3.1–3.7, from the 1851 Census

Employment Classifications: Males

Agriculture, animals and fisheries
Land proprietor; farmer; grazier; farmer's, grazier's, son, grandson, etc.; farm bailiff; agricultural labourer (outdoor); shepherd; farm servant (indoor); others connected with agriculture; woodman; others connected with arboriculture; gardener; nurseryman; others connected with horticulture; horse-dealer; groom, horsekeeper, jockey; farrier, veterinary surgeon; cattle, sheep, dealer, salesman; drover; gamekeeper; vermin destroyer; fisherman; others engaged about animals; cork cutter; others dealing in bark.

Workshops and handicraft
Hairdresser; hatter; tailor; hosier, haberdasher; hose, stocking, manufacture; glover (material not stated); patten, clog maker; umbrella, parasol, stick maker; other providing dress; bookbinder; printer; musical instrument maker; engraver; others employed about pictures and engraving; employed about carving and figures; connected with shows, games, sports; medallists, die sinkers; watchmaker; philosophical instrument makers and dealers; gunsmith; others engaged in manufacture of arms; engine and machine maker; tool-maker; others connected with tools and machines;

saddler; whip-maker; other harness makers; wheelwright; millwright; other implement makers; soap-boiler; tallow-chandler; comb-maker; others dealing in grease, bones, etc.; fellmonger; skinner; currier; tanner; other workers in leather; dealers in feathers, quills; hair manufacture; brush and broom maker; other workers, dealers in hair; woolstapler; stuff manufacture; carpet and rug manufacture; other workers, dealers in wool; silk manufacture; ribbon manufacture; fancy goods manufacture; other workers, dealers in silk; miller; maltster; brewer; oil and colourman; french polisher; other workers, dealers in oils, gums, etc.; sawyer; lath-maker; other wood-workers; cabinet-maker, upholsterer; turner; chair-maker; box-maker; others dealing in wood furniture; cooper; other makers of wood utensils; frame-maker; block and print cutter; other wood tool makers; basket-maker; other workers in cane, rush, straw; ropemaker; sailcloth manufacture; other workers, dealers in hemp; lace manufacture; fustian manufacture; calico, cotton, printer; calico, cotton, dyer; other workers, dealers in flax, cotton; paper-stainer; paper-hanger; other paper workers, dealers; chimney sweeper; marble mason; tobacco-pipe makers and others; other workers in glass; salt makers, dealers; water providers, dealers; workers, dealers in precious stones; goldsmith, silversmith; plater; carver, gilder; other workers in gold and silver; copper manufacture; coppersmith; other workers, dealers in copper; tinman; other workers, dealers in tin; zinc manufacture; other workers, dealers in zinc; other workers, dealers in lead; brassfounder; locksmith, bellhanger; brazier; button-maker; wire, worker, weaver; other workers, dealers in mixed metals; whitesmith; blacksmith; nail manufacture; anchor-smith; boiler-maker; ironmonger; file-maker; cutler; needle manufacture; grinder (branch undefined); other workers, dealers in iron, steel.

Factory
Dyer, scourer, calenderer; engaged in manufacture of chemicals; woollen cloth manufacture; fuller; worsted manufacture; flax, linen manufacture; sugar refiner; cotton manufacture; packer and presser (cotton); paper manufacture; gasworks service; earthenware manufacture; glass manufacture; lead manufacture; white-metal manufacture; wire-maker; iron manufacture.

Transport and communications
Railway engine driver, stoker; others engaged in railway traffic; toll collector; coach, cab owner; livery-stable keeper; coachman (not domestic

servant) guard, postboy; carman, carrier, carter, drayman; omnibus owner, conductor, driver; others engaged in road conveyance; canal service; boat and bargemen; others connected with inland navigation; seaman; pilot; others connected with sea navigation; engaged in warehousing; others connected with storage; messenger, porter (not govt); others employed about messages; coachmaker; others connected with carriage-making; shipwright, shipbuilder; boat, barge builder; others engaged in fitting ships; road labourer; railway labourer;

Mines and quarries
Coal-miner; coal heaver, coal labourer; other workers in coal; stone quarrier; slate quarrier; limestone quarrier, burner; other workers in stone, clay; copper-miner; tin-miner; lead-miner; iron-miner.

'Indefinite occupations'
Labourer (branch undefined); mechanic, manufacturer, shopman (branch undefined); others of indefinite occupations.

Building
Builder; carpenter, joiner; bricklayer; mason, paviour; slater; plasterer; painter, plumber, glazier; others engaged in house construction; timber merchant; other dealers, workers in timber; thatcher; brickmaker.

Retail, foodstuffs and hostelries
Innkeeper; lodging-house keeper; officer of charitable institution; others – boarding and lodging; house proprietor; salesman; auctioneer; commercial traveller; pawnbroker; shopkeeper; hawker, pedlar; other general merchants, dealers; cowkeeper, milkseller; cheesemonger; butcher; provision-curer; poulterer; fishmonger; others dealing in animal food; clothier; woollen draper; silkmercer; greengrocer; corn merchant; flour dealer; baker; confectioner; others dealing in vegetable food; licensed victualler, beershop keeper; wine and spirit merchant; grocer; tobacconist; others dealing in drinks, stimulants; draper; stationer; coal merchant or dealer; earthenware and glass dealer.

Domestic service
Domestic servant (general); domestic servant (coachman); domestic servant (groom); domestic servant (gardener); domestic servant (inn servant).

Professional, clerical and local government
Post office; inland revenue; customs; other government officers; police; union relieving officer; officer of local board; other local officers; East India Service; clergyman; Protestant minister; priests and other religious teachers; barrister; solicitor; other lawyers; physician; surgeon; other medical men; parish clerk; other church officers; law clerk; law court officers and law stationers; druggist; others dealing in drugs etc.; author; editor, writer; others engaged in literature; painter (artist); architect; others engaged in the fine arts; scientific person; music-master; school-master; other teachers; merchant; banker; ship-agent; broker; agent, factor; accountant; commercial clerk; shipowner; publisher, bookseller; others engaged about publications; actor; others engaged about theatres; musician (not teacher); others connected with music; civil engineer; pattern designer; other designers and draughtsmen; surveyor.

Armed forces
Army officer; army half-pay officer; soldier; Chelsea Pensioner; navy officer; navy half-pay officer; seaman, RN; Greenwich pensioner; marine; others engaged in defence.

Employment classifications: Females

Agriculture, animals and fisheries
Farmer; farmer's, grazier's 'wife'; farmer's, grazier's daughter, grand-daughter, etc.; farm servant (indoor); agricultural labourer (outdoor); land proprietor; gardener; others connected with horticulture; engaged about animals; workers, dealers in bark; others connected with agriculture; connected with arboriculture.

Workshops and handicraft
Hatter; straw hat and bonnet maker; furrier; tailor; bonnet-maker; cap-maker; seamstress; shawl manufacture; staymaker; hose, stocking, manufacture; rag gatherer, cutter, dealer; glover (material not stated); shoemaker; shoemaker's wife; umbrella, parasol, stick maker; others providing dress; employed about pictures and engravings; artificial flower-maker; others employed about carving and figures; toy maker, dealer; others connected with shows, games; medallists, die sinkers; philosophical instru-ment makers, dealers; engaged in manufacture of arms; machine makers, dealers; harness makers, dealers; implement makers, dealers; dealers in

grease, bones, etc.; dealers, workers in leather; dealers in feathers, quills; brush, broom maker; other workers, dealers in hair; knitter; stuff manufacture; other workers, dealers in wool; silk manufacture; ribbon manufacture; fancy goods manufacture; embroiderer; other workers, dealers in silk; miller; dealers in oils, gums; workers in wood; cabinet-maker, upholsterer; others dealing in wood furniture; dealers in wood utensils; wood tool makers; straw plait manufacture; others working in cane, rush, straw; hemp manufacture; rope, cordmaker; other workers in hemp; thread manufacture; weaver (material not stated); lace manufacture; fustian manufacture; muslin embroiderer; calico, cotton printer; other workers in flax, cotton; other paper workers, dealers; tobacco-pipe makers and others; glass makers, workers; salt makers, dealers; water providers, dealers; workers, dealers in precious stones; workers, dealers in gold and silver; other workers, dealers in copper; workers, dealers in tin; workers, dealers in zinc; workers, dealers in lead; pin manufacture; button maker; other workers, dealers in brass & mixed metals; nail manufacture; blacksmith; needle manufacture; other workers, dealers in iron, steel.

Factory
Dyer, scourer, calenderer; engaged in manufacture of chemicals; woollen cloth manufacture; worsted manufacture; cotton manufacture; flax, linen manufacture; lint manufacture; paper manufacture; earthenware manufacture.

Transport and communications
Railway attendants; toll collector; carrier, carter; others engaged in road conveyance; in and connected with barges; owners and others connected with ships; engaged in warehousing; employed about messages; carriage makers, dealers; ship, boat, barge builders.

Mines and quarries
Coal-miner; coal labourer; other dealers, workers in coal; workers, dealers in stone, lime, clay; copper-miner.

'Indefinite occupations'
Labourer (branch undefined); shopwoman (branch undefined); other persons of indefinite occupations.

Building
Builders, house decorators; timber dealers, workers.

Retail, foodstuffs and hostelries
Innkeeper; innkeeper's wife; lodging-house keeper; officer of charitable institution; others – boarding and lodging; milliner; hosier, haberdasher; house proprietor; shopkeeper; shopkeeper's wife; hawker, pedlar; other general dealers and agents; cowkeeper, milkseller; butcher; butcher's wife; fishmonger; others dealing in animal food; clothier; greengrocer; baker; confectioner; others dealing in vegetable food; licensed victualler, beershop keeper; licensed victualler; beershop keeper's wife; wine and spirit merchant; grocer; tobacconist; others dealing in drinks, stimulants; draper; stationer; earthenware and glass dealer.

Domestic service
Domestic servant (general); domestic servant (housekeeper); domestic servant (cook); domestic servant (housemaid); domestic servant (nurse); domestic servant (inn servant).

Professional, clerical and local government
Post office; other employed by government; employed by local government; church officers; law court officers; druggist; others dealing in drugs; engaged in literature; engaged in fine arts; scientific persons; music-mistress; schoolmistress; governess; other teachers; nurse (not domestic servant); midwife; merchant; capitalist; bookseller; others engaged about publications; actors and others about theatres; musicians, musical instrument makers; designers.

Further Reading

Much of the literature on child labour in Britain remains dominated by the experiences of children in large industries. The most detailed studies in this respect include B. L. Hutchins and A. Harrison, *A History of Factory Legislation* (1903), A. H. Robson, *The Education of Children Engaged in Industry in England, 1833–1876* (1931) and M. W. Thomas, *The Early Factory Legislation: A Study in Legislative and Administrative Evolution* (1948). The stress on industrial employment is continued in more recent works, including C. Nardinelli, *Child Labor and the Industrial Revolution* (1990), which offers a neo-classical economics approach to the problem of working children, C. Tuttle, *Hard at Work in Factories and Mines: The Economics of Child Labor During the British Industrial Revolution* (1999) and P. Bolin-Hort, *Work, Family and the State: Child Labour and the Organisation of Production in the British Cotton Industry, 1780–1920* (1989). Each of these books contains a great amount of detailed analysis but provides only limited coverage of the broader context of child labour. F. Keeling, *Child Labour in the United Kingdom: A Study of the Development and Administration of the Law Relating to the Employment of Children* (1914) is a pioneering attempt to deal with children in occupations other than those covered by factory and mines legislation and is especially valuable for its discussion of the operation of by-laws relating to children in public entertainments and street trading. I. Pinchbeck, *Women Workers and the Industrial Revolution, 1750–1850* (1930) and E. Hopkins, *Childhood Transformed: Working-Class Children in Nineteenth-Century England* (1994) are invaluable for their discussions of workshop production. P. Horn, *Children's Work and Welfare, 1780–1880s* (1994) provides a valuable but brief synthesis of the child labour market whilst M. Lavalette (ed.) *A Thing of the Past? Child Labour in Britain in the Nineteenth and Twentieth Centuries* (1999) offers an interesting and ambitious project to combine sociological and historical approaches to children's employment.

Works on specific sectors and regions include P. Horn, 'Pillow Lace-Making in Victorian England: The Experience of Oxfordshire', *Textile History*, 3 (1972) and 'Child Workers in the Pillow Lace and Straw Plait Trades of Victorian Buckinghamshire and Bedfordshire', *Historical Journal*, 17 (1974), which demonstrate the enormous importance of child and female labour in domestic industries. The ages and employment conditions of domestic servants are examined in E. Higgs, *Domestic Servants and Households in Rochdale 1851–1871* (1986) and in B. Hill, *Servants: English Domestics in the Eighteenth Century* (1996) whilst the employment of young farm servants is discussed in A. Kussmaul, *Servants in Husbandry in Early Modern England* (1981). For agriculture more generally, W. Hasbach's *A History of the English Agricultural Labourer* (1920) contains sections on the economics of child employment whilst P. Horn, *The Changing Countryside in Victorian and Edwardian England and Wales* (1984) provides an excellent social context to agrarian child labour. Other valuable contributions to the agrarian literature include J. Kitteringham, 'Country Work Girls in Nineteenth-Century England' in R. Samuel (ed.) *Village Life and Labour* (1975), H. V. Speechley, 'Female and Child Agricultural Day Labourers in Somerset, *c*.1685–1870' (PhD thesis, Exeter 1999) and N. Verdon, 'The Employment of Women and Children in Agriculture: A Reassessment of Agricultural Gangs in Nineteenth-Century Norfolk', *Agricultural History Review*, 49 (2001). The important, but often-neglected, subject of family labour in farming is examined in M. Winstanley, 'Industrialization and the Small Farm: Family and Household Economy in Nineteenth-Century Lancashire', *Past and Present*, 152 (1996). Historians of the factory and mines sectors are well represented and include W. H. Hutt, 'The Factory System of the Early Nineteenth Century' in F. A. Hayek (ed.) *Capitalism and the Historians* (1954), C. Nardinelli, 'Child Labor and the Factory Acts', *Journal of Economic History*, 40 (1980) and 'Corporal Punishment and Children's Wages in Nineteenth-Century Britain', *Explorations in Economic History*, 19 (1982), J. Pressley, 'Childhood, Education and Labour: Moral Pressure and the End of the Half-Time System' (PhD. thesis, Lancaster 2000) and P. Kirby, 'The Historic Viability of Child Labour and the Mines Act of 1842' in M. Lavalette (ed.) *A Thing of the Past? Child Labour in Britain in the Nineteenth and Twentieth Centuries* (1999). The institution of apprenticeship is examined in detail in J. Lane, *Apprenticeship in England, 1600–1914* (1996), O. J. Dunlop and R. D. Denman, *English Apprenticeship and Child*

Labour (1912) and D. Simonton, 'Apprenticeship: Training and Gender in Eighteenth-Century England' in M. Berg (ed.) *Markets and Manufacture in Early Industrial Europe* (1991). K. D. M. Snell, *Annals of the Labouring Poor: Social Change and Agrarian England, 1660–1900* (1985) contains chapters on 'The Decline of Apprenticeship' and 'The Apprenticeship of Women'. Snell's article 'The Apprenticeship System in British History: The Fragmentation of a Cultural Institution', *History of Education*, 25 (1996) provides an excellent insight to the relationship between demographic change and the decline of traditional apprenticeship contracts. The apprenticeship of pauper children is discussed in M. D. George, *London Life in the Eighteenth Century* (1925) and in M. B. Rose, 'Social Policy and Business: Parish Apprenticeship and the Early Factory System, 1750–1834', *Business History*, 31 (1989). Few regional studies of child labour exist but by far the most useful is M. Winstanley (ed.) *Working Children in Nineteenth-Century Lancashire* (1995). Urban child labour is discussed at length in a series of works by A. Davin, 'Child Labour, the Working-Class Family, and Domestic Ideology in Nineteenth-Century Britain', *Development and Change*, 13 (1982), 'Working or Helping? London Working-Class Children in the Domestic Economy' in J. Smith, I. Wallerstein and H. Evers (eds) *Households in the World Economy* (1984) and *Growing up Poor: Home, School and Street in London, 1870–1914* (1996).

The influence of household structure upon children's employment has been discussed in research dealing with the household economy such as F. Collier, *The Family Economy of the Working Classes in the Cotton Industry, 1784–1833* ed. R. S. Fitton (1964), M. Anderson, *Family Structure in Nineteenth-Century Lancashire* (1971) and J. S. Lyons, 'Family Response to Economic Decline: Handloom Weavers in Early Nineteenth-Century Lancashire', *Research in Economic History*, 12 (1989), each of which deals with a different aspect of family labour in north-west textiles. Studies of family structure in other sectors include M. W. Dupree, *Family Structure in the Staffordshire Potteries, 1840–1880* (1995) and the range of publications by K. D. M. Snell on the agrarian economy. Theoretical approaches to child and family labour are discussed from an economics point of view in G. S. Becker, 'A Theory of the Allocation of Time', *Economic Journal*, 75 (1965) and from a proto-industrial standpoint in N. McKendrick, 'Home Demand and Economic Growth: A New View of the Role of Women and Children in the Industrial Revolution' in *idem* (ed.) *Historical Perspectives: Studies in English Thought and Society* (1974), J. de Vries, 'The Industrial Revolution and the Industrious Revolution', *Journal of Economic History*, 54 (1994), D. Levine, 'The Demographic Implications of Rural Industrialisation: A Family Reconstitution Study of Shepshed, Leicestershire, 1600–1851', *Social History*, 2 (1976) and 'Industrialisation and the Proletarian Family in England', *Past and Present*, 107 (1985). Other valuable works on children and the household economy include R. Wall, 'The Age at Leaving Home', *Journal of Family History*, 3 (1978) and 'Leaving Home and the Process of Household Formation in Pre-Industrial England', *Continuity and Change*, 2 (1987). S. Horrell and J. Humphries, '"The Exploitation of Little Children": Child Labor and the Family Economy in the Industrial Revolution', *Explorations in Economic History*, 32 (1995) discusses the extent to which child labour might be understood through the analysis of contemporary household accounts. The wider demographic context of childhood can be understood using histories of population and social structure such as E. A. Wrigley and R. S. Schofield, *The Population History of England, 1541–1871* (1989). Useful guides to the major demographic sources include the collection of essays in E. A. Wrigley (ed.) *Nineteenth-Century Society* (1972) and E. Higgs, *A Clearer Sense of the Census* (1996). The latter offers a very clear explanation of what can be achieved using the household schedules of the nineteenth-century censuses. The Irish University Press has published an *Index to British Parliamentary Papers on Children's Employment* which, though not exhaustive in its coverage, provides a very detailed searching aid to the major nineteenth-century state inquiries into child employment. Comprehensive coverage of nineteenth-century parliamentary papers can be found in P. Cockton, *Subject Catalogue of the House of Commons Parliamentary Papers, 1801–1900*, 5 vols (1988). A wide range of working-class testimony is catalogued in J. Burnett, D. Vincent and D. Mayall, *The Autobiography of the Working Class: An Annotated Critical Bibliography, 1790–1945*, 3 vols (Brighton 1986–89). The autobiographers frequently included details of their early lives and labour and this is discussed at greater length in J. Burnett, *Destiny Obscure: Autobiographies of Childhood, Education and Family from the 1820s–1920s* (1982) and in D. Vincent, *Bread, Knowledge and Freedom: A Study of Nineteenth-Century Working-Class Autobiography* (1981).

The popularity of 'childhood' studies has given rise to a number of works which, though not dealing specifically with child labour, provide useful contextual material. H. Cunningham, *Children of the Poor: Representations of Childhood Since the Seventeenth Century* (1991) and *Children and Childhood in Western Society Since 1500* (1995) are useful texts but tend to focus upon middle-class perceptions of childhood. One of the most valuable short introductions to the subject remains P. E. H. Hair, 'Children in

Society, 1850–1980' in T. Barker and M. Drake (eds) *Population and Society in Britain: 1850–1980* (1982) whilst I. Pinchbeck and M. Hewitt, *Children in English Society*, 2 vols (1969; 1973) provides a comprehensive survey of English childhood from Tudor times to the mid-twentieth century. The most recent and well-informed treatment of western childhood may be found in C. Heywood, *A History of Childhood* (2001).

Select Bibliography

Place of publication London unless indicated otherwise.

Aiken, J. *A Description of the Country from Thirty to Forty Miles Round Manchester* (1795).

An Inquiry into the Principle and Tendency of the Bill now Pending in Parliament for Imposing Certain Restrictions on Cotton Factories (1818).

Anderson, M. *Family Structure in Nineteenth-Century Lancashire* (Cambridge, 1971).

Anderson, M. 'Households, Families and Individuals: Some Preliminary Results from the National Sample from the 1851 Census of Great Britain', *Continuity and Change*, 3 (1988).

Anderson, M. 'Marriage Patterns in Victorian Britain: An Analysis Based on Registration District Data for England and Wales', *Journal of Family History*, 1 (1976).

Anderson, M. 'The Social Implications of Demographic Change' in F. M. L. Thompson (ed.) *Cambridge Social History of Britain, 1750–1950*, vol. 2 (Cambridge, 1990).

Anderson, M. 'Sociological History and the Working-Class Family: Smelser Revisited', *Social History*, 1 (1976).

Anderson, M. 'What Can the Mid-Victorian Censuses Tell Us About Variations in Married Women's Employment?', *Local Population Studies*, 62 (1999).

Arch, J. *Joseph Arch: The Story of his Life* (1898; reprinted as *From Ploughtail to Parliament: An Autobiography*, 1986).

Armstrong, W. A. *Farmworkers in England and Wales* (Iowa, 1988).

Armstrong, W. A. 'Rural Population Growth, Systems of Employment and Incomes' in G. E. Mingay (ed.) *The Agrarian History of England and Wales*, vol. 6 (Cambridge, 1989).

Ashton, T. S., and J. Sykes, *The Coal Industry of the Eighteenth Century* (Manchester, 1929).

Bailey, M. 'Demographic Decline in Late Medieval England: Some Thoughts on Recent Research', *Economic History Review*, 2nd ser., 49 (1996).

Bartrip, P. W. J. 'British Government Inspection, 1832–1875: Some Observations', *Historical Journal*, 25 (1982).

Bartrip, P. W. J. 'Success or Failure? The Prosecution of the Early Factory Acts', *Economic History Review*, 2nd ser., 38 (1985).

Bartrip, P. W. J., and P. T. Fenn, 'The Administration of Safety: The Enforcement of the Early Factory Inspectorate, 1844–1864', *Public Administration*, 58 (1980).

Bartrip, P. W. J., and P. T. Fenn, 'The Conventionalization of Factory Crime: A Reassessment', *International Journal of the Sociology of Law*, 8 (1980).

Bartrip, P. W. J., and P. T. Fenn, 'The Evolution of Regulatory Style in the Nineteenth-Century British Factory Inspectorate', *Journal of Law and Society*, 10 (1983).

Becker, G. S. 'A Theory of the Allocation of Time', *Economic Journal*, 75 (Sept. 1965).

Becker, G. S. *A Treatise on the Family* (Cambridge, MA, 1981).

Benson, J. *British Coalminers in the Nineteenth Century: A Social History* (Dublin, 1980).

Berg, M. *The Age of Manufactures* (1985).

Berg, M. 'Women's Work, Mechanisation and the Early Phases of Industrialisation in England' in P. Joyce (ed.) *The Historical Meanings of Work* (Cambridge, 1987).

Berg, M., and P. Hudson, 'Rehabilitating the Industrial Revolution', *Economic History Review*, 2nd ser., 45 (1992).

Blaug, M. 'The Classical Economists and the Factory Acts – A Re-Examination', *Quarterly Journal of Economics*, 72 (1958).

Bolin-Hort, P. *Work, Family and the State: Child Labour and the Organisation of Production in the British Cotton Industry, 1780–1920* (Lund, 1989).

Booth, C. 'Occupations of the People of the United Kingdom, 1801–81', *Journal of the Statistical Society*, 49 (1886).

Boyd, R. N. *Coal Pits and Pitmen: A Short History of the Coal Trade and the Legislation Affecting it* (1892).

Brebner, J. B. 'Laissez-Faire and State Intervention in Nineteenth-Century Britain', *Journal of Economic History Supplement*, 8 (1948).

Burnett, J. *Destiny Obscure: Autobiographies of Childhood, Education and Family from the 1820s–1920s* (1994; first published 1982).

Burnett, J. *Useful Toil: Autobiographies of Working People from the 1820s to the 1920s* (Harmondsworth, 1977).

Burnett, J., D. Vincent, and D. Mayall, *The Autobiography of the Working Class: An Annotated Critical Bibliography, 1790–1945* (3 vols, Brighton, 1986–89).

Burr Litchfield, R. 'The Family and the Mill: Cotton Mill Work, Family Work Patterns, and Fertility in Mid-Victorian Stockport' in A. S. Wohl (ed.) *The Victorian Family: Structure and Stresses* (1978).

Bush, S. J. 'The Technological Development of the English Silk Industry, 1685–1860', M. Phil. thesis (Manchester, 1995).

Buxton, N. K. *The Economic Development of the British Coal Industry from Industrial Revolution to the Present Day* (1978).

Bythell, D. *The Sweated Trades: Outwork in Nineteenth-Century Britain* (1978).

Cargill, W. 'Educational, Criminal, and Social Statistics of Newcastle-upon-Tyne', *Journal of the Statistical Society*, 1 (1838).

Chadwick, E. *Report on the Sanitary Condition of the Labouring Population of Great Britain*, ed. M. W. Flinn (Edinburgh, 1965; first published 1842).

Chaloner, W. H. 'Mrs Trollope and the Early Factory System', *Victorian Studies*, 4 (1960).

Chaloner, W. H. (ed.) 'New Introduction' to W. Dodd, *The Factory System Illustrated: In a Series of Letters to the Rt Hon. Lord Shaftesbury* (1968).

Chapman, S. D. 'Cressbrook and Litton Mills: An Alternative View', *Derbyshire Archaeological Journal*, 89 (1969).

Chapman, S. D. *The Early Factory Masters: The Transition to the Factory System in the Midlands Textile Industry* (Newton Abbot, 1967).

Chapman, S. J. *The Lancashire Cotton Industry: A Study in Economic Development* (Manchester, 1904).

Checkland, S. G. *The Rise of Industrial Society in England, 1815–1885* (1964).

Church, R. A. 'Labour Supply and Innovation, 1800–1860: The Boot and Shoe Industry', *Business History*, 12 (1970).

Clapham, J. H. *An Economic History of Modern Britain*, vols 1 and 2 (Cambridge, 1950; first published 1926).

Clapham, J. H. 'The Spitalfields Acts, 1773–1824', *Economic Journal*, 26 (1916).

Clark, G. 'Factory Discipline', *Journal of Economic History*, 54 (1994).

Clarkson, L. A. *Proto-Industrialization: The First Phase of Industialization?* (1985).

Cockton, P. *Subject Catalogue of the House of Commons Parliamentary Papers, 1801–1900* (5 vols, Cambridge, 1988).

Coleman, B. I. 'The Incidence of Education in Mid-Century' in E. A. Wrigley (ed.) *Nineteenth-Century Society: Essays in the Use of Quantitative Methods for the Study of Social Data* (Cambridge, 1972).

Coleman, D. 'Population' in A. H. Halsey (ed.) *British Social Trends Since 1900* (1988).

Coleman, D. C. *The Economy of England, 1450–1750* (Oxford, 1977).

Coleman, D. C. 'Labour in the English Economy of the Seventeenth Century', *Economic History Review*, 2nd ser., 8 (1955–56).

Collier, F. *The Family Economy of the Working Classes in the Cotton Industry, 1784–1833*, ed. R. S. Fitton (Manchester, 1964).

Collins, E. J. T. 'Harvest Technology and Labour Supply in Britain, 1790–1870', *Economic History Review*, 2nd ser., 22 (1969).

Colls, R. 'Coal, Class and Education in the North-East: A Rejoinder', *Past and Present*, 90 (1981).

Colls, R. '"Oh Happy English Children!": Coal, Class and Education in the North-East', *Past and Present*, 73 (1976).

Coombs, S., and D. Radburn, 'Children and Young People on the Land' in M. Winstanley (ed.) *Working Children in Nineteenth-Century Lancashire* (Preston, 1995).

Corfield, P. J. *The Impact of English Towns, 1700–1800* (Oxford, 1982).

Crowther, M. A. *The Workhouse System, 1834–1929: The History of an English Social Institution* (1981).

Cruickshank, M. *Children and Industry: Child Health and Welfare in North-West Textile Towns During the Nineteenth Century* (Manchester, 1981).

Cunningham, H. *Children and Childhood in Western Society Since 1500* (Harlow, 1995).

Cunningham, H. 'Combating Child Labour: The British Experience' in H. Cunningham and P. P. Viazzo (eds) *Child Labour in Historical Perspective, 1800–1985: Case Studies from Europe, Japan and Colombia* (Florence, 1996).

Cunningham, H. 'The Decline of Child Labour: Labour Markets and Family Economies in Europe and North America Since 1830', *Economic History Review*, 2nd ser., 53 (2000).

Cunningham, H. 'The Employment and Unemployment of Children in England *c*.1680–1851', *Past and Present*, 126 (1990).

Cunningham, H., and P. P. Viazzo, 'Some Issues in the Historical Study of Child Labour' in H. Cunningham and P. P. Viazzo (eds) *Child Labour in Historical Perspective, 1800–1985: Case Studies from Europe, Japan and Colombia* (Florence, 1996).

Daunton, M. J. *House and Home in the Victorian City* (1983).

Davey, H. *Poor Law Settlement and Removal* (1908).

Davies, D. *The Case of Labourers in Husbandry Stated and Considered* (1795).

Davin, A. 'Child Labour, the Working-Class Family, and Domestic Ideology in Nineteenth-Century Britain', *Development and Change*, 13 (1982).

Davin, A. *Growing up Poor: Home, School and Street in London, 1870–1914* (1996).

Davin, A. 'Working or Helping? London Working-Class Children in the Domestic Economy' in J. Smith, I. Wallerstein and H. Evers (eds) *Households in the World Economy* (1984).

Derry, T. K. 'The Repeal of the Apprenticeship Clauses in the Statute of Apprentices', *Economic History Review*, 3 (1931–32).

De Vries, J. 'Between Purchasing Power and the World of Goods: Understanding the Household Economy in Early Modern Europe' in J. Brewer and R. Porter (eds) *Consumption and the World of Goods* (London, 1993).

De Vries, J. 'The Industrial Revolution and the Industrious Revolution', *Journal of Economic History*, 54 (1994).

Digby, A. *Pauper Palaces* (1978).

Dodd, W. *The Factory System Illustrated: In a Series of Letters to the Rt. Hon. Lord Shaftesbury* (1842).

Driver, C. *Tory Radical: The Life of Richard Oastler* (Oxford, 1946).

Duffy, B. 'Coal, Class and Education in the North-East', *Past and Present*, 90 (1981).

Dunlop, O. J., and R. D. Denman, *English Apprenticeship and Child Labour* (1912).

Dupree, M. W. *Family Structure in the Staffordshire Potteries, 1840–1880* (Oxford, 1995).

Eden, Sir F. M. *The State of the Poor, or an History of the Labouring Classes in England* (3 vols, 1797).

Edwards, M. M., and R. Lloyd-Jones, 'N. J. Smelser and the Cotton Factory Family: A Reassessment' in N. B. Harte and K. G. Ponting (eds) *Textile History and Economic History: Essays in Honour of Miss Julia de Lacy Mann* (Manchester, 1973).

Engels, F. *The Condition of the Working Class in England in 1844* (Oxford, 1993; first published 1845).

Evans, G. E. *Ask the Fellows Who Cut the Hay* (1965)

Farnie, D. A. *The English Cotton Industry and the World Market, 1815–1896* (Oxford, 1979).

Felkin, W. *History of the Machine-Wrought Hosiery and Lace Manufacture* (1967; first published 1867).

Fielden, J. *The Curse of the Factory System*, ed. J. T. Ward (1969; first published 1836).

Fisher, F. J. 'Influenza and Inflation in Tudor England', *Economic History Review*, 2nd ser., 18 (1965).

Floud, R., K. Wachter and A. Gregory, *Height, Health and History: Nutritional Status in the United Kingdom, 1750–1980* (Cambridge, 1990).

Fowler, D. *The First Teenagers: The Lifestyle of Young Wage-Earners in Interwar Britain* (1995).

Fyfe, A. *Child Labour* (Cambridge, 1989).

Gardner, P. *The Lost Elementary Schools of Victorian England* (1984).

Gatley, D. A. *Child Workers in Victorian Warrington: The Report of the Children's Employment Commission into Child Labour* (Stoke, 1996).

George, M. D. *London Life in the Eighteenth Century* (Harmondsworth, 1966; first published 1925).

Goldberg, P. J. P. *Women, Work and Life Cycle in a Medieval Economy: Women in York and Yorkshire, 1300–1520* (Oxford, 1992).

Goldstone, J. A. 'The Demographic Revolution in England: A Re-Examination', *Population Studies*, 45 (1986).

Gray, R. 'The Languages of Factory Reform in Britain, *c.* 1830–1860' in P. Joyce (ed.) *The Historical Meanings of Work* (Cambridge, 1987).

Greasley, D. 'The Diffusion of Machine Cutting in the British Coal Industry, 1902–1938', *Explorations in Economic History*, 19 (1982).

Greenwood, A. 'Blind-Alley Labour', *Economic Journal*, 22 (1912).

Greg, W. R. 'Protection of Children in Mines and Collieries', *Westminster Review*, 38 (July, 1842).

Gritt, A. 'The Census and the Servant: A Reassessment of the Decline and Distribution of Farm Service in Early Nineteenth-Century England', *Economic History Review*, 2nd ser., 53 (2000).

Haines, M. R. 'Fertility, Nuptiality, and Occupation: A Study of Coal Mining Populations and Regions in England and Wales in the Mid-Nineteenth Century', *Journal of Interdisciplinary History*, 8 (1977).

Hair, P. E. H. 'Children in Society, 1850–1980' in T. Barker and M. Drake (eds) *Population and Society in Britain, 1850–1980* (1982).

Hair, P. E. H. 'The Lancashire Collier Girl, 1795', *Transactions of the Historic Society of Lancashire and Cheshire*, 120 (1968).

Hair, P. E. H. 'The Social History of the British Coalminers', D. Phil. thesis (Oxford, 1955).

Hallas, C. 'Cottage and Mill: The Textile Industry in Wensleydale and Swaledale', *Textile History*, 21 (1990).

Halsey A. H. (ed.), *British Social Trends Since 1900* (1988).

Hammond, J. L., and B. Hammond, *Lord Shaftesbury* (1923).

Hammond, J. L., and B. Hammond, *The Skilled Labourer, 1760–1832* (1919).

Hammond, J. L., and B. Hammond, *The Town Labourer, 1760–1832: The New Civilisation* (1966; first published 1917).

Hammond, J. L., and B. Hammond, *The Village Labourer, 1760–1832: A Study of the Government of England Before the Reform Bill* (1911).

Hanawalt, B. A. *Growing up in Medieval London: The Experience of Childhood in History* (Oxford, 1993).

Hareven, T. K. 'Recent Research on the History of the Family' in M. Drake (ed.) *Time, Family and Community: Perspectives on Family and Community History* (Oxford, 1994).

Harley, C. K. 'British Industrialization Before 1841: Evidence of Slower Growth During the Industrial Revolution', *Journal of Economic History*, 42 (1982).

Harris, J. *Unemployment and Politics: A Study in English Social Policy* (Oxford, 1972).

Harrison, J. F. C. *The Early Victorians, 1832–51* (1971).

Hartwell, R. M. *The Industrial Revolution and Economic Growth* (1971).

Hasbach, W. *A History of the English Agricultural Labourer* (1920).

Hayek, F. A. *Capitalism and the Historians* (1954).

Heesom, A. J. 'Coal, Class and Education in the North-East', *Past and Present*, 90 (1981).

Heesom, A. J. 'The Coal Mines Act of 1842, Social Reform and Social Control', *Historical Journal*, 24 (1981).

Hendrick, H. *Child Welfare: England, 1872–1989* (1994).

Hendrick, H. *Images of Youth: Age, Class and the Male Youth Problem* (Oxford, 1990).

Henriques, U. R. Q. *Before the Welfare State: Social Administration in Early Industrial Britain* (1979).

Henriques, U. R. Q. *The Early Factory Acts and their Enforcement* (1971).

Hewitt, M. *Wives and Mothers in Victorian England* (1958).

Heywood, C. *A History of Childhood* (Cambridge, 2001).

Heywood, J. S. *Children in Care*, 2nd edn (1965; first published 1959).

Hicks, W. C. R. 'The Education of the Half-Timer', *Economic History: A Supplement of the Economic Journal*, 3 (1939).

Higgs, E. *A Clearer Sense of the Census* (London, 1996).

Higgs, E. *Domestic Servants and Households in Rochdale 1851–1871* (1986).

Higgs, E. *Making Sense of the Census* (London, 1989).

Higgs, E. 'Occupational Censuses and the Agricultural Workforce in Victorian England and Wales', *Economic History Review*, 2nd ser., 48 (1995).

Higgs, E. 'Women, Occupations and Work in the Nineteenth-Century Censuses', *History Workshop*, 23 (1987).

Hill, B. *Servants: English Domestics in the Eighteenth Century* (Oxford, 1996).

Hill, C. *Reformation to Industrial Revolution, 1530–1780* (Harmondsworth, 1969).

Holley, J. D. 'The Two Family Economies of Industrialism: Factory Workers in Victorian Scotland', *Journal of Family History*, 6 (1981).

Honeyman, K. *Women, Gender and Industrialisation in England, 1700–1870* (Basingstoke, 2000).

Hopkins, E. *Childhood Transformed: Working-Class Children in Nineteenth-Century England* (Manchester, 1994).

Hopkins, E. 'Tremenheere's Prize Schemes in the Mining Districts, 1851–1859', *History of Education Society Bulletin*, 15 (1975).

Hopkins, E. 'Working Hours and Conditions During the Industrial Revolution: A Re-Appraisal', *Economic History Review*, 2nd ser., 35 (1982).

Horn, P. *The Changing Countryside in Victorian and Edwardian England and Wales* (1984).

Horn, P. 'Child Workers in the Pillow Lace and Straw Plait Trades of Victorian Buckinghamshire and Bedfordshire', *Historical Journal*, 17 (1974).

Horn, P. *Children's Work and Welfare, 1780–1880s* (Basingstoke, 1994).

Horn, P. 'Pillow Lace-Making in Victorian England: The Experience of Oxfordshire', *Textile History*, 3 (1972).

Horrell, S., and J. Humphries, 'Child Labour and British Industrialisation' in M. Lavalette (ed.) *A Thing of the Past? Child Labour in Britain in the Nineteenth and Twentieth Centuries* (Liverpool, 1999).

Horrell, S., and J. Humphries, '"The Exploitation of Little Children": Child Labor and the Family Economy in the Industrial Revolution', *Explorations in Economic History*, 32 (1995).

Horrell, S., and J. Humphries, 'Old Questions, New Data, and Alternative Perspectives: Families' Living Standards in the Industrial Revolution', *Journal of Economic History*, 52 (1992).

Hudson, P. *The Genesis of Industrial Capital: A Study of the West Riding Wool Textile Industry* (Cambridge, 1986).

Hudson, P. *The Industrial Revolution* (1992).

Humphries, J. 'Female-Headed Households in Early Industrial Britain: The Vanguard of the Proletariat', *Labour History Review* (Spring 1998).

Humphries, J. '"... The Most Free from Objection...": The Sexual Division of Labor and Women's Work in Nineteenth-Century England', *Journal of Economic History*, 47 (1987).

Humphries, J. 'Protective Legislation, the Capitalist State and Working Class Men: The Case of the 1842 Mines Regulation Act', *Feminist Review*, 8 (1981).

Humphries, J. 'Short Stature among Coalmining Children: A Comment', *Economic History Review*, 2nd ser., 50 (1997).

Hunt, E. H. *British Labour History, 1815–1914* (1981).

Hutchins, B. L., and A. Harrison, *A History of Factory Legislation*, 3rd edn (1926; first published 1903).

Hutt, W. H. 'The Factory System of the Early Nineteenth Century' in F. A. Hayek (ed.) *Capitalism and the Historians* (1954).

Inglis, B. *Poverty and the Industrial Revolution* (1972).

Irish University Press, *Index to British Parliamentary Papers on Children's Employment* (Dublin, 1973).

Jackson, R. V. 'Rates of Industrial Growth during the Industrial Revolution', *Economic History Review*, 2nd ser., 45 (1992).

Jenkins, D. T. 'The Factory Returns, 1850–1905', *Textile History*, 9 (1978).

Jenkins, D. T. 'The Validity of the Factory Returns, 1833–1850', *Textile History*, 4 (1973).

Johnson, R. 'Educational Policy and Social Control in Early-Victorian England', *Past and Present*, 49 (1970).

Jones, G. S. *Outcast London* (Harmondsworth, 1984).

Jones, S. R. H. 'Technology, Transaction Costs, and the Transition to Factory Production in the British Silk Industry, 1700–1870', *Journal of Economic History*, 47 (1987).

Jordan, E. 'Female Unemployment in England and Wales, 1851–1911: An Examination of Census Figures for 15–19-year-olds', *Social History*, 13 (1988).

Keeling, F. *Child Labour in the United Kingdom: A Study of the Development and Administration of the Law Relating to the Employment of Children* (1914).

Kenrick, G. S. 'Statistics of the Population in the Parish of Trevethin... and... Part of the District Recently Disturbed', *Journal of the Statistical Society*, 3 (1841).

Kerridge, E. *Textile Manufacturers in Early Modern England* (Manchester, 1985).

Kidd, A. *State, Society and the Poor in Nineteenth-Century England* (Basingstoke, 1999).

Kingsley, C. *The Water Babies* (1863).

Kirby, P. 'Aspects of the Employment of Children in the British Coalmining Industry, 1800–1872', PhD thesis (Sheffield, 1995).

Kirby, P. 'Causes of Short Stature among Coalmining Children, 1823–1850', *Economic History Review*, 2nd ser., 48 (1995).

Kirby, P. 'Height, Urbanisation and Living Standards in the North of England, 1822–1837', *Manchester Working Papers in Economic and Social History*, 35 (1996).

Kirby, P. 'The Historic Viability of Child Labour and the Mines Act of 1842' in M. Lavalette (ed.) *A Thing of the Past? Child Labour in Britain in the Nineteenth and Twentieth Centuries* (Liverpool, 1999).

Kirby, P. 'How Many Children were "Unemployed" in Eighteenth- and Nineteenth-Century England?', *Past and Present* (forthcoming).

Kirby, P. 'Short Stature among Coalmining Children: A Rejoinder', *Economic History Review*, 2nd ser., 50 (1997).

Kirby, P., and J. E. Oeppen, 'The Child Labour Market in English and Welsh Agriculture, *c.* 1750–1851' (forthcoming).

Kitteringham, J. 'Country Work Girls in Nineteenth-Century England' in R. Samuel (ed.) *Village Life and Labour* (1975).

Knowles, L. C. A. *Industrial and Commercial Revolutions* (1930).

Knox, W. W. 'British Apprenticeship, 1800–1914', PhD. thesis (Edinburgh, 1980).

Kovacevic, I. and S. B. Kanner, 'Blue Book into Novel: The Forgotten Industrial Fiction of Charlotte Elizabeth Tonna', *Nineteenth Century Fiction*, 25 (1970).

Kussmaul, A. 'The Ambiguous Mobility of Farm Servants', *Economic History Review*, 2nd ser., 34 (1981).

Kussmaul, A. *Servants in Husbandry in Early Modern England* (Cambridge, 1981).

Lane, J. *Apprenticeship in England, 1600–1914* (1996).

Lane, J. 'Apprenticeship in Warwickshire Cotton Mills, 1790–1830', *Textile History*, 10 (1979).

Langton, J. 'The Industrial Revolution and the Regional Geography of England', *Transactions of the Institute of British Geographers*, 9 (1984).

Laslett, P. *The World We Have Lost* (1965).

Laslett, P. *Family Life and Illicit Love in Earlier Generations* (1977).

Lavalette, M. 'Conclusion' in M. Lavalette (ed.) *A Thing of the Past? Child Labour in Britain in the Nineteenth and Twentieth Centuries* (Liverpool, 1999).

Lavalette, M. 'The Changing Form of Child Labour *circa* 1880–1918: The Growth of "Out of School" Work' in Lavalette (ed.) *A Thing of the Past* (*vide supra*).

Lawson, J., and H. Silver, *A Social History of Education in England* (1973).

Lazonick, W. 'Industrial Relations and Technical Change: The Case of the Self-Acting Mule', *Cambridge Journal of Economics*, 3 (1979).

Levine, D. 'The Demographic Implications of Rural Industrialisation: A Family Reconstitution Study of Shepshed, Leicestershire, 1600–1851', *Social History*, 1 (1976).

Levine, D. 'Industrialisation and the Proletarian Family in England', *Past and Present*, 107 (1985).

Lindert, P. H. 'English Occupations, 1670–1811', *Journal of Economic History*, 40 (1980).

Lindert, P. H. *Fertility and Scarcity in America* (Princeton, NJ, 1978).

Lindert, P. H., and J. G. Williamson, 'English Workers' Living Standards During the Industrial Revolution: A New Look', *Economic History Review*, 2nd ser., 36 (1983).

Lyons, J. S. 'Family Response to Economic Decline: Handloom Weavers in Early Nineteenth-Century Lancashire', *Research in Economic History*, 12 (1989).

MacDonagh, O. *Early Victorian Government* (1977).

Mackenzie, M. H. 'Cressbrook and Litton Mills, 1779–1835', *Derbyshire Archaeological Journal*, 88 (1968).

Mackenzie, M. H. 'Cressbrook and Litton Mills: A Reply', *Derbyshire Archaeological Journal*, 90 (1970).

Mackenzie, M. H. 'Cressbrook Mill, 1810–1835', *Derbyshire Archaeological Journal*, 90 (1970).

MacKinnon, M. 'Living Standards, 1870–1914' in R. Floud and D. N. McCloskey (eds) *The Economic History of Britain Since 1700*, vol. 2 (Cambridge, 1994).

Malthus, T. R. *An Essay on the Principle of Population* (1798).

Marvel, H. P. 'Factory Regulation: A Reinterpretation of Early English Experience', *Journal of Law and Economics*, 20 (1977).

Mathias, P. 'Labour and the Process of Industrialization in the First Phases of British Industrialization' in P. Mathias and J. A. Davis (eds) *The Nature of Industrialization, Vol. 3. Enterprise and Labour: From the Eighteenth Century to the Present* (Oxford, 1996).

McKendrick, N. 'Home Demand and Economic Growth: A New View of the Role of Women and Children in the Industrial Revolution' in *idem* (ed.) *Historical Perspectives: Studies in English Thought and Society* (1974).

Medick, H. 'The Proto-Industrial Family Economy: The Structural Function of Household and Family during the Transition from Peasant to Industrial Capitalism', *Social History*, 1 (1976).

Mendels, F. 'Family Forms in Historic Europe: A Review Article', *Social History*, 11 (1986).

Mendels, F. 'Proto-Industrialisation: The First Phase of the Process of Industrialization', *Journal of Economic History*, 32 (1972).

Minge-Kalman, W. 'The Industrial Revolution and the European Family: The Institutionalization of "Childhood" as a Market for Family Labor', *Comparative Studies in Society and History*, 20 (1978).

Mitch, D. F. *The Rise of Popular Literacy in Victorian England: the Influence of Private Choice and Public Policy* (Philadelphia, PA, 1992).

Mitch, D. F. 'The Role of Human Capital in the First Industrial Revolution' in J. Mokyr (ed.) *The British Industrial Revolution: An Economic Perspective* (Boulder, CO, 1993).

Mitchell, B. R. *British Historical Statistics* (Cambridge, 1988).

Mitchison, R. 'Scotland, 1750–1850' in F. M. L. Thompson (ed.) *The Cambridge Social History of Britain, 1750–1950*, vol. 1 (Cambridge, 1990).

Morgan, D. H. 'The Place of Harvesters in Nineteenth-Century Village Life' in R. Samuel (ed.) *Village Life and Labour* (1975).

Musson, A. E. 'Robert Blincoe and the Early Factory System', *Trade Union and Social History* (1974).

Nardinelli, C. 'Child Labor and the Factory Acts', *Journal of Economic History*, 40 (1980).

Nardinelli, C. *Child Labor and the Industrial Revolution* (Bloomington, IN, 1990).

Nardinelli, C. 'Corporal Punishment and Children's Wages in Nineteenth-Century Britain', *Explorations in Economic History*, 19 (1982).

Nardinelli, C. 'The Successful Prosecution of the Factory Acts: A Suggested Explanation', *Economic History Review*, 2nd ser., 38 (1985).

Neff, W. *Victorian Working Women* (1929).

Nutt, T. W. 'Illegitimacy and the Poor Law in Nineteenth-Century England', MA thesis (Manchester, 2000).

Ogden, J. *A Description of Manchester by a Native of the Town*, reprinted as *Manchester a Hundred Years Ago*, ed. W. E. A. Axon (1887).

Parr, J. *Labouring Children: British Immigrant Apprentices to Canada, 1869–1924* (1980).

Paterson, C. S. 'From Fever to Digestive Disease: Approaches to the Problem of Factory Ill-Health in Britain, 1784–1833', PhD thesis (British Columbia, 1995).

Peacock, A. E. 'The Successful Prosecution of the Factory Acts, 1833–55', *Economic History Review*, 2nd ser., 37 (1984).

Perkin, H. *The Origins of Modern English Society, 1780–1880* (1969).

Phillips, G. L. *England's Climbing-Boys: A History of the Long Struggle to Abolish Child Labor in Chimney-Sweeping* (Boston, MA, 1949).

Pinchbeck, I. *Women Workers and the Industrial Revolution, 1750–1850* (1930).
Pinchbeck, I., and M. Hewitt, *Children in English Society* (2 vols, 1969; 1973).
Pollard, S. 'Factory Discipline in the Industrial Revolution', *Economic History Review*, 2nd ser., 16 (1963–64).
Pollard, S. *The Genesis of Modern Management* (1965).
Pollard, S. *Peaceful Conquest* (Oxford, 1981).
Pressley, J. 'Childhood, Education and Labour: Moral Pressure and the End of the Half-Time System', PhD thesis (Lancaster, 2000).
Prothero, I. J. *Artisans and Politics in Early Nineteenth-Century London* (Folkestone, 1979).
Radcliffe, W. *The Origin of Power-Loom Weaving* (1828).
Richards, E. 'Women in the British Economy Since About 1700: An Interpretation', *History*, 59 (1974).
Roberts, C. 'The Physical Requirements of Factory Children', *Journal of the Statistical Society*, 39 (1876).
Roberts, E. *Women's Work, 1840–1940* (Cambridge, 1988).
Roberts, M. 'Sickles and Scythes: Women's Work and Men's Work at Harvest Time', *History Workshop*, 7 (1979).
Roberts, R. *The Classic Slum: Salford Life in the First Quarter of the Century* (1973; first published 1971).
Robson, A. H. *The Education of Children Engaged in Industry in England, 1833–1876* (1931).
Rose, M. B. *The Gregs of Quarry Bank Mill* (Cambridge, 1986).
Rose, M. B. 'Social Policy and Business: Parish Apprenticeship and the Early Factory System, 1750–1834', *Business History*, 31 (1989).
Rostow, W. W. 'Business Cycles, Harvests and Politics', *Journal of Economic History*, 1 (1941).
Royston Pike, E. *Human Documents of the Industrial Revolution* (1966).
Rule, J. *The Experience of Labour in Eighteenth-Century English Industry* (New York, 1981).
Saito, O. 'Children's Work, Industrialism and the Family Economy in Japan, 1872–1926' in H. Cunninghamand P. P. Viazzo (eds) *Child Labour in Historical Perspective, 1800–1985: Case Studies from Europe, Japan and Colombia* (Florence, 1996).
Saito, O. 'Labour Supply Behaviour of the Poor in the English Industrial Revolution', *Journal of European Economic History*, 10 (1981).
Samuel, R. 'Mechanisation and Hand Labour in Industrializing Britain' in L. R. Berlanstein (ed.) *The Industrial Revolution and Work in Nineteenth-Century Europe* (1992).
Samuel, R. 'Village Labour', *Village Life and Labour* (1975).
Sanderson, M. 'Education and the Factory in Industrial Lancashire, 1780–1840', *Economic History Review*, 2nd ser., 20 (1967).
Saunders, E. *The Teeth, a Test of Age, Considered with Reference to the Factory Children* (1837).
Schofield, R. S. 'Dimensions of Illiteracy, 1750–1850', *Explorations in Economic History*, 10 (1973).
Schwarz, L. 'English Servants and their Employers during the Eighteenth and Nineteenth Centuries', *Economic History Review*, 2nd ser., 52 (1999).

Seccombe, W. *Weathering the Storm: Working-Class Families from the Industrial Revolution to the Fertility Decline* (1993).

Shahar, S. *Childhood in the Middle Ages* (1990).

Shammas, C. 'Food Expenditures and Economic Well-Being in Early Modern England', *Journal of Economic History*, 43 (1983).

Simonton, D. 'Apprenticeship: Training and Gender in Eighteenth-Century England' in M. Berg (ed.) *Markets and Manufacture in Early Industrial Europe* (1991).

Smart, W. *Economic Annals of the Nineteenth Century* (1917).

Smelser, N. J. *Social Change in the Industrial Revolution* (1959).

Smelser, N. J. 'Sociological History: The Industrial Revolution and the British Working-Class Family', *Journal of Social History*, 1 (1967–68).

Snell, K. D. M. 'Agricultural Seasonal Unemployment, the Standard of Living, and Women's Work in the South and East, 1690–1860', *Economic History Review*, 2nd ser., 34 (1981).

Snell, K. D. M. *Annals of the Labouring Poor: Social Change and Agrarian England, 1660–1900* (Cambridge, 1985).

Snell, K. D. M. 'The Apprenticeship System in British History: The Fragmentation of a Cultural Institution', *History of Education*, 25 (1996).

Snell, K. D. M. 'The Standard of Living, Social Relations, the Family and Labour Mobility in South-Eastern and Western Counties, 1700–1860', PhD thesis (Cambridge, 1979).

Snell, K. D. M. 'The Sunday-School Movement in England and Wales: Child Labour, Denominational Control and Working-Class Culture', *Past and Present*, 164 (1999).

Snell, K. D. M., and Millar, J. 'Lone-Parent Families and the Welfare State: Past and Present', *Continuity and Change*, 2 (1987).

Speechley, H. V. 'Female and Child Agricultural Day Labourers in Somerset, c.1685–1870', PhD thesis (Exeter, 1999).

Spenceley, G. F. R. 'The English Pillow Lace Industry, 1840–80: A Rural Industry in Competition with Machinery', *Business History*, 19 (1977).

Stephens, W. B. *Education in Britain, 1750–1914* (Basingstoke, 1998).

Stephens, W. B. *Education, Literacy and Society, 1830–70* (Manchester, 1987).

Stone, L. *The Family, Sex and Marriage in England, 1500–1800* (1979).

Strange, K. H. *The Climbing Boys: A Study of Sweeps' Apprentices, 1773–1875* (1982).

Styles, J. 'Manufacturing, Consumption and Design in Eighteenth-Century England' in J. Brewer and R. Porter (eds) *Consumption and the World of Goods* (1993).

Tanner, J. M. 'The Secular Trend toward Earlier Maturity', *Education and Physical Growth* (1961).

Tawney, R. H. 'The Economics of Boy Labour', *Economic Journal*, 19 (1909).

Taylor, A. J. 'Labour Productivity and Technological Innovation in the British Coal Industry, 1850–1914', *Economic History Review*, 2nd ser., 14 (1961–62).

Thomas, M. W. *The Early Factory Legislation: A Study in Legislative and Administrative Evolution* (1948).

Thompson, E. P. 'History's March to the Foot of the Page', *The Times Literary Supplement* (6 May 1965).

Thompson, E. P. *The Making of the English Working Class* (Harmondsworth, 1968; first published 1963).

Tillott, P. M. 'Sources of Inaccuracy in the 1851 and 1861 Censuses' in E. A. Wrigley (ed.) *Nineteenth-Century Society: Essays in the Use of Quantitative Methods for the Study of Social Data* (Cambridge, 1972).

Tranter, N. L. 'The Labour Supply, 1780–1860' in R. Floud and D. McCloskey (eds) *The Economic History of Britain since 1700*, vol. 1 (Cambridge, 1981).

Trollope, F. *The Life and Adventures of Michael Armstrong, the Factory Boy* (1839–40).

Tuttle, C. *Hard at Work in Factories and Mines: The Economics of Child Labor During the British Industrial Revolution* (Boulder, CO, 1999).

Urwick, E. J. (ed.) *Studies of Boy Life in our Cities* (1904).

Verdon, N. 'The Employment of Women and Children in Agriculture: A Reassessment of Agricultural Gangs in Nineteenth-Century Norfolk', *Agricultural History Review*, 49 (2001).

Vincent, D. *Bread, Knowledge and Freedom: A Study of Nineteenth-Century Working-Class Autobiography* (1981).

Vincent, D. *Literacy and Popular Culture: England, 1750–1914* (Cambridge, 1989).

Vlassoff, M. 'Labour Demand and Economic Utility of Children: A Case Study in Rural India', *Population Studies*, 33 (1979).

Wagner, G. *Children of the Empire* (1982).

Walker, K. O. 'The Classical Economists and the Factory Acts', *Journal of Economic History*, 1 (1941).

Wall, R. 'The Age at Leaving Home', *Journal of Family History*, 3 (1978).

Wall, R. 'Leaving Home and the Process of Household Formation in Pre-Industrial England', *Continuity and Change*, 2 (1987).

Wall, R. 'Some Implications of the Earnings, Income and Expenditure Patterns of Married Women in Populations in the Past' in J. Henderson and R. Wall (eds) *Poor Women and Children in the European Past* (1994).

Wall, R. 'Work, Welfare and the Family: An Illustration of the Adaptive Family Economy', in L. Bonfield, R. M. Smith and K. Wrightson (eds) *The World We Have Gained* (Oxford, 1986).

Walvin, J. *A Child's World: A Social History of English Childhood, 1800–1914* (Harmondsworth, 1982).

Weiner, M. *The Child and the State in India* (Princeton, NJ, 1991).

West, E. G. *Education and the Industrial Revolution* (1975).

Wing, C. *Evils of the Factory System Exposed* (1836).

Winstanley, M. 'The Factory Workforce' in M. B. Rose (ed.) *The Lancashire Cotton Industry: A History Since 1700* (Preston, 1996).

Winstanley, M. 'Industrialization and the Small Farm: Family and Household Economy in Nineteenth-Century Lancashire', *Past and Present*, 152 (1996).

Winstanley, M. (ed.) *Working Children in Nineteenth-Century Lancashire* (Preston, 1995).

Woodward, D. 'The Background to the Statute of Artificers: The Genesis of Labour Policy, 1558–63', *Economic History Review*, 2nd ser., 33 (1980).

Worship, V. 'Cotton Factory or Workhouse: Poor Law Assisted Migration from Buckinghamshire to Northern England, 1835–7', *Family and Community History*, 3 (2000), pp. 33–48.

Wright, H. 'Sowerby Parish Apprentices', *Tranactions of the Halifax Antiquarian Society* (1934).

Wrigley, E. A. *Continuity, Chance and Change: The Character of the Industrial Revolution in England* (Cambridge, 1988).

Wrigley, E. A. (ed.) *Nineteenth-Century Society* (Cambridge, 1972).

Wrigley, E. A. 'Men on the Land and Men in the Countryside: Employment in Agriculture in Early Nineteenth-Century England' in L. Bonfield, R. M. Smith and K. Wrightson (eds) *The World We Have Gained* (Oxford, 1986).

Wrigley, E. A., and R. S. Schofield, *The Population History of England, 1541–1871* (Cambridge, 1981).

Zucchi, J. E. *The Little Slaves of the Harp: Italian Child Street Musicians in Nineteenth-Century Paris, London and New York* (Montreal, 1992).

Index

Printed in the United States
22447LVS00001B/156